SOUTHWEST PASSAGE

SOUTHWEST PASSAGE

The Inside Story of
Southwest Airlines' Formative Years

LAMAR MUSE

EAKIN PRESS ⬥ Austin, Texas

FIRST EDITION
Copyright © 2002
By Lamar Muse
Published in the United States of America
By Eakin Press
A Division of Sunbelt Media, Inc.
P.O. Drawer 90159 ⌕ Austin, Texas 78709-0159
email: sales@eakinpress.com
⌨ website: www.eakinpress.com ⌨
ALL RIGHTS RESERVED.
1 2 3 4 5 6 7 8 9
1-57168-790-4 HB
1-57168-739-4 PB

Library of Congress Cataloging-in-Publication Data
Muse, Lamar, 1920–
    Southwest passage : the inside story of Southwest Airlines' forma-
tive years / Lamar Muse.–1st ed.
        p.   cm.
    Includes index.
    ISBN 1-57168-790-4 (hardbound) — ISBN 1-57168-739-4 (pbk.)
    1. Southwest Airlines Co.–Management. 2. Airlines–United States-
Management. 3. Muse, Lamar, 1920– 4. Chief executive officers-
United States–Biography. I. Title: How Lamar Muse founded South-
west Airlines. II. Title.
HE9803.S68   2002
387.7'092–dc21   2002015315

CONTENTS

ACKNOWLEDGMENTS
AND DEDICATION

While this book is a memoir of my early life and business career, it would be impossible to name the hundreds of people who influenced it, who gave a helping hand, who pointed out my weaknesses, who encouraged me, and who made my life the joy that it has been. Inevitably, naming names will slight very deserving people, but I do wish to recognize those who contributed so much to the actual writing of this book and its subsequent publication.

My ex-wife Pat recognized that I had a story to tell and badgered me into sitting down at my computer and starting to type, after which I just couldn't stop. I spent the summer and early fall of the year 2000 alone on my boat, the *Holy Moses*, at my friends Sven and Kathy Stokke's dock in Pender Harbour, British Columbia, working from ten to fourteen hours a day at my Dell computer. My very best friend, Dr. Ben Dlin, took an interest in my work and guided me to Betty C. Keller of Quintessential Literary Services, located in Sechelt, B.C. Betty took my clumsy words and drivel, eliminated much of the foul language, changed phrasing, and moved sentences and paragraphs to where they should have been in the first place, until we wound up with a manuscript that we were both proud of and considered worthy of presenting to a publisher.

Since the Harvard Business School had always been so interested in what I was doing at Southwest Airlines and had authored several case studies (one of which, the $13 War, was their most popular and most copied of all case studies), they got first shot at it. They loved the manuscript but had a policy against printing memoirs. Harvard pointed me to John Wylie & Sons in New York, who they felt would jump at the opportunity. Wylie's chief editor read it, loved it, and passed it on to the other departments for final approval. Their marketing department rejected it on the basis that so much had already been written about Southwest Airlines that the book would not sell. Obviously, their marketing department either didn't read the book, just assuming it to be more of the same drivel they had seen before, or did read the book and never realized it is a totally different story from earlier, convoluted tales of Southwest's history.

I was discouraged and about ready to pitch the whole project. While having lunch one day with my long-time friend Harold Simmons in Dallas, I mentioned that I had written a memoir that nobody seemed interested in publishing. He wanted to read it. I gave him a floppy disk containing the manuscript. The very next day he had had his secretary print it out for him. He had read it, loved it, and said the story, particularly the major portion about how I built the most profitable airline that ever existed, needed to be published and if nobody else would do it, he would pay to have it done. Harold asked permission to send the manuscript to a man he had assisted many years ago, a famous writer of aviation-related books, Mr. John J. Nance, out in Tacoma, Washington, who, incidentally, is ABC Television's aviation expert.

As it turned out, John recognized this story's value, and one morning, while I was having breakfast with him in Tacoma, he remembered a small publishing company in Austin, Texas, that had published many books by Texans about Texas and said that I should get in touch with Ed Eakin, owner of Eakin Press. I did and a few days later had a very pleasant lunch with Mr. Eakin and his lovely wife, Charlene. After lunch, I presented him a copy of the manuscript to read and make a decision as to whether to proceed. He reached behind his desk for a blank publishing agreement form and started filling out his part of it, saying that with what he already knew about my career in the airline business, together with what Mr. Nance had related to him about the book, he didn't need to read it to know he wanted to publish it. That took guts, and I admire people with the guts to make a decision and just know instinctively that is the right decision. Ed died suddenly last February from heart failure. His daughter, Virginia Messer, has taken over as president of Eakin Press and appears to be a chip off the old block.

I therefore dedicate this book to the memory of two great men who had the guts to make a decision. One is Wesley West of Houston, who trusted me with the startup funds to make Southwest Airlines a reality and who said, "If Braniff Airways gives us too much trouble, we will just buy the bastards." You will read more about him throughout the book. And the other, of course, is Ed Eakin, who made it possible for the story of the formative years of Southwest Airlines to be told, hopefully to tens of thousands of real and would-be entrepreneurs.

Lamar Muse

INTRODUCTION

If you should happen to be browsing in a bookstore and pick up this volume, wondering who the heck this author is, well, here I am. A kid who barely got through the public school system of Palestine, Texas, more interested in the nine-piece dance band, in which he played third alto sax and clarinet, than in readin', writin', and 'rithmetic. Only by happenstance did I go to college, where I fell in love with accounting and finance. I took a couple of marketing courses, which piqued my interest, and I made good grades for three years, though I didn't stick around long enough to even get an undergraduate degree.

I ended up working for Price Waterhouse & Co. for some years both before and after service in the army during World War II. I was hired by the fledgling Trans-Texas Airways (TTA) as its chief financial officer in 1948 and spent the balance of my business career in the commercial aviation industry as a senior executive. After resigning from TTA in 1960, other positions followed, with: American Airlines, as assistant VP–corporate planning, 1960–61; Southern Airways, as VP–finance, 1962–65; Central Airlines, as president and CEO, 1965–67; Universal Airlines, in the same capacity, 1967–69; Southwest Airlines, as co-founder, president, and CEO, plus chairman of the executive committee, 1970–78; and finally Muse Air, initially as chairman of the board, and finally as chairman plus president and CEO, 1981–85. On June 30, 1985, shortly after celebrating my sixty-fifth birthday, Herb Kelleher, then president of Southwest Airlines, and I consummated the sale of Muse Air to Southwest. I had earlier participated in founding Southwest and subsequently, as its chief executive officer, guided the airline to fame and fortune during its formative years. So, as you can imagine, this book will have quite a bit to say about the airline industry in general and Southwest Airlines in particular.

Ever since leaving Southwest Airlines on March 28, 1978, just about everybody familiar with my career has remarked, "Lamar, you ought to write a book." Two decades-plus later, I've done it. When I mentioned my new project to John Eichner, a friend and business associate of forty-seven years, he remarked that I'd better have a good team of lawyers, referring of course to my revelations about the Southwest years. Rest assured, dear reader, my files more than substantiate the subjects covered in the Southwest chapters—from Southwest's first flight to my unplanned departure on March 28, 1978.

I would expect Bill Franklin and Bud Herring, business associates and good friends, to be a storehouse of knowledge all the way from the twelve years at TTA through and including my eight years at Southwest. My former wife Barbara and my four kids will have their slant on certain events, which often are at divergence from the way I saw things. Then there are Ben, Camille, Carole Ann, Ed, Ellen, Ernie, Hal, Harold, Herb, Herman, Jack, Jan, Jerry, Jess, John, Karen, Marcy, Nedra, Ron, Shad, and Sherry. Those are the folks still alive, and they know who they are.

Some awfully good people who are no longer with us had a vital effect on my life and career. First and foremost were my parents, Hiram and Nan Muse, after whom the new YMCA in Palestine is named. Then there's Miss Ida Stephens, my fourth-grade teacher. She caught me cheating on a test and convinced me never to do that again by informing my dad, who gave me a spanking I won't forget, saying they would have to burn the damn schoolhouse down to ever get me out of it. Would you believe the old Lamar (no relation) Elementary School building in Palestine, Texas, burned to the ground that summer of 1930?

Lots of other people influenced my life. I always looked upon A.V. (Pop) Mims, treasurer of the I-GN Railroad and father of my friends Trow and Bud, as my second dad. Dr. Bergen, president of Southwestern University, was the sole reason for me being exposed to some higher education. Juanice, my ever-loving first wife, stuck with me when we moved from Houston to Westport, Connecticut, back to Houston, to Atlanta, Georgia, to Dallas, to Ann Arbor, Michigan, to Conroe, Texas, and then back to Dallas, where she died of lung cancer. Larry Lamping and Reb Burke at Price Waterhouse & Co., and Charley Oursler and Bill Hogan at American Airlines should not be forgotten. Frank Hulse at Southern Airways convinced me to return to the airline industry, and Jack Bradford had the confidence to give me my first CEO job at Central Airlines. Last, but certainly not least, John B. Connally was my true and enduring friend, and Harold Simmons, who is still very much alive, made it possible to salvage enough of Muse Air to make it an attractive acquisition for Southwest Airlines.

In this book I am going to write about my life and my business principles. You'll find that I believe organizations thrive under the leadership of a benevolent dictator. Committees create mediocrity. Our present government, for instance, is nothing more than a great big committee, which is not altogether bad; it pretty well ensures that nothing really horrible occurs. But at the same time, it guarantees that nothing really super, such as the financial success of Southwest Airlines, does, either.

So don't put this book down just yet. Read on, my friend — I've got a lot to say!

1. AIR SOUTHWEST –

Only a Dream

Air Southwest began when Rollin W. King (the W is for White, of White Motors, the truck manufacturer of Cleveland, Ohio), a late-1950s graduate of the Harvard Business School and possessor of a commercial pilot's license, found himself losing money operating a one-plane air-taxi service out of San Antonio to such metropolises as Uvalde and Eagle Pass, Texas. Rollin, like hundreds of other aviation-minded people, dreamed of a scheduled airline operating exclusively in what we Texans call the Golden Triangle: Dallas on the north, Houston on the southeast, and San Antonio on the southwest. Distances are 227 miles from Dallas's Love Field to Houston's Intercontinental Airport (241 to its Hobby Airport), 251 miles from Love Field to San Antonio, and 190 miles from Houston to San Antonio. The difference between Rollin and the other dreamers was that Rollin didn't just dream about it. He did something about it, to his everlasting credit, thus proving himself the true entrepreneur.

In 1945 the Texas legislature had created the Texas Aeronautics Commission (TAC), then reorganized it in 1961 to empower it to, among other things, issue Certificates of Public Convenience and Necessity for intrastate airlines. King viewed this

1

as an opportunity. He went to Herbert D. Kelleher, a young lawyer transplanted from New Jersey, who had married Joan Negley, a prominent and well-to-do young lady of San Antonio, where Kelleher had recently joined a law practice. I don't doubt one bit that during the course of their ensuing discussion, one of them sketched that Golden Triangle on a cocktail napkin. Seems logical. Kelleher, after initially saying Rollin was nuts, later came around to appreciate the idea. He solicited the support of John Peace, a well-known San Antonio attorney who had the ability to open all the important doors in the state of Texas.

An application was filed with the TAC for the proposed service, and when a hearing examiner was duly appointed, he promptly called for a public hearing on the matter. At the hearing in late 1967, Braniff Airways, Texas International Airlines, and Continental Airlines all appeared in opposition to the proposed service, but the examiner, anxious to have a real airline utilizing large equipment under the TAC's jurisdiction, found in favor of the applicant—King's Air Southwest. That ruling was followed by oral arguments before the members of the commission, who unanimously agreed with the earlier finding of the examiner. Subsequently, the TAC members voted to grant the requested authority and issue the necessary certificate for operation of *intrastate* air service between the three major Texas cities: Dallas, Houston, and San Antonio. The carriers with whom the new company would be competing in the marketplace all held *interstate* certificates issued by the Civil Aeronautics Board in Washington, D.C. There is a big difference, as will be seen in due course.

The very next day, February 21, 1968, the three opposition airlines went to Texas District Court Judge Betts, who issued a temporary restraining order, suspending the TAC action, and this wound up keeping the case in court for the next two-plus years. Subsequent judgments adverse to Air Southwest and the TAC action came down in both Betts' district court and the State Court of Appeals. After the second negative decision by the Texas courts, the Air Southwest board was ready to throw in the towel, but by then Kelleher had done such a good job of originally selling the concept to the TAC that he had even sold himself on it. He told the board that he was going to take the case on to the Texas Supreme Court and that the company owed him no more attorney fees until such time as he got the favorable decision he knew the case deserved. Obviously, Kelleher was overjoyed, for both personal and financial reasons, when the Supreme Court unanimously reversed the two lower courts' flawed decisions. This was in September 1970, after which the opposing carriers appealed to the U.S. Supreme Court in Washington, D.C., where on December 7 they were denied a hearing.

It was at this point that I got involved with what was then Air Southwest. After being fired as president and CEO of Universal Airlines in Detroit the previous October, I was receiving my semimonthly paychecks on schedule and would continue to do so for the next two years. I was spending a lot of time on the golf course at Panorama Country Club and doing a little fishing. My wife Juanice and I also took a couple of trips to Las Vegas, but I guess at age forty-nine I was just too young to quit being productive, and frankly, I was bored stiff. Here I was, doing nothing, though I was in the prime of life, a certified public accountant with five years of public accounting experience and twenty-two years' experience in the airline industry. I had served as chief financial officer for two airlines, corporate planning officer for one, and president and CEO of two others.

Each day I devoured the morning *Houston Post,* the afternoon *Houston Chronicle,* and the *Wall Street Journal,* and I studied *BusinessWeek* and *Forbes* as soon as they arrived. One morning in September 1970, my eye caught a little blurb in one of the papers reporting on the Texas Supreme Court's reversal of the lower courts' ruling for an outfit called Air Southwest, mentioning that the company had an office in San Antonio and referring to a Mr. Rollin King.

I called to compliment Mr. King on the favorable decision by the Texas Supreme Court. He knew who I was and said that, as a matter of fact, they had been inquiring as to my whereabouts. It was arranged that Juanice and I would go to San Antonio the next weekend, at which time we met Herb and Joan Kelleher, as well as John Peace. After a brief discussion, it was generally agreed that at the appropriate time I would be elected president and CEO by the company's board of directors and would become a member of the board and chairman of its executive committee. In the interim, I would informally plan some of the many steps that had to be taken before service could begin.

Rollin King showed me an eight-page document he had prepared outlining the operating plan that had been presented during the TAC hearings and for which the board of directors had granted him 150,000 shares of Air Southwest common stock. To me, 150,000 shares seemed a little steep for a skimpy eight-page document. Herb Kelleher claims that Rollin King contributed other property besides the eight-page plan, although I have no idea what it could have been. Upon examining the stock records, I noted that Rollin had passed on 50,000 shares each to Herb Kelleher and John Peace. I later learned the price was $.01 per share. In my opinion, this whole deal looked as if it had been designed to get some stock out to Kelleher and Peace without the knowledge of the other directors. Herb Kelleher claims that the transfer of Rollin's 50,000 shares to him had nothing to do with the initial issuance and was a "subsequent development." The stock was restricted and its market value questionable, and while in hindsight I could have been suspicious, at the time I was (1) naive and (2) extremely anxious at age fifty to be doing something productive again.

The plan outlined in King's eight pages provided for the company to purchase three of American Airlines' Lockheed Electra L-188 turboprop aircraft, which would be operated on four daily roundtrips between Dallas and Houston, two trips between Dallas and San Antonio, and one trip between Houston and San Antonio. My only comment: "You've got to be kidding!" Their response: "Well, we only have a limited amount of funds," or something to that effect. There was never a truer statement.

Around the time of the hearings before the TAC in 1968, John Peace had opened a number of doors in the state to sell approximately $400,000 of common stock in pops of 3,333 shares for $10,000, or $3 per share. That list of purchasers could well have substituted for "Who's Who in Texas." The money Peace raised had gone primarily to Herb Kelleher for legal fees and expenses, and to Rollin King for salary and expenses. Some had also gone for a secretary for King, rental on a small office at the San Antonio Airport, and a local advertising agency that got a fee for preparing some exhibits for Air Southwest's route case before the TAC examiner, and I believe there was also an expert-witness fee for somebody.

As it turned out, John Peace and his heirs never got to share in the massive bounty that Southwest Airlines eventually produced. He died in 1972 without ever, so far as I know, billing the company a dime for the many hours he expended for its survival in those early days. It has always been my understanding that Herb Kelleher purchased Peace's 50,000 shares from his widow, Ruby. Mr. Kelleher denies that. Since it still would have been unregistered stock, she would have had difficulty disposing of it in the open market, so, if I'm correct, I am sure the price was right.

I spent the balance of 1970 pretty much just dreaming about the wonderful opportunity presented to me of starting with an almost clean sheet of paper to build an air-transportation company from scratch. I would not be confronted with all the embedded problems of companies I had joined in the past, or the problems I was unable to control because I wasn't the boss. I had spent my entire career building toward this opportunity, and if it proved to be a success, I would get the credit. If it failed, I was ready to accept the full blame. I began compiling a list of the things that were going to have to be accomplished before the first plane could take to the air.

2. BEGINNINGS –

My Immediate Family

The real beginning of this whole story of my involvement in the airline industry goes right back to the birth of my parents. My dad, Hiram Marion Muse, was born in a house that stood on the bank of Ioni Creek, near Slocum in Anderson County, Texas, on January 28, 1879. My dad always swore that he could remember the first time he ever saw sunlight. It was when he was one week old and his sister, Azalee, took him out on the front porch. He firmly believed this, whether anybody else did or not. A full-time job on his father's farm took the place of school after the sixth grade, a tradeoff that I understand was quite common in those days. At age sixteen he decided there had to be something in the world more exciting and profitable than farm labor, so he rode his horse bareback twelve miles north to Palestine.

A peaceful town of about 13,000 souls, Palestine was a division point on the International–Great Northern Railroad (I-GN). The general office of the I-GN was located there, as was a large engine- and car-repair facility, known as a roundhouse. The town was home to many train crews operating in three directions from Palestine: to Longview, Houston, and Taylor, Texas. Dad told the I-GN Railroad trainmaster that he was eighteen, the minimum hiring age, and went to work for the railroad as a fireman. The I-GN later became a major component of the Missouri Pacific Lines (MoPac), now merged into the Union Pacific Railroad.

Dad was promoted to engineer some years later and celebrated his promotion by buying the first motorcar in Palestine, a Stanley Steamer, on which he installed a steam-locomotive whistle. Since the whistle caused horses to bolt and run, the Palestine City Council passed a law, still on the books, commanding that there shall be no blowing of train whistles on city streets. Meanwhile, Dad had so much trouble keeping the Stanley Steamer running that he traded it off to a Mr. Prather, who ran a bicycle shop on Avenue A, for a brand-new bicycle.

According to stories told me by his peers, Dad was a gay blade as a young man. For one thing, he was quite a hypnotist. He would do tricks at parties with the other guests as subjects, sometimes using them to find hidden objects. One story I heard from several sources was that Dad instructed a hypnotized partygoer that his feet would stick to the sidewalk at the Bratton Drug Store corner when he walked home from the party that night. Late that night, some folks awakened Dad to go downtown and let the poor man loose from where he was stuck in front of Bratton's so he could go home and get some sleep. When I asked Dad to prove his skill by hypnotizing me, he had said he had lost the power many years earlier when he tried to have his best subject explore Heaven. He told me that when he made that effort, instructing the subject to enter the pearly gates, a big light flashed in the sky and he was never able to hypnotize anyone again. (Now, please don't somebody try to sell me the Brooklyn Bridge.)

My dad was a gruff, stern taskmaster, and everybody who ever knew him says that I am his spittin' image. He had most of the people in Palestine not afraid of him, but wary and respectful. In other words, watch out—he might bite. But I knew him to be a kind, considerate, softhearted gentleman. I sat next to him in church many times and watched tears slide down his chin and heard him sigh. He was the kind of guy who helped others without any fanfare. My friend Randolph lived just outside the city limits and, as there were no public schools out in the county in those days, he had to bring a $10 tuition fee to the city school the first of every month in order to attend. Randolph did not show up at school the first day one month, and I related this to my dad. The next morning, he told me to get in the car instead of riding my bicycle to school, and we went out to Randolph's house by the Texas State Railroad tracks and picked him up for school. Dad gave him the $10 for the teacher. Randolph was just a good kid whose family was in financial trouble and needed a little help.

Eventually, with his seniority, Dad could bid a trip down to Houston in the morning and back to Palestine that afternoon with every other day off and be home every night. He always wanted to be productive, however, and since he was a pretty good carpenter and enjoyed building houses, he built several nice five-room brick homes around our neighborhood and rented them out for $25 a month. His one helper, besides me, was a fine black man named John, whose wife, Mary, cleaned and cooked for our family. John prepared the lots for building, put in the foundations, mixed concrete, and did all the heavy and dirty work. He would say to me when I would miss a nail while hammering, "Lamar, the directions on the keg say hit the nail on the head." When we would finish a task he would say, "Good enough fer who it's fer." The average cost of the houses Dad built was about $1,700, including the lot. With a house renting for $25, that's about 1.5 percent return on your investment each month. Try getting that today!

My mother, Nan Durst Urquhart, was born in Tyler, Texas, some eighteen years after my father on July 7, 1895. My mother's father—the only one of my grandparents still living when I came into the world—had been pastor of the First Methodist Church in Tyler when she was born. She was the seventh of nine children, including two older brothers who had drowned in a flooded creek that runs by the present-day medical center in Tyler. Of her surviving siblings, three sisters and one brother were older than her, and one sister and one brother were younger. After graduating from high school, she became a teacher in Goose Creek (now Baytown), Texas, for two years. Then she went on to Houston, where she became chief accountant for the one-store operation of Foley Brothers Dry Goods Company, next door to the old First National Bank on Main Street near Buffalo Bayou.

By this time, Dad was bidding trips that originated out of the big city of Houston, where the lights were brighter and the girls prettier. He met my mother in Houston, courted her, and married her in 1918. They settled down in a house located at 302 Estelle Street, three blocks off Harrisburg Boulevard in the east end of Houston. It was about five blocks from the old Ford Motor Company Model-T assembly plant. The smell of the black paint they put on those cars was so strong that sometimes we could smell the fumes from our house. In due course, I was born June 4, 1920, in the house's front bedroom. I was the first-born, followed three years later by my brother, Kindred Henry (Ken), and another seven years later my little sister, Marian Kate.

My mother's distant ancestors were the Urquharts of Ross and Cromarty County in northern Scotland, and Grandpa — whose full name was Henry Bascom Urquhart — was very proud of his namesake and his forebears' famed Urquhart Castle. He had been in the first graduating class of Vanderbilt University in Nashville, Tennessee. He lived most of his last twenty-five years with our family, finally passing away at the age of ninety-six, and spent most of those years researching biblical facts and fantasies and writing articles for various Methodist publications. I never saw him that he didn't look like he just stepped out of a bandbox.

My mother's brother Tim was the top Dodge car salesman in the state of Texas. Her younger brother, Lamar, a wholesale tire distributor, was shot dead in the early 1930s in the process of picking up a "lady of the street" on Congress Avenue in Houston. Mother's sisters were Aunt Sister (that's all I ever knew to call her), Aunt Zue, Aunt Nell, and Aunt Adalina. They were all good, simple people, and the highlight of the last three's lives was a two-week trip to Europe that I sent them on in late 1969 so they could visit the ancestral family home at Cromarty. They also visited London, Amsterdam, Paris, and Rome and flew the entire trip first-class, courtesy of KLM Airlines and my friend Harry Bradley.

My mother was the most wonderful, most loving, and happiest woman I ever knew. And I was not the only one who thought so. Our house was the meeting place for all my friends. They loved to come over because they felt welcome and comfortable there.

9

Mom would prepare a basket and take us on a picnic at least once every week. Her pineapple-and-cheese sandwiches on round slices of bread were to die for. She was a big woman, weighing two hundred pounds, and when she would laugh, which was often, her stomach would just shake. She had a nickname for everybody. When my best friend, Hal Holland, would show up, she would always say, "Here comes Tall-Dark-and-Handsome."

As small children, my siblings and I would get in bed with Mom and Dad every morning. When it was time to get moving, she would always sing an old World War I song that went, "Oh, how I hate to get up in the morrrrrrninggggg." Mother suffered from high blood pressure and had to take medicine daily, but she kept the coffee pot going all day, drinking coffee rather than eating, to fight her weight problem. On New Year's Day, 1947, she suffered a cerebral hemorrhage, and she died an untimely death eleven days later at the age of fifty-one. Having been an accountant herself, she had been so proud that by that time her eldest son was associated with the number-one public accounting firm in the world, at least in her eyes, and had kept pressing me to take the Certified Public Accountant examinations to become a CPA, her own lifelong dream.

Ken, my younger brother, became a career pilot in the air force, flying B-24s in Italy during World War II, P-51s in the Korean War, and later planning all in-country air operations in Vietnam. After Vietnam, he was director of operations for headquarters, Air University Command, at Maxwell Air Force Base in Montgomery, Alabama. When he retired after thirty years of military service, he became director of aviation for the City of Montgomery for another ten years. Now he plays golf at least every other day at Arrowhead Country Club in Montgomery. His family consists of his wife, Ruth, and two children. One is a senior officer at a Montgomery bank, and the other is an official in Washington with the Environmental Protection Agency.

Marian, my sister, never left Palestine. She married, about fifty years ago, R. E. Thompson, a contractor who built a respectable percentage of the homes in Palestine, and she is still putting up with the old codger. They have three children, all doing well as a sales manager, a computer programmer, and a school administrator.

3. BEGINNINGS —

My School Years

My first paying job, at age nine, was going house-to-house selling the *Saturday Evening Post* every week around our neighborhood in Houston. I got 2 cents of the nickel price for each magazine. Once a month I sold the *Ladies Home Journal* for 15 cents, of which I kept a whole nickel. My first political experience was when I accompanied Dad to the corner grocery store down on Harrisburg Boulevard in Houston, where he voted for Al Smith, the Democratic nominee for president, against Herbert Hoover in 1928. That was the first year since Reconstruction that Texas voted Republican.

During the 1920s, as Dad's rising seniority allowed him to bid better trips, we moved up and down the railroad track between Houston and Palestine, including periods in Huntsville and Spring, Texas. In Huntsville I was allowed to ride on the engine with Dad for his daily trips on what was called the "Huntsville Tap," making four roundtrips a day over the ten-mile track to meet the passenger trains running on the I-GN main line at Phelps. Occasionally, when there was a light load, Dad would let me put my hand on the throttle and slowly pull it back for a gradual start of the whole train, one car at a time, as

11

the slack was taken up between each car. Just maybe that is where I got my uncontrollable desire to run things. The only thing I remember about the few months we lived in Spring is that when we arrived by car from Palestine at the house Dad had rented, I was just about to pee in my pants. I ran all through the house looking for the bathroom, but to no avail. Then Dad led me out to the back end of the lot, where there was a small building with a quarter-moon cut out of the door: "Go to it, son!" In 1930 we moved back to Palestine for the last time, since by then Dad had enough seniority to bid any trip from any base on the I-GN he wanted.

I learned early on that saving was an important part of living. From the time I sold the *Saturday Evening Post* in Houston at age nine, one-half of every dime I made had gone to my mom, who put it in a savings account. My dad had bought a $1,000, twenty-year-pay insurance policy on my life from Lefty Martin—high school teacher, first baseman on the Palestine Pals baseball team, as well as an agent for Seaboard Life Insurance Company (now American General Life of Houston). Dad had paid the first year's premium on it but made it clear to me that it was my responsibility to make all future annual payments. This was in 1931, when my only income was the few nickels I brought home from selling the *Palestine Daily Herald.* I lay in bed many a night crying because I was afraid I would never be able to save the annual premium of $19.14 over the period of a year and thus would cause my policy to lapse into default. I didn't quite know what *default* meant, but it sure sounded terrible.

About this time, the City of Palestine cleared some flat land on top of a hill about five miles west of the town, short of the Trinity River on the road to Austin, and started calling it the Palestine Municipal Airport. Pretty soon, word started spreading that some barnstormers were bringing a new ten-passenger Ford Tri-Motor airplane to the field the next Sunday and that they were going to take passengers on a trip over the town of Palestine for a buck a head. Our family went out there to see the excitement, and my dad, without too much badgering, agreed to take my brother Ken and me for a trip on that huge plane. Mother stayed on the ground with our little sister. The main things I remember about the trip were that the plane was equipped with wicker seats, and that the noise of those three engines trying to get off that sandy hill was louder than a speeding steam locomotive. I've often wondered if that short flight had anything to do with my subsequent career in the airline industry and Ken's career in the air force.

In 1932, during the depths of the Great Depression, some government agency decided that Palestine ought to have a municipal band. With a New Deal government grant, a band director was hired (as I recall, his name was Buddy Lively), who also gave music instruction to young and old for 50 cents a lesson on the second floor of the old, condemned Dilley Building. Dad bought me a silver clarinet for $27, and I started taking music lessons. A month later, I was playing next-to-last chair in the municipal band.

Then, in 1934, Pop Mims, who was treasurer of the I-GN, organized a dance band. He played the bass horn, and his two sons, Bud and Trow, played the trumpet and tenor sax, respectively. Their next-door neighbor, my friend Hal Holland, also played the trumpet. Horace Owens, who lived across town, played a pretty mean alto sax, and O. B. Davis was a great drummer. A nice little boy named Billy Montana played piano. (Anybody who played piano as a teenager was considered a sissy in those days.) Most of us were just thirteen to fifteen years old.

Before long we had a great nine-piece swingin' dance band that became famous all over East Texas. We charged $27 for a three-hour dance, which amounted to $3, or $1 per hour, for each of us. Given that the original minimum wage of 30 cents per hour was not even in existence at that point, we were in high cotton, with money in our pockets. In 1936 Billy was replaced at the piano by a man twenty years our senior, Leland Adams, who had returned to Palestine after a number of years playing piano and arranging music for several larger traveling dance bands. We were so much better with the addition of his light jazz touch and the special arrangements he wrote for us that we doubled our prices, with Leland getting a double cut. By that time, in addition to going to school and playing in the dance band, I also played in the school band, and I continued to sell the *Palestine Daily Herald* on downtown streets after school (keeping two cents per copy). I also made deliveries for the Tri-Oaks Grocery every Saturday, earning $1.50 for a twelve-hour day, 7:00 A.M. to 7:00 P.M. As a result of all this work, I never had much time to get into trouble or, for that matter, to have much fun during my high school years.

In any case, throughout high school and even in college, I was so ugly (skinny, freckled, and an introvert) that my nickname was "Ug." I had two long, protruding front teeth that didn't help my appearance. Things improved a little before I became a teenager when I fell on the steel handle of a little red wagon and shortened one tooth. The other suffered the same fate when I walked into a swinging baseball bat. The family dentist filed down the remnants of both teeth to normal length, and I was one step closer to losing the nickname "Ug."

I spent many hours in the YMCA gym and swimming pool, the only one in town. It was an exceptionally nice one, owned and operated by the railroad and dedicated to improving the quality of life for—and the quality of—the young people who grew up in Palestine. The hospital was also railroad-owned and -operated, it being important to the older generation; my father spent the last four years of his life there suffering from hardening of the arteries—no doubt due to eating hot biscuits, cream gravy, sausage, and eggs every single morning of his long life.

When the I-GN was consolidated into the MoPac during the early 1950s, the hospital was moved to St. Louis, MoPac's headquarters. About that same time, the YMCA burned to the ground. A feeble effort was made to replace it with a totally inadequate building on the far north side of town, and it served as best it could for several decades. However, a beautiful new YMCA, named the "Hiram and Nan Muse YMCA," was completed in 1999, thanks to the efforts of many local citizens, companies, and foundations, and this new facility has helped quadruple the organization's membership. It definitely improves the quality of life for all the citizens of that area, which was my goal in making the substantial donation that got the ball rolling back in 1995.

The Great Depression of the 1930s hardly affected Palestine, due to the discovery of the East Texas oil fields in 1929. In that era there were no pipelines from those fields to the refineries on

14

the Gulf Coast. The oil was carried instead by the MoPac, which ran right through Kilgore, the center of the oil field, to Palestine, and then to Houston and on to the refineries: the Humble refinery in Baytown, Amoco in Texas City, Shell in Pasadena, and Gulf in Port Arthur. One long freight train right after another came through Palestine, with most of them stalling on Palestine Hill. We would hear the freight engines chugging up the hill, all the while getting slower and slower until they would just give up and stop. A few seconds later we would hear four long whistles signaling the station to send a yard-engine down the track to help them get into town.

In those days, there were always many unfortunate people riding the rails looking for work, and quite often they would leave a freight train when it stalled on the hill and walk the streets in search of a handout. My wonderful mother never turned down a person who came to the kitchen door in quest of a free meal. Even if she didn't have anything prepared, she would put something together for each one of them. Some people said the hobos would mark the curb to indicate a soft touch, but I never believed it — particularly since we didn't have a curb.

In 1931 the love of my life was Loraine Garrett, a stately and beautiful blonde whose dad was the Ford dealer in Palestine. She had a younger brother named Max whom I played with all the time just so I could be in her vicinity. I never got up the nerve to tell her I was in love with her. Then at age fourteen came Elizabeth Stafford, daughter of the Buick dealer. (I loved cars.) I got a 50-cent allowance on Dad's paydays, the 14th and 28th of each month, so every other Saturday I would take Elizabeth to the movie. The admission was 10 cents. After the show we would go to Murphy's Drug up on the Courthouse Square for an ice cream soda, which cost 15 cents, and there went my whole allowance, but it was worth it. (Remember, my name was "Ug.") After a while, Elizabeth got to thinking she was an actress, started running with an older crowd, and no longer had time for me.

In 1990, some fifty-five years later, both Elizabeth and I were named Distinguished Alumni of Palestine High School — me a C student, she an A student. We both spoke to the student body at an assembly. I raised the roof off the building with cheers after telling them that I had been so homely they called me "Ug," and how beautiful Elizabeth had been, and that I never even got to kiss her. Then I said, by gosh, I wanted to kiss her right then and there. And so I did. I also told them to be kind to wallflowers and those people we now call "nerds," because they just might find themselves working for one of them someday.

After Elizabeth, there came in fast succession Betty Jane Weeks, Mary Ellen Wynn, and Nedra Hoyt. Betty Jane and Mary Ellen were passing flirtations, but the mutual love and respect between Nedra Hoyt and myself has lasted through her marriage of fifty-plus years to my friend Jack Roquemore, and through all of my marriages. She is what keeps me going back to Palestine and supporting charities in my hometown after all these years.

Back then, public schools consisted of eleven grades — five in grade school, three in junior high or middle school, and three in senior high school. I graduated from Palestine High School on my seventeenth birthday, June 4, 1937, without ever giving a thought to going to college. The high school yearbook says beside my name and ugly puss, "A senior quite sedate, about that there is no debate."

That summer my best friend, Hal Holland, and I utilized our dads' railroad-pass authority to take a trip through the western part of our nation. We each had a $20 bill to make the trip on, but before we boarded our train that night, each of our dads gave us another $5 bill, with the strict understanding that it was for emergencies only. We were not to spend it otherwise.

We had coach seats and slept on the train each night. We went first to Colorado Springs and laid over a day to take a limo up Pikes Peak. Next stop was Salt Lake City. At the Mormon Tabernacle, a guide dropped a pin on a slanted board, and as it rolled down the plank, the acoustics were so fine that from the opposite end of that huge edifice we heard it drop and roll. From there we took the Feather River Route train to Oakland, California, and a ferry across to San Francisco. The train stopped along the way at the bottom of the Royal Gorge so passengers could look way up from the riverbed at the highest expansion bridge in the world. I learned much later that one of my directors at Southwest Airlines, John Murchison, and his brother

Clint owned that bridge and charged tolls for traffic to cross it. Small world!

In San Francisco we spent a day seeing all the sights we could afford and were ready for a night in a bed, but rather than check in to a hotel, we shared a single upper berth in the Pullman car on the overnight train to Los Angeles. My aunt Alice ran a boarding house there and had previously agreed to put us up and feed us for a whole week.

The late 1930s was a time when swing music was played everywhere, and you could dance all night to great bands broadcasting on the radio from famous ballrooms across the country. It just happened that Benny Goodman was making a name for himself and his band at the Palomar Dance Hall in downtown L.A. The general admission was 50 cents per person, and you didn't even have to buy a Coke if you didn't want to. Hal and I stood in front of the bandstand for five hours listening to Benny, with Harry James on trumpet, Gene Krupa on drums, Teddy Wilson on piano, Lionel Hampton on vibes, Helen Forrest singing, and all the rest of his great nineteen–piece band. It was only the next year that Benny and the same band tore the roof off Carnegie Hall with "Sing, Sing, Sing."

While in L.A, we just had to go to the Coconut Grove at the Biltmore Hotel, a few blocks from my aunt's big boarding house. We hated to spend the money for the required meal at the club, because the entertainment was by Hal Kemp's Orchestra, which we considered to be strictly "Mickey Mouse." But we went anyway, bought the cheapest thing on the menu, and were able to say we had been to "the world-famous Coconut Grove." Another day we caught the boat to Catalina and heard Jan Garber at the island's casino. He played sweet, slow music for all the old folks, as Lawrence Welk did a few decades later.

Toward the end of the week, we were ready to hear some good music again, so we decided to go back to the Palomar for another session with the man, Benny Goodman. This time we invited my aunt's granddaughter, Maxine, my second cousin, to go with us. She was a good-looking gal with flowing black hair. Up until that time I had always played music for dances and had never really learned how to dance myself. But that was my night to learn. My cousin and I danced every piece. She was an excellent dancer and a good teacher, and that was the night I quit being a wallflower. I wasn't ugly anymore—even though friends still called me "Ug." This was a big turning point in my young life, and when we got back to Texas, I gained a reputation as one of the best dancers available, and all the gals asked me to dance with them, rather than the other way around. I had gained confidence, all because of learning to dance with Maxine.

When we returned to Palestine, both Hal and I still had that $5 emergency fund, along with some small change, in our pockets. Both of our dads complimented us for our frugality and permitted us to keep the money.

One hot afternoon in early August of that same summer, our dance band was out in Pop Mims' barn practicing some new tunes, such as "Cheek to Cheek," "Sophisticated Lady," and "White Heat," when an old Ford came to a stop out in front. An elderly gentleman got out of the car, came inside, sat down, and listened to us play. This wasn't so unusual, since passersby often came in to hear our practice sessions. When we finished, he praised our music. He pointed out that five of us had just graduated from high school the previous June and asked about our college plans. We, of course, told him there were none. Then he told us just who and what he was, and that he had come to Palestine just to hear our band.

He was Dr. John William Bergen, president of Southwestern University in Georgetown, Texas. Would we five graduates be interested in attending the fall semester at Southwestern—on full scholarship? If so, we would be the new nucleus of Southwestern's marching and concert band, which produced an annual traveling show called "The Pigskin Review." He told us that the band was being conducted by Tom Johnson, who had made the swing 180-cadence marching band at SMU world-famous with their halftime show at the 1935 Rose Bowl. Upon learning that Georgetown was only thirty miles north of Austin, the home of the University of Texas, which had a big demand for dance bands, we looked at each other and said, "Why not? That just might be our entry to being a big-time traveling band." So, within a period of a couple hours, we went from no thought of ever going to college to being signed up to enter the following month. It was a bigger deal for all of us than we realized at the moment. Our parents were ecstatic to hear the news that evening.

All five of us — Hal Holland, Trow Mims, Horace Owens, O. B. Davis, and myself — went to Southwestern for the next two years. The same year we arrived, a great musician named Garner Clarke came to finish his education at Southwestern after several years as first trumpet in big-name bands. We formed a new band that had Garner fronting it with his great trumpet, backed up by four saxes and four rhythm players. The lineup produced a really fabulous, unusual sound. The only bad thing was that it left my friend Hal Holland out. We all regretted that very much.

It wasn't till my sophomore year that I really got interested in learning for the first time in my life. I loved accounting, and the marketing courses I took were so exciting that I made A's in both, the first I had ever earned. After two years, however, I had taken all of the business courses Southwestern had to offer, and, along with all the others except Horace, decided to transfer to the University of Texas in Austin. Hal, Trow, and O. B. were accepted, but UT rejected me because my high school English marks had all been C's. Texas Christian University in Fort Worth was willing to take me, though, and they offered advanced accounting and auditing courses, marketing, and business math. Horace stayed on at Southwestern for his degree.

After graduation, O. B. went back to Palestine and worked as the office manager for Texas Power & Light until his death at an early age. Horace owned and operated a retail tire store in Palestine for many years. Hal became a geologist, working for Humble (now Exxon) in Corpus Christi for many years, and then as an independent in Mineral Wells and later in Houston. Trow became a surgeon and has spent his professional life practicing in Hereford, Texas.

I didn't graduate. When I was ready to begin my senior year, my kid brother, Ken, was due to commence college. Since Dad couldn't afford to send two kids to school at the same time, I laid out my senior year so Ken could get started, fully intending to return after one year. But as so often happens, life interrupted.

4. BEGINNINGS—

The Route to the Airlines

Back home in Palestine, I was hired as a jobber. I drove a big, long, two-ton Dodge panel truck, selling cigarettes, cigars, chewing tobacco, snuff, and all varieties of candy and gum for George Pessoney of the Pessoney Candy Company. I traveled different routes each day throughout East Texas. During this period there was an abrupt change in my love life. From the summer of 1939 through my junior year at TCU and after returning to Palestine, I had been crazy about Catherine Crittenden, a cute little thing with the prettiest round face and silkiest black hair you ever saw. My best friend, that tall, dark, and handsome Hal Holland, finally took her away from me, though. Then I started dating Juanice Gunn, a great dancer with gorgeous legs.

One evening I was coming back into Palestine in my panel truck when the left front wheel came off as I was barreling down a hill and hugging a curve at about 70 mph. I darn near went over a steep cliff before I got the thing stopped. It was a close call, but my only thought when I came to a stop was how much I craved being close to Juanice at that moment. I hitched a ride to town, got my dad's car, picked up Juanice, and took her with me as I led the wrecker to the scene of the accident. I proposed to her that night, quit my peddling job, and headed to Houston, where I could get a real job with a future so Juanice and I could get married.

My first job in Houston was as the cashier for the Fehr Baking Company (Fairmaid Bread & Cakes). As opposed to just one driver-salesman at the candy company (me), there were 150 on the road for Fairmaid, and my responsibility was the other end of what I had been doing in Palestine for Pessoney. Instead of being the driver/salesman, I was the guy to whom the Fairmaid drivers reported each evening with their settlement sheets, inventory return forms, cash, checks and credit slips — all of which had to balance.

During the depression, Juanice's father struggled to make a living, running drug stores in Palestine and Jacksonville, primarily selling prescription liquor and wine out the back door. In those days, they had an old has-been doctor sitting right by the back door writing out the prescriptions, so as to comply with the new laws as a result of the end of Prohibition. But, having previously been a railroad conductor, Mr. Gunn got the itch for the rails again and took a job with the Southern Pacific in California. When he went out there in early 1941, Juanice and her mother moved to Houston. Mrs. Gunn ran a boarding house, and I and my friend Slick Kelly, who worked at the Folgers Coffee plant, were her main customers. Six months into my new job, Juanice and I decided we had waited long enough. We secretly got married on June 21, 1941, pressing into service as witnesses my friend Slick and a lady who worked with Juanice in her new job at the Trinity Universal Life Insurance Company.

You've heard about people getting married on a shoestring. Let me tell you, ours was the shortest shoestring you ever saw. Even at "big city" wages and with a recent raise, I was only making $22.50 a week at the bakery while Juanice was making $50 a month as a private secretary to the manager of Trinity. I had to borrow $10 from my boss to pay the preacher, who married us at St. Paul Methodist Church on South Main. We bought Juanice's wedding ring for $80, payable in installments of $8 per month for ten months. I sold my Conn alto sax and my Selmer

21

clarinet and flute to the Parker Music Company for $25 cash; over the course of my high school and college band days, I had paid nearly a thousand dollars for those instruments, but at that stage of life, the $25 was more important. We rented a furnished apartment just three blocks from the bakery for $42 a month; the rent and the ring payment of $8 consumed Juanice's monthly check. We had a high time spending my $22.50 a week for all of our other expenses.

Then, in January 1942, I received a call from Ray Jordan, a principal at Price Waterhouse & Company, saying that I had been recommended to them as a prospective applicant for employment by Mr. A.V. (Pop) Mims. I arranged an interview for that same afternoon and was hired as a junior accountant on their audit staff, starting at a whopping $130 per month. They gave me an expense advance of $100, deposited to my new bank account at Second National Bank near their offices at 711 Esperson Building, and a first-class railroad ticket to Dallas. I had instructions to report to Mr. Huck Underwood, manager of the audit that Price Waterhouse was performing at Oil Well Supply Company, a division of U.S. Steel, one of the firm's clients.

It was an uplifting and wonderful experience to have been recommended to Price Waterhouse by the man I always considered to be my "second dad," and then, after being interviewed by the leading public accounting firm of the world, to be accepted for employment that very same day and given an enormous pay raise. And when I was ushered to my swivel seat in the lounge car of the Sunbeam, the SP's crack train between Houston and Dallas, the attendant asked what I would like to drink. I was flying high with both feet on the ground!

After introducing myself to Mr. Underwood and meeting the other members of the audit crew, I was told I could start by checking the bank account reconciliation previously prepared by employees of Oil Well Supply. Having just opened my very first personal bank account with my expense advance the previous day, I hardly knew what he meant—particularly when I saw the stacks of canceled checks lying all over the desk assigned to me. It took me a while, but I pretended the work was old hat and ultimately figured it all out. Over the next couple of years, I learned all the things they don't teach you in college business courses, became a senior accountant, ran audit jobs myself, got to share in the annual June 30 bonuses, and soon figured out that I more than earned the miserable salary they paid me. (Please note my change of attitude.) I even got to perform the annual audit of the I-GN records in Palestine for several years as the audit manager — the local-boy-makes-good angle.

By the last half of 1942, I was making just enough so that Juanice could quit her job, and that winter we spent three months living at the Pontchartrain Hotel on St. Charles Street in New Orleans while I was participating in audits of PW clients in the area. Besides paying for the hotel, the company covered all my meals. That was high living for a country boy, but since we had a suite with kitchenette, we fixed most of our own meals and used my accumulated meal allowances to go out on the town occasionally. One of our favorite places was a dark little bar down in the French Quarter where a great trio played: Al Hirt on trumpet, Pete Fountain on clarinet, and a good drummer whose name I can't remember. The horn players were quite a pair, with Al weighing at least 250 pounds standing alongside diminutive Pete. If somebody had told me then that thirty-eight years later I would be hiring Pete Fountain and his group to entertain my friends and business associates, I would have said they were nuts.

World War II interrupted my nascent career with PW in September 1943. I will be the first to admit that serving my country in the military did not excite me, but fortunately, since I was married and a bit older, the situation overseas had to get pretty bad before I was called up. I didn't volunteer until the draft board was breathing hard down my neck, and I only did so then to have a chance of selecting the branch of the military I would join. I tried for the Coast Guard, but they turned me down, saying that my poor eyesight would be a menace to navigation. I wound up as a buck-ass private in the engineers (Company D, 361st Engineer Regiment), but at least I avoided the infantry, where most of the draftees ended up.

From my very first day in the service, all I was ever looking for was an honorable discharge. I spent a year in training at Camp Claiborne in Monroe, Louisiana, and then shipped overseas during September 1944. Our outfit went over on the *New Amsterdam* of the Holland-America Line, unescorted. There were

10,000 GIs on that ship, which was designed for about 900, and Uncle Sam paid the ship's owners first-class fare of $1,000 for each of us. Our company slept in hammocks strung up on the port promenade deck, which had been only halfway closed off from the weather. The first day out, I played poker for almost twenty-four hours and made a couple of hundred dollars. Then I decided I should quit while I was ahead and sent the money to Juanice by Western Union from the ship's wireless room.

For the rest of the voyage, I sat around feeling sorry for myself, because I assumed I was going to get my ass shot off, and I got deathly seasick. I stayed sick for eight days, eating absolutely nothing, until one morning somebody said, "I see land!" It was the cliffs on the northern coast of Scotland, probably twenty-five miles away. The water was still just as rough as it had ever been, but instantaneously I was no longer seasick and felt so hungry I could have eaten a mule on the hoof. I decided right then that seasickness was strictly in the mind, and I have proved it over the past twenty years on my fifty-three-foot yacht, the *Holy Moses*, during which time I have never been seasick.

Leaving the ship in the Firth of Clyde, we boarded a troop train that took us overnight to Southampton, England. We crossed the English Channel to Omaha Beach, going ashore in landing craft that dropped their ramps in several feet of water, leaving us practically swimming to shore with full backpacks, gas masks, steel helmets, and M-1 rifles. We traversed that entire beach of deep sand, two steps forward while slipping back one, over to some trails that ascended to the crest of the tall cliffs that those jerks in HQ expected us to climb with all that equipment.

The further we went, the louder the cursing and complaining about our screwed-up army became. That is, until we neared the top of the cliff. The closer I got to it, the quieter things became up ahead of me. Then I saw why. As I stuck my head over the edge, I saw that there was nothing but white crosses, thousands of them, all the way to the horizon. D-Day had been only three months earlier. Nobody had anything to say for several hours after that experience. We bivouacked for the next forty-eight hours in an apple orchard, where we subsisted on C-rations and, of course, apples fixed every way imaginable, while we awaited trucks to transport us to our permanent assignment.

24

We spent the next few months maintaining the Red Ball Route, which was the road that supplies traveled to reach the front lines from the port of Cherbourg, France. Subsequent to that assignment, we moved our operation to the construction site of an army hospital near Reims, France. The duty I remember best during that period was hitching up a trailer to my jeep and making a run over to Épernay every Saturday morning to pick up a load of Mum's Champagne for the officers (less one bottle, of course, for me). Since duties of this sort were making no marked difference in the outcome of the war effort, and the Battle of the Bulge was underway, I and numerous others were transferred to fighting outfits in February 1945.

I joined a tank destroyer group located near Heidelberg, Germany, but was still well behind the front lines. Without once having seen an enemy tank, in early May of 1945 I finally got a three-day pass and went to Paris. While I was there, two events of some significance occurred: the Germans threw in the towel, and I got word that my first child had been born on May 11 at the Palestine Sanitarium on Neches Street in Palestine. Mother and daughter were doing just great. I had shipped out nine months earlier, the day after a rushed twenty-four-hour trip home from the training camp in Louisiana to see Juanice for what I feared might just be the last time. We had finally been successful in fertilizing the egg that became our first-born child, Linda Diane Muse.

In August 1945 our outfit was ordered to Marseilles so we could board a ship that would take us directly to the Pacific theater of operations for further wartime duty. Our company commander had appropriated a beautiful 1937 Mercedes-Benz, a four-door convertible touring sedan once used by high-ranking German officers, and I was assigned to drive him to Marseilles at the head of our convoy.

Just days before we were scheduled to leave Marseilles for the Pacific, we all wildly celebrated V-Day, hoping against hope that the Japanese surrender would mean we were going to go home rather than on to Japan. But the army remained firm; our unit was still destined for Japan to be a part of the occupation forces. However, fortunately for us, the navy transport on which all our equipment had been loaded was suddenly reassigned to Boston, Massachusetts. Since they couldn't retrieve our equipment without completely unloading the ship, our outfit was also reassigned stateside to ultimate discharge, rather than, at the minimum, a six-month stretch in Japan.

The afternoon our ship departed for home, I drove the Mercedes down the pier to the side of the navy transport. The company commander, staff officers, and I got out of that classic Mercedes and walked up the gangplank, just leaving her on the pier with the keys lying on the driver's seat. I have often wondered whatever became of that beautiful automobile. I returned to the States in October 1945 and got an immediate leave for thirty days. As it happened, the birthdate of our first-born child had been just one day before the cutoff to qualify for the twelve "discharge points" each dependent child was worth to servicemen returning stateside. So it seemed the gods were with me, and the army cut me loose. If my outfit's gear hadn't been so deep in the hold, or if Diane had been born one day later, I might have been in for another year or so. I had survived the war untouched.

In addition to the $200 salary Price Waterhouse paid me upon returning from the military in December 1945, I received $90 per month from Uncle Sam from the on-the-job training program that Congress made into law after World War II. At PW, this was a wonderful opportunity. I attended regularly scheduled classes every week, conducted by partners and managers, with a lot of homework. The course was designed to prepare all the returning veterans at PW for successful completion of the four-part Certified Public Accountant exam necessary for a state CPA professional license. I passed three of the four parts the first time I took them: accounting theory, accounting practice, and auditing. But I did not pass the easiest part — business law — until after I left PW.

After spending approximately five years in public accounting, a guy needs to make a decision as to whether he should stick with it and go for a partnership in a major firm or take his varied experience into commercial accounting. I was inclined to be an introvert, and a public accounting firm partner is expected to be a glad-hander, mix and mingle with the country club set, and bring in new business. That did not seem to be my cup of tea, so I spent my 1948 vacation looking for a position with opportunity and more money. Two positions were offered to me: comptroller of a large wholesale grocery concern in Houston or secretary-treasurer of a fledgling new airline. Trans-Texas Airways (TTA) had begun flight operations less than a year before, on October 11, 1947, flying a small fleet of DC-3 aircraft on three routes: Houston to San Antonio via Victoria, Houston to Dallas via Palestine, and Dallas to San Angelo via Fort Worth and Brownwood. I decided the airline job would be more fun and should have much more growth potential.

5. THE AIRLINE YEARS —

Trans-Texas Airways

When I joined Trans-Texas in July 1948, R. Earl McKaughan was controlling stockholder and president, Henry (Hank) Erdmann was VP-operations, Howard Whatley ran maintenance, Leon Hassler and Dick N. Richards shared the chief pilot duties, Phil Reid was VP-personnel, Harry Bradley handled purchasing and stores, and Cliff Ewens was VP-sales. I can't remember who headed up ground operations, but Bud Herring and Bill Franklin were the guys who made the operation tick.

Trans-Texas was one of fourteen so-called "local service carriers" certificated by the Civil Aeronautics Board (CAB) after World War II to serve smaller communities throughout the continental United States. The local service carriers' primary mission was to feed traffic to the "trunk" airlines from smaller cities not served by those major carriers. The idea was that they would be initially subsidized through "mail pay" administered by the CAB but actually paid by the U.S. Postal Service. The bureaucrats dreamed of the local service carriers someday reaching a state of self-sufficiency. (Like Amtrak. Ha!) The thirteen other carriers were, from east to west, Mohawk, Allegheny, Piedmont, Southern, Lake Central, North Central, Ozark, Central, Pioneer, Frontier, Bonanza, Pacific, and West Coast.

Mohawk, Lake Central, and then Piedmont were acquired by Allegheny (nicknamed "Agony"), which became the USAir Group. Ozark joined up with Trans World Airlines and then watched TWA swoon into bankruptcy as a result of its rape by Carl Ichan during the late 1980s, and its subsequent absorption by American Airlines. Jack Bradford, controlling stockholder of Central, sold out to RKO General, which owned control of Frontier, with Frontier being the surviving company. (Frontier itself had been an amalgamation of three smaller carriers named Monarch, Challenger, and Arizona airlines.) Frontier eventually also headed for the bankruptcy courts and was subsequently picked up by Texas Air, the holding company for Texas International — formerly Trans-Texas — and later Continental Airlines.

Pioneer bought Martin 202 equipment; when the CAB disallowed the additional operating cost of these larger planes, they had to sell out to Continental. The best thing acquired by Continental in that transaction was Pioneer's VP-sales, one Harding G. Lawrence, who became Continental's executive VP and then moved on to Braniff as president and CEO in 1965.

Bonanza, Pacific, and West Coast merged into a new company called Air West. Howard Hughes later purchased it, when he was buying up everything in Las Vegas, and renamed it Hughes Air West. When Hughes' fortunes turned sour, North Central bought the company, changed its name to Republic, added Southern to their stable, and then merged the whole shootin' match into Northwest Airlines.

In 1966 Earl McKaughan, still president and controlling shareholder of Trans-Texas (which by that time had acquired such nicknames as "Tree-Top" and "Teeter-Totter"), sold that company to a group headed by Carl Pohlad of Minneapolis, who changed the name to Texas International Airlines (TI). Pohlad and his then-manager, Frank Lorenzo, also bought up effective control of National Airlines and immediately unloaded it onto Pan American at a nice profit, then bought bankrupt Eastern Airlines (stripping the remaining meat off its bones as Ichan had done with TWA), and wound up buying Continental. They merged Continental into TI, but the company assumed Continental's good name. Thus, over a couple of decades the entire local service industry except for Trans-Texas, which is now

Continental, and USAir (Allegheny, Mohawk, Lake Central, and Piedmont), which is in bankruptcy, has disappeared either into the court system or into the bowels of a major trunk carrier.

In the fall of 1948, a few months after joining TTA, I had occasion to wonder whether I had made the right decision when the Civil Aeronautics Board issued an order instituting a proceeding (investigation) to determine if the agency should cancel the company's Certificate of Public Convenience and Necessity. This certificate authorized the granting of federal mail pay subsidies, and without it, the company would be out of business. The reason for the investigation? Low passenger response to the service being offered. TTA was the only local carrier ever issued such an order, but the investigation wound up favorable to the company, and as fate would have it, save for USAir, it is the only one still in business today, even though it's now called Continental.

In February 1949, by virtue of my passing the final business law portion of the CPA exam — having sat up most of the previous night digesting a high school business-law textbook — and becoming professionally licensed as a CPA, McKaughan gave me a 50 percent raise, from $400 per month to $600. My CPA license and raise were a direct result of the GI Bill and the expert tutelage our PW partners and managers had provided the returning veterans. I was now in high cotton and went out and bought my family a television set. It replaced the little round-screen Zenith set McKaughan had given me the previous Christmas when he had bought his family a new one. My favorite program at that time was John Daly's national news, a forerunner of *The Huntley-Brinkley Report*.

At TTA I saw my function and principal contribution as bringing about stringent cost control and making the most of the complicated subsidy initiatives administered by the mail-rate staff of the CAB. The CAB paid these subsidies in two ways — under a temporary rate order or a permanent rate order, and the entire local service industry strove to stay on temporary rates because this would guarantee that they would never have large losses. However, with the risk factor removed, they would never enjoy any meaningful profits, either.

TTA, however, badly needed to be able to operate in such a

manner as to maximize the positive effect of the subsidy program—in other words, get the most out of Uncle Sam under the regulations then in effect. Therefore, with the stringent cost and operating controls instituted after my arrival, we strove to operate under a permanent mail rate order on the assumption that we could beat the mutually agreed-upon forecasts presumed by a permanent rate order and thus make—or even exceed—the reasonable 12 percent return on invested capital incorporated into all permanent rate orders. As a result, of the total federal income taxes paid by the entire local service industry during the twelve-year period I was at TTA, we paid 95 percent thereof, with Pacific Airways in California paying the other 5 percent. All the others lost money.

TTA was continually involved in new route proceedings, and it fell to my lot to prepare the exhibits for filing with the CAB in support of our applications. These applications were presented to the CAB as "cases" with witnesses in much the same manner as a court case. Other carriers competing for the same route awards that we wanted were our adversaries. It was in connection with this responsibility that I came in close contact with people who broadened my perspective on life and career.

First was Jimmy Allred, former governor of Texas and later a federal judge, whom my dad and I had listened to when he made a campaign speech on the steps of the Anderson County Courthouse one fall evening in the early '30s. Although I was only a child then, he impressed me as a good and honest man, and I was proud that my father voted for him. When I joined TTA, he was the company's general counsel and, of course, was our legal representative at the hearings. I spent many hours with him, explaining our objectives in the case and the exhibits supporting those objectives, both before and during hearings and oral argument.

Earl McKaughan always judged a set of exhibits by how many volumes it took to contain them and their total depth in inches when stacked on a table. I, on the other hand, was a guy who always got right to the point, explained what I wanted, why I wanted it, and what I would do with it if I had it. I could, therefore, present the whole rate or route case before the CAB with a dozen pages or so. Since this was not to McKaughan's liking, Judge Allred helped me out by introducing me to an old friend of his in Austin, Dr. Bob Montgomery, head of the economics department at the University of Texas. Bob was capable of writing hundreds of pages about the cities and towns we proposed to serve and the historic significance of the routes by which we proposed to serve them, and that was how we satisfied Earl McKaughan's criteria for a good set of exhibits. When Bob would get on the stand to support his work, I would promise a free dinner to opposing counsel to get them not to just pass the witness but to ask him a couple of leading questions. That way he could expound and feel as though he was earning his fee for appearing as our witness.

Jimmy Allred was rather liberal, and Bob Montgomery was radically liberal, and some of their liberalism rubbed off on me. Bob was so liberal, in fact, that there were members of the Texas legislature who wanted him fired from the University of Texas system. And one day, when the university was under discussion on the floor of the Senate, one outraged senator was relating what he had supposedly heard Bob—who wore his hair extremely long and full—say the previous Saturday morning at a local Austin barbershop. The good senator was interrupted by another member who claimed a point of order. The story could not possibly be true, he said, because Bob Montgomery had never been in a barbershop during his entire life. After great applause, the matter under discussion was tabled.

When Harry Truman nominated Jimmy Allred to be a federal judge for South Texas in Corpus Christi, he had to close his law office, but he made two wonderful recommendations to the company. First, he proposed that we take in his young and handsome assistant, Jack K. Ayer, as our VP-legal, and second, that we retain a young, upcoming, brilliant, and very handsome Austin attorney named John B. Connally as our outside counsel to represent us in all future route cases.

I am not an attorney and have never studied the subject any more than just enough to pass the business-law portion of the CPA exam, but I have always felt that I was a better lawyer than nine out of ten of those who hang their shingles (and hide behind them). Only three lawyers with whom I have had a close working relationship fall outside of that heap. The first is John B. Connally, TTA's general counsel from the early to late fifties, when John decided to go full time with Sid Richardson in Fort Worth. This was before he ran for governor of Texas. The second is Herbert D. Kelleher, my general counsel at Southwest Airlines from its beginning until my departure from that company in 1978. The third is Jack Hauer of Akin, Gump, Strauss, Hauer & Feld, whom we retained to represent Southwest before U.S. District Judge William M. Taylor Jr. in the Love Field case. All three had the ability to quickly understand and analyze a problem and come up with the brilliant defense it required.

I remember one evening, probably in 1953, while John Connally, Bob Montgomery, and I were having dinner, talking to them about a concept that pricked their interest. I pointed out to them how many different credit cards we all had in our pocketbooks — an average of two oil company cards, four or five department store cards, a long-distance calling card, and often two or three fancy restaurant credit cards, plus, of course, our Air Travel Cards. Why didn't somebody issue a single card that would eliminate all those individual cards? They could charge a small annual fee for the issuance of the card and retain a percentage of each charge equal to the vendors' actual internal cost of handling the original charge and subsequent collection. The profit would come from the economy of scale that one would realize from combining the thousands of different credit centers into one organization, plus the float that could be maintained in the payment schedule. John was particularly excited about the idea; unfortunately, we were all so damn busy that we let it slide. A couple of years later, here comes Diners Club, followed by American Express, MasterCard, and Visa. Another good idea down the drain.

During my twelve TTA years, I devoted almost all my time to my career and very little to my family, even though it had grown by two. Our second child, and only son, was born September 29, 1949. We chose to name him Michael Lamar. I wouldn't name anyone "Marion," which is my first name. Eighteen months later to the day, Deborah Ann (Debbie) was born on March 29, 1951. She was known to tell everybody she met, "My Mommy and Daddy didn't ask for me, but now they wouldn't take a million bucks for me." Juanice was a wonderful mother, and it fell to her lot to do most of the child-rearing. About the only rest she got from the kids was on Saturday mornings when I would take them with me to the office. They would attack the Marchant calculators and Underwood adding machines, and they loved to play with the IBM punch-card machines, which made small rectangular holes in pasteboard cards that had one corner cut off so you could see if one got turned upside down or backward in a stack. The cards were used to enter transactions into the IBM tabulating machines, which predated modern computers — a primitive form of today's "memory." When the office force would show up on Monday mornings, they always knew who had been there over the weekend.

By 1960 Trans-Texas had long since proved its right to stay in business; it had grown from three DC-3s to thirty, and we decided that the time had come to acquire larger planes to handle the traffic being generated and to be generated. The only thing available that we felt financially comfortable acquiring was used equipment from the trunk lines. For several reasons we decided that we should go after the Convair 240, which was being phased out by American Airlines. It was a superior aircraft to the competing Martin 404 used for the sort of routes and load factors we had at TTA, and it could be obtained at a much lower capital cost than more recent Convair models then available. The clincher was my close association with Charlie Oursler, who was the American Airlines officer responsible for disposition of surplus aircraft. At the time, I was president of the Airline Finance and Accounting Conference of the Air Transport Association, largely because Charlie Oursler had promoted me for that honor. We had a mutual admiration society going.

McKaughan appointed Jack Ayer, our VP-legal, and me to go to New York and negotiate a deal for up to twenty-five of American's Convair 240s, with staggered deliveries. We spent the better part of two days negotiating with Charlie, covering arrangements for spare parts, engines, and propellers, and coming to a handshake on a price of $200,000 per aircraft with spare equipment. We were overjoyed, because when we left Houston we had figured we were going to have to pay up to $250,000 per plane. I told Charlie we would be back the next morning to sign a letter of intent after clearing it by phone with McKaughan that evening as a formality and courtesy. He had given us the authority to negotiate the best deal we could, and we certainly felt we had done that.

Jack and I decided we would celebrate with cocktails and a fine dinner at the Waldorf. But first we rushed to our hotel room to call our boss to give him the good news. His response?

"Well, come on home, boys. That's just not good enough."

"Excuse me, what did you say?"

"You heard me. Come on home!"

Instead of going out to dinner, we just sat in the room and got drunker than skunks. I was ashamed to go back to American's offices the next morning, so I just called Charlie and told him what had happened, and we headed back to Houston on the next flight. On the way back I decided that my integrity would not permit me to be a party to such shenanigans, so upon arrival at my office I dictated my letter of resignation to my secretary and had it hand-delivered to McKaughan. I knew he would be hard-pressed to find a better deal than the one we had negotiated. Sure enough, the following week he sent Jack back to New York alone and they signed a deal with some insignificant adjustment; neither Jack nor I can even remember at this late date what it was. It was just a token gesture by American to be done with the matter.

6. THE AIRLINE YEARS —

Path to American Airlines

I left TTA on June 30, 1960, after the Convair fiasco, not knowing what was coming next. Almost immediately, I got a contract to do a marketing study for Fairchild Aircraft in Hagerstown, Maryland. My mission was to find out why they were not selling more of their F-27 aircraft to the local service carriers. These relatively modern, high-wing, forty-passenger aircraft, powered by the Rolls Royce Dart turboprop engine, were only being used by three of the fourteen local service carriers: Piedmont, Bonanza, and West Coast. At Trans-Texas we had never seriously considered the airplane because of its high capital and operating costs on our short routes. Additionally, the data that Fairchild presented to the carriers left much to be desired with regard to payload capability. I couldn't do anything for Fairchild relative to capital and operating costs, but I did design a presentation that showed the aircraft in a much better light from the standpoint of payload. In other words, it was not nearly as bad as it appeared. I can't claim that my redesign of the presentation got them any new sales. Probably, like most other consultant fees, it was just money down the drain.

Immediately thereafter, I spent a month in Las Vegas installing the same cost control system for Bonanza Airlines that I had so successfully developed and used at TTA. Then I consulted with the Conference of Local Service Airlines in Washington on a new concept to pay the carriers' subsidies by what would be called a "class rate," which would be a permanent, as opposed to temporary, rate for the entire local service industry. While I was in Washington on the class rate project, the hangar at Hobby Airport in Houston, in which Trans-Texas general offices were housed, caught fire and burned to the ground as a result of a fuel tank explosion across the street. I was glad there was a known cause; otherwise they might have suspected me.

I heard that my friend Charlie Oursler was looking for me. He wanted me to come to American, at that time the nation's largest airline, as assistant VP-planning, to install the airline's very first long-range planning group, a recommendation to the company by its management consultants, McKinsey & Company. Charlie's boss, executive VP-finance Bill Hogan, and I agreed on a starting salary of $20,000 per year beginning October 1, 1960. I set out for New York City.

Charlie lived in Westport, Connecticut, and commuted into NYC on the New Haven Railroad every day. With our three children, that seemed to be the right location for us, too. In the village of Greens Farms I took a one-year lease on a nineteenth-century carriage house that had been converted into a home. It sat on two acres of landscaped grounds, with a pond (frozen over in winter) and creek in the back yard.

The three kids and I drove to Connecticut from Houston in our new 1960 Ford convertible, giving Juanice a much-needed rest as we made our way north. We picked her up at Idlewild (now John F. Kennedy) Airport on a snowy Sunday morning in early November and drove to our new home in Greens Farms, stopping first at the local service station for gas. As the owner of the station was cleaning the windshield, Juanice lowered her window and asked the nice gentleman in her pleasing Texas drawl, "Do y'all sell snow tires?" The man threw his chamois up in the air with a flourish and replied, "Sho nuff, honey, we sell

37

snow tires." Without blinking an eye, Juanice said right back to him, "Well, how much is *four* of them?" With that exchange, we were introduced to winter in the Northeast. Incidentally, we did buy and have installed two new snow tires. A few months later I was telling this story to three American officers with whom I was having lunch. I remarked that I didn't have a Texas accent like Juanice did, whereupon three loud hoots came from the group.

We soon found the insulation in that very old carriage house to be totally inadequate, and only a tremendous amount of heating oil kept us from freezing to death—a new experience for us. And it didn't take but a couple months of commuting—with Juanice having to drive me to the station at 6:45 A.M. and pick me up when I got off the 6:25 P.M. one-stop express from the city back to Greens Farms—for me to confide to her that if I believed for one minute I would have to live like that for the rest of my life, I just might seriously consider suicide. Having to wait all week for Saturday and Sunday just to spend time with my kids was not for me.

It also didn't take me long to realize that it was a hell of a lot more fun to be a big fish in a little pond than a little fish in a big pond. I was never really able to do very much relative to long-range planning at American, because Bill Hogan had a war going on with Marion Sadler, executive VP-marketing, and Hogan drafted me as his point man in this war. The real problem was that some of the people in Sadler's camp, namely Mel Brenner, VP-schedules, and his right-hand man, Earl Ditmars, came up with what I thought were the dumbest ideas for operating an airline that I ever heard. Hogan and I lost most of our internal battles to Sadler's camp after C. R. Smith, American's president, decided to restructure the company's executive leadership; while continuing to serve as chairman of the board and CEO, he gave up the presidency to Sadler. But we gave them a good fight nevertheless, and time proved us to be right on all counts.

American had a bad habit of ordering twenty-five of just about every transport aircraft model introduced without too much thought beforehand. Some were good buys. But some were not, such as the Convair 990, the BAC 111-400, the Boeing 727-100, the Boeing 720, and worst of all, the Boeing 747-100.

The Convair 990, with its streamlined, narrow body, was a slightly faster and quieter design than competing models, but it would not permit six-abreast seating, thus ensuring higher seat-mile costs than comparable Boeing and Douglas equipment. Brenner and Ditmars' answer to that problem was a plan to use the 990 primarily as a first-class airplane with four-abreast seating. But these first-class seats would not be as wide and comfortable as in the competition's luxury section. Having virtually all-first-class seating also meant that it would be nearly impossible to interchange the aircraft when necessary with others in the fleet. American finally decided to reduce its initial order, and the airplanes for which delivery had been accepted were put on the market for resale while still practically brand-new.

The powers at American ordered the BAC 111-400s to replace their old Convair 240s, many of which had been bought by TTA. They also ordered highly inefficient Boeing 727-100s, strictly because the flight department over at Eastern Airlines had unwisely convinced their management to order that airplane. Pilots loved it, of course, because it performed like a fighter plane and plowed up runways. At American, the finance and planning departments were encouraging Boeing, through Dan Palmer, our sales representative there, to speed up introduction of their planned two-engine 737, a real short-haul beauty, in lieu of committing the assembly line to more of these three-engine 727-100s, until they could perfect the vastly superior 727-200, a stretched version of the earlier model that made great economic sense. However, the 727-200 was still on the drawing boards awaiting the development of more powerful Pratt & Whitney engines, as was the 737, which would have been the perfect replacement for the Convair 240s and would have been preferable to the 727-100, as well. But Boeing had a backlog of orders from Eastern and Pan American and was hell-bent on turning out 727-100s. This decision permitted Douglas to steal the entire market for short-haul jet aircraft for a full decade with the DC-9-10, -30, and -50 models.

The Boeing 720 was the same story. It was nothing but a 707 with a section cut out of the fuselage and, consequently, thirty fewer seats. It would fly farther than the 707, but range wasn't a problem on any of American's domestic routes, so they were just stuck with twenty-five less-efficient aircraft. The Boeing 747-100 was the reverse of this story. It came long after I had left American, and once again, they ordered twenty-five of them without any conception of how in the world they were going to utilize them. In stage lengths of 2,500 miles or less, the airplane's seat-mile costs were no lower than the smaller-capacity Douglas DC-8-60 series operated by other carriers. Therefore, to operate them profitably on the vast majority of American's routes, they either had to generate twice as many passengers per flight or cut the number of actual flights operated in a given market by at least 50 percent, forcing passengers to deal with a less convenient schedule. The first scenario was impossible at the regulated fares American (and other airlines) had to charge; the market simply could not be expanded. The second was highly undesirable because it would definitely lose traffic to the competition, which could offer convenience to passengers through higher frequency. As a result, those 747s went up for sale at bargain-basement prices long before American even took delivery of the last white elephant of their twenty-five-plane order.

The really big internal fight while I was at American, however, was over the company's response to Eastern Airlines' establishment of their revolutionary hourly, no-reserved-seat shuttle between Washington, New York's LaGuardia Airport, and Boston. Eastern guaranteed that any passenger who showed up in time to board any scheduled shuttle flight would be accommodated without waiting another hour for the next shuttle, even if the plane was fully loaded. For just one overflow passenger, Eastern would immediately put another plane and crew into service to honor the guarantee. Positioning extra aircraft and paying standby crews to fly them at three different airports just to back up the guarantee could quickly eat up the potential profits from such an innovative service.

It was the belief on our side of American's executive offices that, instead of duplicating Eastern's guaranteed-seat shuttle, we would be better advised to offer the same hourly service but give a free seat on the next flight to any passenger whom we could not accommodate. To the extent that we could forecast certain hours or days when flights might end up substantially "oversold," we could position equipment and crews to handle those overflow passengers profitably. But at borderline times, we would simply offer free, guaranteed seats on the next flight to the few passengers we could not accommodate. Many passengers would be businessmen on expense accounts and would have little interest in saving money, rather than time, with our free-seat offer, but invariably we would have passengers paying their own way who would jump at the chance to get their fare returned and arrive at their destination just one hour later than originally planned. We figured that enough of those folks would give up their seats in exchange for a refund in order to satisfy the expense-account crowd. This clever scheme was akin to the way airlines today handle intentional "overselling" of flights, which sometimes have a lower "no-show" factor than contemplated, forcing gate agents to offer passengers special compensation so they will relinquish seats in favor of others.

However, the marketing staff thought this was a stupid idea. They felt the only way American could keep shuttle-market passengers from flocking to Eastern was to offer a fancier product. Their vision of such a product was a first-class meal for every passenger, with linen, fine wines, and desert on each and every flight, be it mealtime, midmorning service, cocktail hour, or even late evening. These first-class meals and beverages for shuttle-market passengers would be served graciously on a flight that was at cruising altitude for no more than fifteen minutes. In the first place, it was impossible. What's more, it was imprudent. The passengers did not want it, it was expensive—and it was just stupid. Ninety days after instituting this new service, American abandoned the two highest-volume routes in the nation to Eastern entirely, because the load factor percentages on the routes were running in the 20s; with the expensive meals they were serving, American needed to be running in the 80s. The routes were simply handed to Eastern on a silver platter.

Struggles of this kind, in which I had to sit by and watch the organization do great damage to itself like a person bent on self-mutilation, were fast instilling in me a burning desire to run my own show. Otherwise, I feared I was going to be eaten up by stomach ulcers. In the end it was these pitched battles (which for the most part were so damn stupid), together with the daily commute from Greens Farms, that made my mind up for me. In

October 1961 I walked into Bill Hogan's office and told him I was fed up with American Airlines and New York City and wanted to resign. His response was, "I can understand that, but you can't leave until you find a replacement satisfactory to me." Knowing that my good friend John Eichner, who was still running marketing down in Houston for TTA, was very unhappy with his situation, I was on the phone to him within the hour. I knew that, even though his experience was as a salesman, he had a great analytical mind (almost as good as mine!).

I told John to get his tail up to New York, that I was going to liberate him from the mess he was participating in down there and introduce him to an even bigger mess in New York, but with lots more money. He came, he interviewed, and he took over my position, concurrent with the end of my one-year lease on the Greens Farms house. I moved my family back to Houston, intending to spend the winter there, but by January 1962 I was heading to Atlanta to become VP-finance of Southern Airways, the local service airline then serving the southeastern section of the United States.

It was only a few years later that Marion Sadler resigned as president of American, publicly stating that his reason for leaving was one John Eichner. When John learned that C. R. Smith was pleading with Sadler to return, he knew that his days were numbered, so he accepted a management position with the aviation-consulting firm of Simat & Helliesen, which thereafter was named Simat, Helliesen & Eichner. Which just goes to show that I picked a good man for Bill Hogan.

7. THE AIRLINE YEARS —

Southern Gentlemen

Southern's top management consisted of Frank Hulse, president and founder of the company; Graydon Hall, VP-marketing; Bill McGill, VP-operations; and myself as VP-finance. Although we were all roughly the same age, I was the only one who could hardly be considered a "southern gentleman." They had all been born and raised in the Deep South and played the part, speaking with southern drawls, always acting exceedingly gracious, avoiding controversy at all costs, and never making tough decisions without a degree of compromise.

When I joined the company, Southern had been experiencing a bitter strike by the Airline Pilots Association (ALPA) for over two years, and replacement pilots were being picketed at every major city served by the company. A few months after my arrival, and the day before ALPA's annual meeting in Miami, the company received an order from the Civil Aeronautics Board: The airline must resolve the labor controversy within the next thirty days or face revocation of its Certificate of Public Convenience and Necessity — no ifs, ands, or buts.

I began to think I was snake-bit. Two certificate-revocation proceedings had been instituted during the entire history of commercial aviation, and in both cases I had just been employed by the affected company a few months beforehand. In this case, because of the entrenched hostility between the parties, it was left up to the company's attorney and me to meet with the displaced ALPA pilot group and arrange some kind of agreement.

The bitterest part of the bargaining was what was to become of the non-ALPA replacement pilots who had saved the company from disaster, apparently just for the future benefit of the striking pilots. The result was not a happy one. The original pilot group reassumed their former positions on the seniority list as of the date of the strike, and the replacement pilots were slotted into that list based on their seniority with the company. Since the company had actually grown substantially during the period of the strike and many of the striking pilots had taken jobs elsewhere, we could take the remaining strikers back and still keep all but the very lowest-seniority replacement pilots.

However, we now had former first officers who had not flown in more than two years suddenly being able to bid on the captain's seat while current, experienced captains had to accept jobs as first officers. The training and retraining costs to properly qualify all pilots for the duties each would now be performing was a major cost factor for the company, only partially offset by the complete capitulation of the union on pay and benefit issues. In fact, the ALPA pilots came back to work on the exact terms that were offered by the company at the time they went out on strike some two years earlier, with no retroactive pay or accrued seniority for the strike period whatsoever.

My family stayed in Houston throughout that winter, with me flying home every weekend. Then, at the end of the school year, we purchased a two-story home on a secluded cul-de-sac on Beverly Lane in north Atlanta and made the move in early June 1962, with the full intention of raising our three children in that beautiful city and spending the rest of our lives there. We joined the Cherokee Town and Country Club, bought the kids a beautiful black Tennessee walking horse, and found Juanice a black poodle, which we named Tia for "Tia Maria," a libation that she favored.

My three-plus years at Southern were generally very pleasant, as Frank, Graydon, and Bill were all such consummate southern gentlemen, but from time to time I was somewhat frustrated because the group was anything but aggressive. We could have acquired two new routes opened up by the CAB but let these opportunities pass us by. One, through North and South Carolina from Atlanta, was ceded to Piedmont Airlines without a whimper, just because Frank Hulse and Tom Davis, president of Piedmont, were good friends. The other, across southern Louisiana from New Orleans to Houston, was lost to TTA because they wouldn't let me fight for it.

By the time I arrived at Southern, the CAB had instituted the "class rate" for the local service industry along the lines I had recommended as a consultant to the Conference of Local Service Airlines after I left TTA. As opposed to the temporary and permanent individual carrier rates previously in effect, this was a permanent rate order for the entire local service industry. It was based on several factors, each with a monetary value—such as plane-miles, available seat-miles, number of daily/weekly departures, passengers enplaned, and revenue passenger miles—that was applicable to all thirteen remaining carriers, Pioneer having been previously merged with Continental. Thus, the entire industry would be on the same rate-structure formula until such time as changing conditions made revisions and establishment of a new class rate necessary. The trick was to understand precisely the workings of the class rate order and gear your carrier's operation (primarily frequencies between various points on the system) to maximize your subsidy payment and net income. Together, we at Southern did a good job and, beginning in 1962, converted the company's historic losses or minimal profits to the highest return on investment in the industry.

In early 1964 Jack Bradford, a wealthy oilman from Midland, Texas, who had recently bought control of Central Airlines, headquartered in Fort Worth, Texas, contacted me to see if I would come to Central as number-two man there. He already had a president for the airline. Since I had little confidence in the man who would be my boss, I turned it down, but it got me to thinking that I was ready for a top position, and if it didn't come within a year at Southern, I would be ready to move on. That meant that I needed to bring in a person under me who could, in a reasonably short time, take over my responsibilities as VP-finance and CFO. An executive-search firm in Chicago lined up five applicants for me to interview in Chicago one day. One of them was the perfect applicant: Tom Grojean, a senior accountant in the Chicago office of my old employer, Price Waterhouse. He was a good Catholic, married with three children and one in the hangar, obviously quick, aggressive, decisive, and very intelligent. Just what the doctor ordered for slow, sleepy Southern.

I had Tom fly down to Atlanta to meet our management team and just look around. All the officers seemed to like him. Then our VP-personnel took him downtown to meet the company psychiatrist (whom I had never heard of before), apparently to take some tests. Before he returned to Chicago that same afternoon, we agreed that he would give two weeks' notice to PW and move his family to Atlanta. The next morning, after Tom had given notice, our VP-personnel called me to say that I would not be able to hire the applicant, since the psychiatrist had rejected him. I said, "What the hell are you talking about? I've already hired him, and he has given his employer two weeks' notice."

"Well, I'm sorry, but that is the way it is."

I immediately went to Frank Hulse's office to get the matter resolved. To my utter amazement, Frank sided with the VP-personnel, saying we were paying the good doctor a fancy fee and we just had to follow his advice. It seemed the doctor had turned Tom down for the very reasons I hired him: he was too smart, aggressive, and decisive. The doctor didn't think Tom's personality would fit with the Southern Airways culture. I tried to explain to Frank that this was exactly what Southern needed a shot of. His only response was to let him think about it. I immediately called Tom, told him the problem, and asked him to try and extend the notice period from two weeks to "indefinite." The PW partners were more than happy to oblige, as they were very upset about losing Tom anyway, and this might give them a chance to retain him.

After two weeks with no decision from Frank, I told him we just had to do something right away. He suggested that we have Tom fly to Birmingham, Alabama, and be interviewed by an industrial psychologist he knew named Dr. James Tanner, as long as we could agree in advance that his decision would be binding on us both. I said fine and sent Tom to Birmingham the next day. About 4:00 P.M. I got a call from Dr. Tanner, whom I had never met. He said, "I guess I don't understand the problem, Mr. Muse. Why are y'all not hiring this guy if you need him?" After only a few minutes' conversation with him, Dr. Tanner knew that Tom was exactly what Southern Airways management group needed. I told him to please hang up, call Frank immediately, and say exactly the same thing to him. Two weeks later, Tom and his family were in Atlanta in time for Christmas in their new home. After that incident, I never quite had the respect for my boss that I should have had, and I was very excited when Jack Bradford called again, this time offering me the job of president and CEO of Central Airlines. I accepted effective May 1, 1965.

During the next two years, my choice for Southern's new comptroller, Tom Grojean, made such a reputation in the industry as Southern's chief financial officer that he was offered the position of comptroller at Flying Tiger Airlines in Los Angeles with a 100 percent increase in salary. While working for them, he negotiated Flying Tiger's purchase of National Tank Car Company, which had its headquarters in Chicago. The company then sent him back to Chicago to run the new subsidiary at a salary twelve times what he had been making when he left Chicago to join Southern. Sometime later he was called back to Los Angeles to be president of Flying Tiger. This was the man who hadn't been good enough to work for Southern Airways, according to the company's high-priced psychiatrist. Since that time, I haven't had much respect for psychiatrists, except for one of my very best friends, Dr. Ben Dlin, my "Jewish psychiatrist from Philadelphia," who knows what he's talking about. Incidentally, his book, entitled *Country Doctor*, was published in October 2000 in a hardback edition.

8. THE AIRLINE YEARS —

Yippee, Number One!

On the morning of May 1, 1965, Jack Bradford, the controlling stockholder and chairman of the board of Central Airlines, accompanied me to Central's corporate headquarters at Greater Southwest Airport, which was operated by the City of Fort Worth but was located midway between Fort Worth and Dallas. He introduced me to the assembled officers and top supervisors of the company, all of whom were, I'm sure, as wary of me as I was of them. They were probably also very concerned about their jobs. I was not an accomplished public speaker at this stage of my life—nor am I now for that matter—but at least I have every confidence that I know more about my subject than does my audience.

Nervous as I was, I reviewed my background for them, told them I understood the precarious condition the company was in—large losses with the stock trading at $1.50 per share—but that I had yet to be associated with an airline that was not the top producer and profit-maker of the industry. As number one at Central, as opposed to number two or three at Southern and Trans-Texas, I assured them that with their help I was going to be president of the very best and most profitable local service carrier in the industry or bust a gut trying.

I announced that two new senior officers would be joining the company as soon as they completed commitments to their present employers. They were Bob Sicard, then the head of the Federal Aviation Administration's (FAA) training school in Oklahoma City, and Bud Herring, a VP at TTA in Houston. Both would be in the office of the president, with Sicard being responsible for flight, dispatch, and maintenance operations, and Herring having responsibility for in-flight service and all ground operations. Central's Harold Salfen would continue as VP-sales, with direct responsibility for all marketing and sales activity systemwide. Additionally, Chet Lundstrom would continue in the position of treasurer, with responsibility for all accounting, budgeting, tax, and insurance matters. I explained that Sicard and Herring would be pretty much running their own show, but that I planned to be in Salfen and Lundstrom's faces much more than they would probably like because we had some major hurdles to overcome in all phases of our marketing program, with particular reference to pricing. Additionally, within the next thirty days I wanted an operating budget for cost control similar to the one I had created so successfully at TTA and Southern.

I further told the group that Central was held in low regard by the rest of the industry, by the cities and states the company operated in, and by present and potential customers. It was not something they particularly liked hearing, but they knew it to be the truth. As the first step in restoring the company to profitability, I felt it essential to invest the funds necessary to give the corporation an entirely new image. To begin the transformation, I had retained Ernest G. Mantz Associates of Dallas to put a new face on Central, with a new logo, new paint design on all flight and ground equipment, new uniforms for employees, and even new stationery. Since the company's advertising dollars were, in my opinion, being largely wasted, new advertising agencies would be asked to submit proposals. We would consider and apply for new routes, and we would make major schedule changes designed to complement the class-subsidy rate currently in effect. We would immediately start pushing the refurbished Convair 600 turboprop aircraft scheduled to arrive in the next few months, and for at least the next six months they could forget about eight-hour days and five-day weeks. I set our six-month goal as being solidly profitable, carrying at least 25 percent more passengers, and getting financial recognition by at least tripling the market price of our stock.

The next morning when I arrived at the office, I was pleased to see the employee parking lot a whole lot fuller than it had been the previous morning. Things were already beginning to move at a faster pace. I spent most of the second day interviewing young ladies to be my private secretary. I settled on a bright, quick-witted, sharp-tongued young woman named Dorothy Burke, who was married to an Arlington, Texas, detective and had no children. We found we were very much alike: both result-oriented and always eager to get on to the next task or project. I only had one problem with her over the two-plus years I was at Central. She hated to file. She always eventually produced what I had asked for from the files, but it sometimes took longer than seemed reasonable. I used to accuse her of having only two files: an in-file and an out-file. I was never convinced that this wasn't the case.

After getting things moving the first week, I took a couple of days to find living quarters for my family, who were planning to join me as soon as school was out in Atlanta the following month. I settled on a lovely home in north Dallas that had been on the market by the builder for nearly a year. Located on a corner lot at 3705 Shadycliff, one block from the Northwood Country Club, it had four bedrooms, five and a half baths (his-and-hers baths in the master suite, no less), a nice-sized entry, living and dining rooms, a big den, a kitchen with breakfast area, a double garage, extensive landscaping, and a circular driveway. It was half as big again as our home in Atlanta and just beautiful. We made a deal to buy it for $56,000 with only $6,000 down. Juanice and the three kids were thrilled and could hardly wait for school to be out. My friends Clyde Skeen, executive VP of Ling-Temco-Vought, and Dick Richards, former chief pilot at TTA and now one of the larger home builders in the Northwood Addition, sponsored me for a membership in the Northwood Club, and we actually had that membership before the summer was over. Not that I had any time to enjoy it, but Juanice and the kids sure put it to good use.

It quickly became apparent that Harold Salfen was extremely loyal to the founder and original president of Central Airlines, Keith Kayle, who was no longer a supporter of the company, despite his substantial minority stock-holdings. I could understand Harold's divided loyalties but could not tolerate that kind of situation, and it was mutually agreed that he should go on to other ventures, which he did very successfully as a travel agent. Dick Elliott, a young man from Mohawk Airlines in New York, who was full of piss and vinegar and anxious to run his own show, was exactly the kind of person I was looking for to replace Salfen as VP-sales. So Elliott and I made a deal, at which time things started popping and heads rolling in that area of the operation. Chet Lundstrom, our treasurer, was a hard-working, solid citizen who in the past had just lacked supervision; I was more than willing to provide it, and he turned out to be a valuable officer.

When I got into the books and financial situation of the company, I found mass disorder. Things were even worse than they had appeared to be when I arrived. As a result, one of the first things I did was terminate Central's public accountants, Arthur Young & Co., and replace them with my accounting alma mater, Price Waterhouse. First we got control of our costs by determining the where and why of all spending with a lot of "nos" thrown in, did some rescheduling to maximize the benefits of the CAB's new subsidy class-rate order, and instituted the new corporate-image program as expeditiously as possible. Tracy Locke was selected to create and produce our advertising.

I visited most cities we served in Texas, Oklahoma, Arkansas, Missouri, Kansas, and Colorado, trying to find the cause of the poor traffic we suffered. I talked with travel agents, chambers of commerce, civic groups, and business clubs. As had been the case at both TTA and Southern, most Central passengers flew just one or at most two flight legs, such as Dallas to Fort Smith, Arkansas, or Dallas to Fayetteville, Arkansas, via Fort Smith—routes on which we experienced little or no competition other than the private automobile. But on longer hauls, such as Dallas to St. Louis or Kansas City, routes also served by the trunk carriers offering nonstop flights, we had hardly any business, as would be expected.

As a result of what I learned on my tour of the system, we

made more schedule changes and instituted a new, systemwide roundtrip fare that equaled the one-way fare between any two points on the system plus a flat $10. This had the effect of dramatically reducing the fare per-mile flown as the distance between the points of origin and destination increased, and when it caught on, with the help of our systemwide advertising, the passenger loads began a steady climb. We gained a good number of new long-haul passengers from Little Rock or St. Louis on the east, for example, to Denver on the west, even with as many as four or five stops along the way. For people who thought more of their pocketbooks than their time, the lower fare made the extra stops worthwhile. As expected, business travelers continued to opt for the convenience of the trunk carriers' nonstop flights, since they weren't paying the bill. Most of the passengers handled by local service airlines had interline tickets connecting them to or from the major long-haul trunk carriers at terminal points. What we were doing with our innovative roundtrip fare, which was not available for interline traffic, substantially increased our internally generated business, but it still represented less than half our total passenger revenues.

I had wanted to try this "plus $10" concept at both Trans-Texas and Southern, but the legal and marketing people insisted that the CAB would never approve a tariff filing that infringed on the trunk carriers' territory. I had never been able to get across to them that it wouldn't infringe; it would just create new business that was now going by private automobile, bus, or not at all. Paradoxically, in today's world the highly restricted, advance-purchase roundtrip tickets that are available on a limited basis at fares even lower than regular one-way fares are the offspring of our original concept of one-way plus $10 with no restrictions.

In 1965 Central turned its first profit in some years. But about this time there was an extended strike by American Airlines pilots, which shut that company down for several weeks, and since a high percentage of our interline traffic connected to American, our loads went to pot. However, within days we were able to dedicate two of our newly acquired Convair 600s to the military charter market, primarily carrying reserves from their hometowns to their summer training camps. Selfishly, we hated to see the strike end, because those two airplanes were producing more profits in charter service for the military's summer encampments than they ever did in scheduled service.

Fortunately for me, I remembered sometime during the spring of 1966 that on June 21 Juanice and I would be celebrating our silver wedding anniversary. I really wanted to do something special for that momentous occasion, as I needed to offset the many hours and days I had been away trying to make a mink coat out of the sow's ear that Central had been for so long. After swearing Dorothy to secrecy, the planning started. We decided on a whole weekend of activities, beginning at 6:00 P.M. on Friday at the Lancers Club atop the LTV Tower in downtown Dallas for cocktails, dinner, and dancing until the place closed. On Saturday, guests could play golf or tennis at the Northwood Club or go shopping. Saturday evening, we would serve cocktails and steaks with all the trimmings at our house on Shadycliff Drive. Sunday morning, everybody would come back for bloody marys and a beautifully served catered brunch before departing for home. The weekend was a total surprise to Juanice and gained me many brownie points. The guests included our closest friends from every part of the country. We were flattered that every person invited was in attendance.

My time at Central was particularly good for my health and my mental attitude. The stomach ulcers I had developed while working for Southern just seemed to disappear after I arrived at Central. A couple of months later, I had forgotten I ever had them. This convinced me that it is not what you eat that causes ulcers, it is what is eating you. However, my officers at Central kidded me by saying that I had just passed my ulcers over to them.

In 1966 Central reported the highest return on invested capital of any of the remaining thirteen local service carriers. But apparently we had done our job too well for our own good, because in early 1967 Jack Bradford advised me that he was going to sell his majority ownership in the company. He got $14 cash per share—quite an improvement on the $1.50 at which the company's shares had been trading when I arrived on the scene some two years earlier. The buyer was RKO General Corporation, which also owned control of Frontier Airlines. Frontier was headquartered in Denver and was very eager to enter the Dallas–Fort Worth market.

The merger was effective as of September 30, 1967. It is interesting to note that for the calendar year 1967, Frontier Airlines reported a lower net profit for the combined Central/Frontier operation than Central had for the first nine months of that year by itself. In other words, Frontier, under the management of its egotistical president, Lou Diamond, had actually lost money during 1967.

By this time, though, I was already out of there. I guess Diamond had feared that if I joined the merged company, I would have wound up with his job sooner or later, so I was literally offered the position of assistant treasurer in charge of the stockroom—not particularly my cup of tea. When I left, the one thing I did take with me was the very expensive and beautiful Romwebber furniture I had purchased for my office after the company became profitable. Since there weren't going to be two presidents at Frontier, they had no use for the collection. I offered a thousand dollars for it, and they took it. It was good riddance for them, and for me it has been thirty-seven years of enjoyment. I've always considered it my good luck charm. That complete Romwebber collection has been moved nine times since then, and it is still beautiful.

I had never taken a single day of vacation at Central Airlines, and since I now had absolutely no interest in the company's welfare, I took off most of the month of September 1967. Our good friends Dick and Paula Richards flew with Juanice and me to northern Italy and Switzerland for a little R and R. We had a ball and got back in time for me to report to my new position in Michigan on October 1, 1967, just one day after the merger of Central into Frontier, a sad day for most of Central's employees.

My only gain for parlaying Jack Bradford's $1 million investment—which hadn't been worth a tinker's damn when I arrived at Central—to an asset worth $8 million two years later was my option to purchase 10,000 shares of Central's common stock. While Mr. Bradford got cash for his stock from RKO General, the public stockholders of the company received convertible debentures issued by Frontier. Their value was based on the price of $14 per share that Bradford had received. Since my debentures arose from options, they were not a registered security and were not saleable for two years; Frontier's general counsel would release them for sale or conversion after the holding period. But Frontier continued to lose more and more throughout 1968–69. When, in late 1969, Diamond finally permitted his counsel to release my bonds for sale in the open market, they were down 75 percent from their original market value.

9. THE AIRLINE YEARS—

Any Port in a Storm

In the early part of the twentieth century, a man named Matthews put together a very large warehouse and stevedoring operation called Universal in New York Harbor. It was very profitable, and eventually his three sons and one daughter inherited the company. All four were on the board, but Don Matthews was the chairman and ran the show for the benefit of himself and his siblings. The operation was a cash cow: among other things, they had bought—lock, stock, and barrel—the Hamilton Watch Company, previously famous for making railroad watches with big, bold-face numerals. I remember that one of those fine watches had been my dad's proudest possession.

I have found that quite a few people with substantial amounts of investment capital seem to cherish a dream of owning an airline. (I remember how excited I had been back in 1948 just to go to work for one!) In 1966 Don Matthews had heard about an airline operation for sale in Detroit; it was owned by the Zantop brothers and naturally was called Zantop Airlines. Without very much investigation or knowledge of the industry, Don gave the Zantops $1 million for their company, the same amount Bradford had paid for control of Central. Gene Zerkel, who had previously worked for the Zantops, continued to run the day-to-day operation for the Matthews, and Don appointed his brother Dick to monitor the operation as VP-personnel while he himself served as the airline's board chairman, making an occasional visit to Detroit.

After a year's operation, he came to the realization that his $1 million investment had already lost $2 million, and thus it was time to do *something*, even if it was wrong. Apparently, somebody told him that I just might be available to head up the company, since Central was being merged into Frontier and there was nothing in the merged company for me. With three kids and a big house payment, I obviously needed the work and was therefore a willing listener when Don contacted me. After he related some details of the three operating divisions of the company and its 100-plus freight aircraft, I told him I was interested. Headquarters was at Willow Run Airport, which would permit me and my family to live in Ann Arbor, Michigan, a college town, rather than in Detroit.

My requirements, which the Matthews immediately met, were a five-year employment contract with minimum annual pay of $50,000 per year, plus 5 percent of the company as a signing bonus. I'd had my fill of stock options. I wanted to own something tangible that I could grow by my own efforts. There was so much opportunity at the newly named Universal Airlines, there was never a doubt in my mind that I could make the company profitable and do it—for the first time—without a federal subsidy.

Rushing to find a new house before the next school term was not as important as it had been with previous moves, since our daughter Diane had graduated from SMU and was working for Braniff Airways and living on her own, and Mike was in college at Vanderbilt in Nashville, Tennessee. Debbie, still in high school and an excellent student who stayed way ahead of her class, would be in college soon anyway. I didn't want to buy a house in Michigan, because I had a feeling that Universal was not going to be my life's work, and I wanted to keep my options open. Yet there were no available apartments large enough to satisfy our requirements, so I rented two adjoining apartments and had some walls knocked out to make them into a single unit. We now had two distinct, though small, kitchens, and we made a bar out of one of them. Two years later, when we gave up the apartments, it was pretty expensive restoring them to their original design.

Universal had some intriguing aspects to it. First, it had its headquarters at Willow Run Airport in the string of cavernous hangars in which the Ford Motor Company had built most of the B-25 bombers used in Europe and the Pacific during World War II. Essentially a "charter" freight carrier, Universal held a special exemption from the Civil Aeronautics Board that allowed them to commingle, on the same flights, air freight from several shippers—specifically the Big Three automobile companies, General Motors, Ford, and Chrysler.

The operation involved almost a hundred freighter aircraft. They included the old C-46, built during World War II by Curtiss Aircraft; the *Argosy,* a British-built high-wing aircraft with a tail that opened up for fast loading and unloading; a few DC-4s; many DC-6s; and several DC-7s, all built by Douglas Aircraft. Each night, seven nights a week, planes would leave airports near Big Three automobile assembly plants across the nation loaded with automobile parts from those plants or from parts manufacturers in the same area supplying the Big Three. The flights were scheduled to arrive about midnight at Willow Run. For the next four hours, freight was shuffled from one plane to another, or onto trucks that would deliver it to Big Three plants in the Detroit–Willow Run–Flint area. The same aircraft would then load up with freight from those plants and local parts manufacturers that was destined for the outlying destinations. Then the fleet would depart for the airports from which they had come earlier that night and disgorge their cargo in the early-morning hours. Generally, they would wait there for the next night's beehive of activity. This was years before anybody ever dreamed of the hub-and-spoke air express operations "pioneered" by FedEx in Memphis.

To understand the scale of this nightly affair, consider that at that time, United Airlines' scheduled air-freight operation at O'Hare Field in Chicago was thought to be the world's largest, with one million pounds per night. Universal's Willow Run charter operation averaged about two million pounds of air-freight per night, twice as much. This operation was a very good indicator of the efficiency of the Big Three auto companies, by virtue of the quantity of freight each tendered for shipment. Had those companies done a perfect job of scheduling and delivering all necessary parts to each assembly plant by truck or rail so they could maintain a steady, uninterrupted production of vehicles, they would have had no need for Universal's air-freight service. So who was Universal's biggest customer? Chrysler! Who was its smallest customer? Ford! Remember, this was 1967–68; Chrysler became a totally different company, thanks largely to Lee Iaccoca, but currently seems to be back in the soup after its acquisition by Daimler.

Universal's second area of operation was the provision of aircraft and flight crews under annual contract to the navy to run their entire scheduled freight operation, called "Quick-Trans." The service provided was between navy bases all the way from New England, along the East and Gulf coasts, to the Dallas Naval Air Station, then to San Diego and up the Pacific Coast to the Seattle area, and points in between. Some schedules operated on a direct transcontinental basis via the Great Lakes rather than along the southern route. Additionally, the company had annual contracts to participate in the air force's "LogAir" scheduled air-freight operation between various air bases, handling about one-third of that system's flight operations. Finally, the company had a Certificate of Public Convenience and Necessity as a supplemental carrier to operate passenger charter flights within the fifty states and Mexico. While there were no operations being conducted in this division at the time of my arrival, the company had five McDonnell Douglas DC-9s and two stretch DC-8-61 aircraft on order.

It became apparent to me from my first day that neither the management nor the owners had ever been supplied with financial statements or reports outlining the operations of the company's various components. All they knew was that they were losing money. They had no idea where or why. After a couple weeks of burning the midnight oil, I had the accounting system whipped into shape so that we could get some October figures that were meaningful. Although everybody had assumed that the automobile-parts freight division was profitable, it certainly had not been so that month and probably hadn't been for some time.

A cursory examination of the freight floor one night told me that the principal characteristic of most of our freight was its odd shape, which meant it took up a lot of room in the airplane but didn't weigh very much. Many of these items took up so much space, it forced the company to fly an extra section even though the initial flight was not grossed out by weight. However, the company was billing the automobile manufacturers only on the basis of weight. Being totally unfamiliar with the freight business, I asked if there wasn't some way we could get compensated for that extra space. The answer: "Yeah, that's called 'weight or cube,' whichever rate is higher."

"Don't we have cube (space) rates?"

"No, sir. One has never been filed with the CAB."

A new tariff was filed the next day, and the automobile companies were notified. The result was that many high-cube items, which the manufacturers had shipped for pure convenience at our expense, now found a less costly way to go. Those parts that were "must-go" with Universal got billed accordingly. Magically, the auto freight operation started showing a profit.

My analysis of the market for 100-passenger DC-9-30 aircraft in domestic charter service indicated that Universal would have a hard time making a buck with a five-airplane fleet. About the only major market they could serve would be into and out of Las Vegas, which historically is a low-yield market. On the other hand, the DC-8-61s could be operated worldwide in lucrative military charters, with the holes in their schedules filled by civilian charters to Las Vegas and Hawaii. Fortunately, I was able to convince the board of directors to let me cancel the DC-9 order before it cost us big money. McDonnell Douglas was glad to get the aircraft back, as several scheduled carriers were clamoring for delivery positions at higher prices than our contract offered.

The two DC-8-61s were only a few months away from delivery. I had a good man named Milt Page in charge of booking these aircraft for charters six months to a year in advance, but I didn't have anybody who could establish a department to manage the operation of these brand-new, highly sophisticated, globe-circling aircraft. However, I knew that Bud Herring had gone back to his former employer when Central merged into Frontier, and I figured he would be ideal for the top job in that area if I could talk him into leaving Texas. It was not hard at all. He was unhappy in his situation at what was by then called "Texas International," a name change brought on by the company's acquisition of a route from McAllen, Texas, to Tampico, Mexico.

While the passenger charter division turned out to be profitable, it was a hair-raising experience that could have brought back my ulcers if I had let it. I could not afford to let a $25,000,000 piece of equipment and its flight crews sit around idle for even one day, because the interest alone on the financing for the equipment and spare parts was more than $6,000 per day. Keeping that from happening, given that some of these sleazy tour operators would book a charter six months to a year in advance and then cancel out a week or two before the charter date, kept us on pins and needles all the time. Nevertheless, despite all the problems, during my first year at Universal we made $2 million instead of losing $2 million. In my second year, which was the first full year of operation with the DC-8-61s, we doubled that profit to $4 million.

During that second year, we got wind that Overseas National, a supplemental carrier with charter authority to Europe (which we lacked), was buying up Lockheed Electra L-188 aircraft all around the country. They intended to convert them to freighters for the purpose of taking our QuickTrans contract away from us at the next annual contract letting. We sure didn't want that to happen, but if we just sat there with our old DC-7s, we were liable to lose it.

I knew that the very best-maintained Electra fleet in the world were the eight aircraft equipped with Hamilton Standard square-tipped propellers operated by KLM on their European routes. It was entirely possible that, with the right approach, that fleet might be available to us. My old friend Harry Bradley, who had been in charge of purchasing and stores at TTA, was now owner and president of Houston Aviation Products Company, a major supplier of aircraft parts to KLM and a close friend of their director of purchasing, who also handled the disposal of surplus equipment. "Brad" was one of KLM's best customers for surplus.

Even though Brad would buy surplus from KLM by the pound and sell the same surplus back to them by the piece, sometimes at a hundred times what he paid for it, he stayed on good terms with them. I got Brad to make a trip to Amsterdam with me. We played around for a couple days, and I offered KLM $5 million for the fleet, including all spare engines, props, and parts, as well as an Electra Link Trainer. Lo and behold, they took it. Having learned my lesson with TTA, I didn't have to go back to the boss for approval—I already had it in my pocket. We contracted with Lockheed to convert the fleet to cargo at their Ontario, California, retrofit facility, and we had the new fleet ready at bidding time for the new QuickTrans contract. We won it hands down, and Overseas National, which knew nothing about the freight business, had a hard time keeping their Electras busy.

As Universal was privately held, we operated for the first year I was with the company pretty much on a shoestring. The Matthews wanted to retain an 80 percent interest in the company for tax reasons but were willing to issue new stock amounting to 15 percent of the total shares outstanding. We therefore had a public offering in early 1969 at $21 per share (as compared to the $1 per share that the Matthews had paid the Zantops). This cash infusion helped tremendously by letting us get loan financing for the full cost of the Electra fleet and its conversion. The only fly in the ointment was that the Chemical Bank in New York required both Don Matthews and me to sign the note personally. It was the dumbest action of my entire business career.

Since Universal was one of the largest operators of freighter aircraft in the world, Dan Houghton, chairman and CEO of Lockheed Corporation, invited me and my whole family to attend the rollout of the first C5A freighter aircraft at their plant in Marietta, Georgia. While there, he and I discussed the feasibility of a commercial model of the C5A. The major changes from the military version would have to be the elimination of the features that made it capable of operating from short dirt fields, utilizing that weight-saving to include a full-length passenger cabin on top for say, 200 passengers. The cavernous interior would be retained and stretched in length as much as aerodynamically feasible. I envisioned the interior reconfigured to house two side-by-side rows of containers at floor level, and two side-by-side rows of passenger cars above the containers, with the flexibility to substitute four more side-by-side rows of passenger vehicles in lieu of all or some of the container rows. It was exciting to even think about these freight trains of the sky flying initially from Newark Airport in the late evening nonstop to Los Angeles, San Francisco, and Seattle loaded primarily with containers and topped off with private automobiles and their passengers, and then the next day returning to Newark with a primary load of private automobiles and passengers, topped off with containers.

Not long after that, Lockheed announced the development of the L-500, a commercial version of the C5A that would carry up to 200 passengers as well as cargo. We really got busy then on fleshing out our concept of how the L-500 should be utilized, and, for the first time in CAB history, simultaneously filed our application for a Certificate of Public Convenience and Necessity. We made a full presentation to the five CAB board members assembled for the specific purpose of seeing our "to scale" model with containers, cars, and people and hearing the full presentation of our planned operation, which by this time included service to Atlanta, Chicago, Dallas, and Detroit.

What happened that such an innovative service never came to fruition? At the same time we were pushing for the L-500, Lockheed had already spent billions on the development of the L-1011 passenger jet. And one day Dan Houghton himself arrived at our facility at Willow Run Airport in his personal Lockheed JetStar Executive aircraft to advise me that he had just come from a Lockheed board meeting where they had made the decision that they were not financially capable of continuing to develop two aircraft models at the same time. Since the L-1011 was so much further along in the development stage, the board had decided to abandon the L-500 project. While I could understand their reasoning, it seemed to me that with Douglas's DC-10 and Boeing's 747 dominating the market, something as innovative as the L-500 might have a better chance of becoming a profitable product. I strongly suspected that the fact that the L-500 would be built in Georgia, while the L-1011 would be built in California, had carried undue weight with their board of directors. Anyway, that ended the one exciting development that I had seen while with Universal. As it turned out, the L-1011 was a disaster for Lockheed. They lost billions on the project.

Owner Don Matthews came to me with what he thought was a brand-new idea: If we can make so much money with DC-8-61s, he said, just think how much we could make with Boeing 747s. He wanted to get approval at the upcoming board meeting to purchase two 747s at about $40 million each. I told him that I wasn't as enthusiastic about such a move as he was, but that I would check the figures out before the board meeting. The only thing I really needed to know was the direct flight cost per seat-mile at various stage lengths, as compared to our DC-8-61s. This would make a decision on the feasibility of his idea very simple.

What I learned was that the seat-mile costs for the 747, at stage lengths up to 2,500 miles, were almost identical to those of the aircraft we were currently flying. Beyond 2,500 miles, the costs got significantly lower, but in our operation we very seldom flew a segment of more than 2,500 miles. This was the same problem that American Airlines had faced when they foolishly bought 747s. At Universal, it was already hard enough putting together 251 people who desired to go to the same place on the same day and time and then return to their starting point at the same time. It would be just that much harder to round up 438 people to do it. It was a very simple equation, just as most things really are when properly analyzed.

By the date of the board meeting, Don had whipped himself into a frenzy of enthusiasm for his idea. After he had made his proposal to the board, he asked if I had thought any more about this great opportunity. I explained to the board my position on the matter, and they voted to put the matter off for further study so as not to embarrass Don. I assumed that the matter was dead, but a couple of months later, immediately preceding the next board meeting at Willow Run, the ax fell. Don came into my office, shut the door, and told me the board was going to approve the purchase of the Boeing 747s. Since I could not support that decision, he said they were going to name my assistant, Glenn

Hickerson, president of the company. In other words, "Good Day, Mr. Muse." I told him that was his prerogative, but I also suggested that he discuss his decision with his attorney and have him call me. Not for a couple of weeks, though, because I was taking a well-earned vacation. And I walked out of the office, climbed into the almost brand-new Lincoln Mark III company car I drove, and left the facility.

Our youngest daughter, Debbie, had graduated from high school the previous spring and been accepted at Vanderbilt, where her brother, Mike, would be a junior that year. They and Juanice were in Nashville for registration for the new school year. I went home, packed a few clothes, and headed for Nashville in that Mark III. I arrived there the next morning in time to join the family for breakfast, much to their surprise. When I told them the latest news, their principal concern was, "Well, Daddy, does that mean we are not going to college this year?" I assured them that were not the situation. I explained that I was very happy about the turn of events and reminded them that I had an ironclad employment agreement and that I owned 5 percent of the company — facts that Don had obviously failed to consider. My main concern was that he might want to rescind my dismissal when he got around to putting his brain in gear. I much preferred the company to honor my employment contract without me having to show up for work and make some kind of cash settlement on my unregistered 5 percent ownership interest. And this is exactly what they did a couple weeks later when Juanice and I returned to Ann Arbor.

Incidentally, since Hickerson was a Californian, his first action was to move the company's headquarters to Oakland, 2,000 miles away from Universal's extremely profitable auto freight operation. The excuse? To be closer to Boeing in anticipation of delivery of Universal's two 747s, one of which came really quickly when Braniff got smart and canceled its order for a second 747. To make a long story short, a little over a year after my departure, the company filed for bankruptcy, causing me to suddenly remember that I had cosigned that note at the Chemical Bank for the Electra fleet.

Right quickly, I transferred just about everything I owned to Juanice and waited for the sheriff to arrive. I later learned that it had been necessary for Universal to make several amendments to the loan agreement during the period after I left, and since they hadn't arranged for my approval, I was released from liability. A couple of years later, I ran into Don Matthews' secretary on Main Street in Dallas. Since she was strictly a NYC girl, I asked what in the world she was doing there, and she told me that the Chemical Bank had totally wiped out the Matthews' family fortune. She and Don had moved to Dallas, where he was now selling life insurance. Did I want to buy any?

After leaving Universal, for the first time I had enough capital that I could, if I wanted to, retire comfortably for the rest of my life. We moved back to Texas, bought property at the Panorama Country Club near Houston—adjoining lots on the eighteenth fairway—leased a very nice apartment in Conroe close to the club, bought a golf cart, and planned to take it easy till we decided what was next on the menu. And that next menu item would turn out to include the most exciting and rewarding eight years of my business career.

10. THE LUV YEARS —

Preoperating Period

In January 1971, the board of directors of Air Southwest met and made me a director, president, CEO, and chairman of its executive committee, which consisted of Herb Kelleher, Rollin W. King, John Peace, and myself. The other three board members were Robert (Bob) Strauss, Chuck Kuhn, and John Murchison, all important citizens of Dallas. They all wanted to know when I thought we could begin service. I responded with, "Gentlemen, that question is kind of like asking how long is a rope. Right now we have a little over $100 in the bank and over $100,000 of past-due attorneys' fees and accrued salaries. We own a couple desks and chairs and maybe one file cabinet. That's a long way from launching aircraft with paying passengers. But if we don't run into impossible obstacles, I'd say sometime this summer."

In an effort to conserve cash, as well as keep costs as low as possible, I recommended that the board set my salary at $30,000 per year, with an additional $30,000 in deferred compensation bearing simple interest of 5 percent. This was all set forth in a three-year employment agreement effective from January 1, 1971. It was further agreed that I would take all my cash salary in common stock at $3 per share during the airline's preinaugural period, and I advised the board that I would offer all other officers the same opportunity to take common stock in lieu of salary at the same price. Those who accepted did their heirs a great service, as it made them rich.

The first thing I did after taking over the chair was to suggest a name change for our new airline. Since Air Southwest sounded to me like some Mickey Mouse, third-level carrier, I convinced the board to change the name to "Southwest Airlines Co." I then discussed with the board the three-part financing plan I had in mind. First, I calculated that it was going to take close to $1 million to bring us to actual startup; this was what I called "walking-around money." Therefore, I envisioned issuing subordinated convertible debentures (with warrants) in the amount of $1,250,000 (my startup estimate plus a cushion) at, say, 7 percent interest. These would be payable two years from date of issue or from the proceeds of any public offering successfully completed prior to the end of such a two-year period. Second, prior to the inauguration of any service, I wanted to have a public offering of common stock to produce a minimum of $6 million, to be used principally as a war fund to cover losses during our initial operating period. We needed to make this offering before we actually started operations or, faced with our initial losses, the public would never buy the shares. Finally, I expected either to lease aircraft or to purchase them with 100 percent financing. My general approach was acceptable, since nobody else had any thoughts on the subject. However, I got the impression that some of the board members I had not previously met thought I was blowing smoke. We would see about that!

Top priority in my plan was to get the debenture offering subscribed and closed so we would have our walking-around money and be able to accomplish the thousand and one things essential for an early-summer startup. Herb and I went to see our mutual friend John B. Connally, who, after his terms as governor of the great state of Texas, had accepted a partnership in Houston at the state's leading law firm, Vinson & Elkins. Our mission was to convince him that Southwest Airlines would someday be a client his firm would be proud to have. Specifically, we wanted the services of their corporate finance department, headed up by Bill Fleming, to prepare the debenture offering of $1,250,000 for us. I needed to peddle it at the very earliest date possible, as my American Express card was getting pretty heavy. We also asked them to prepare a registration statement for filing with the Securities and Exchange Commission regarding our public offering of common stock. John was optimistic about our plans, and since both Herb and I had mutual admiration societies going with him, obtaining his firm's representation was a piece of cake. After a nice lunch, John took us right down to Bill Fleming's office, introduced us, saying the firm "wants to work with these boys," and told him to do a good job so we would be able to pay their fees.

In New York at that time there was a small underwriting firm by the name of Auchincloss, Parker & Redpath, with which I had very good relations going back some twenty years. This firm, through one of its senior officers, Todd Alexander, was the only one on Wall Street that would touch the local service airline industry with a ten-foot pole. I went to New York with my pitch, received a favorable reception, and wound up with a conditional commitment to head up the underwriting effort for our initial public offering (IPO) in the range of $6-7 million, as well as a promise to search for investors for the planned debenture offering. A good selling point was that we had lined up Bill Fleming of Vinson & Elkins for our SEC work.

Meanwhile, my very first executive decision had been controversial. Since we were going to be flying initially from Dallas to Houston and from Dallas to San Antonio, and since most future service to points in Texas would be primarily from Dallas, I determined that company headquarters should be in Dallas, not San Antonio. Where Rollin and Herb lived was of no consequence, and neither Rollin's prior promises to utilize space nor his offers of employment to people in that city were binding commitments. We had to be headquartered in Dallas, and that is where I went to start organizing the company.

While reading all those newspapers during my "retirement," I had been struck by the originality and hard-hitting copy of an advertising program that introduced a new brand of beer called Faubaucher, produced by Jax Beer of New Orleans. Upon investigation, I determined that a Dallas advertising group, the Bloom Agency, had produced the Faubaucher story.

I wanted to invite that agency, as well as Tracy Locke, the agency that had done such a wonderful job for me at Central Airlines back in 1965, to present proposals for Southwest's account. When I mentioned this to Rollin and Herb, I was told that the advertising account had already been promised to an agency Rollin had worked with in the past. They suggested we go ahead with their choice for the first year, and then if it wasn't working out, we could make a change.

I explained that we did not have the luxury of waiting a full year to get it right. There could be no trial and error; it had to be right from the very first day, because the competition from Braniff and Texas International was going to be unbelievable. Our overall presentation to the public in the early months was going to be critical. We had to present ourselves as a class outfit made up of professionals who knew their business, flew equipment that was safe and comfortable, and provided enthusiastic and courteous service to the public. And these facts had to be told to travelers in such a way that they would be champing at the bit to give us a try. Additionally, with our headquarters in Dallas, it would be far preferable to have a Dallas agency. I did agree, though, to meet with the agency representative in KLM's private club at Houston Intercontinental Airport. Before the meeting, I had decided to let them participate fully in the bidding in competition with the Bloom Agency and Tracy Locke, even though privately I didn't give them much chance of success. However, their representative's main pitch was that if they got the account, he would see to it that both Rollin and I would be $10,000 richer. As politely as I knew how—which probably wasn't very polite—I ended the meeting without offering him a chance to compete.

This left Tracy Locke and the Bloom Agency still in the running. However, the only good thing Frontier Airlines president Lou Diamond had done when Central was merged into Frontier was keep Central's advertising agency and fire his own. Thus, Tracy Locke had to get Diamond's approval to bid on another airline account. Being the jerk he was, he refused permission. Tracy Locke would have been well advised to tell Diamond to stick it and go after the account full blast, since they had the inside track, but I guess they didn't have the guts to take a chance on Southwest actually being successful. The old bird-in-the-hand concept, I guess, but they wouldn't have been the only ones with that opinion.

The Bloom Agency was now in line for our account. In advising them that the account was theirs, we were totally honest with Sam and Bob Bloom. I said I was really impressed with their work for Jax Beer, but we were without funds. They would have to work on a credit basis while building a program for us. I told them I had plans for raising funds but could not give any assurance yet that I would be successful. They agreed to proceed on faith, largely because they thought we had a good business plan that would be ultimately successful, and they wanted to be a part of it. They understood that they were to work in conjunction with Bud Mantz of Ernest G. Mantz Associates, who would be doing our corporate-image work, hopefully as successfully as that firm had done it for me at both Central and Universal Airlines.

In the meantime, as I negotiated with financial and advertising agencies, we were also searching out our various department heads. Selection of our top management group was essential in getting the nitty-gritty things moving, such as preparing operating manuals for inspection and approval by the Federal Aviation Administration (FAA). We were extremely fortunate in this area, because there was a serious airline depression at the time and many good people were looking for employment. Rollin did a great job of coming up with Jack Vidal and Don Ogden, as well as chief dispatcher Harold Riley. Jack Vidal had until recently been the manager in charge of line maintenance in Dallas for Braniff Airways. Fortunately for both Jack and Southwest, Braniff had let him go: I particularly felt that having been let go by Braniff was just about the best recommendation a person could have. He became our VP–aircraft maintenance.

Don Ogden was sixty years old as of February 1, 1971, and thus had been forced to retire from American Airlines as one of their chief pilots and director of systemwide cockpit standardization for all of American's flight crews. On that day of his retirement from American, he was named VP–flight operations for Southwest, a position he held with great distinction for the next sixteen years, finally retiring at the ripe old age of seventy-six. He deserves much of the credit for Southwest's excellent safety record, it being the only major airline in the world without a passenger fatality. Very deservedly, one of Southwest's aircraft is named for Don.

Another recently displaced Braniff employee was Dick Elliott, who had been my "full of piss and vinegar" VP-sales at Central Airlines and subsequently district sales manager of the Dallas–Fort Worth area for Braniff. Unfortunately, Dick had developed a drinking problem. I told him at the time of his interview for employment at Southwest that the top job in marketing and public relations was his so long as he conducted himself in such a manner as to make me proud of him. But I told him to be forewarned that there would be no second chances. The very first time that he embarrassed the company as a result of his recognized problem, he would be out. He did a wonderful job of organizing his department, being our go-between with the Bloom Agency, and handling a thousand other details of getting started.

Bill Franklin, who had earlier been fired from Texas International, was unhappy with his position at Frontier Airlines in Denver and anxious to return to Texas. I was equally anxious for a good ground operations officer and, as far as I was concerned, Bill was the best there was. It was not hard to convince him that he should be our VP–ground operations. Doug Lane, who had handled purchasing and stores at Trans-Texas for a number of years and had joined me in the same capacity at Universal Airlines, was more than happy to leave the Oakland, California, area and return to his native Texas to join our hoped-for new airline. Fred Rigby filled out the team as chief accountant. He was assisted, and later replaced by, my chief accountant at Trans-Texas, Herman Farr, who was also elected treasurer.

Meanwhile, Auchincloss, Parker & Redpath had only been successful in placing $100,000 of the debenture offering with two of their customers in upper New York State. It became my lot to start knocking on doors to get the remaining $1,150,000 placed. My first step was committing to the purchase of $50,000 myself. I felt my own commitment was an important sales tool. I then went to John Murchison, one of our directors. Without too much coaxing, he committed to a subscription of $50,000 for himself and $50,000 for his wife, Lupe. Bud Mantz, my corporate-image

72

guy, had a friend, Van Calvin Ellis, who he thought might be interested due to the recent sale of his family's business to General Foods, making him that company's second-largest stockholder. Bud got me an appointment with Ellis and, like Murchison, he subscribed $100,000 worth without too much talk. Then the cheese began to bind.

I flew out to Midland, Texas, to get Jack Bradford to put some of his gains from the sale of Central Airlines into my new venture but to my great surprise and disappointment was rebuffed. He did suggest that I talk to the Leonard brothers, who owned a big department store in Fort Worth, and I got a kind of tentative commitment from them for $50,000 each. Another investor promised us $50,000, but that deal was mighty shaky. And even if it came through, I still had $750,000 left to raise.

Two of Juanice's and my closest friends were Carl and Vaudine Sudbury, and Vaudine just happened to be the personal secretary to Hugh Roy Cullen, one of Houston's richest oilmen and bankers. Vaudine got me an appointment with the man at her company who handled Cullen's personal investments, and I went to him with high hopes. He listened very courteously to my pitch, but at the end he advised me that it was his policy to pass on initial offerings such as this and then pick them up in the after-market at substantially reduced prices. It would have been nice of him to have informed me of that at the outset, but I guess he was just honoring the boss's secretary's request.

After numerous other dry runs, including a pitch to my longtime friend Herm Ruppel, who was business manager for A. Pollard Simons, one of Dallas's wealthier individuals, and an unsuccessful session with Lamar Hunt, I stopped at the Houston office of Schneider, Bernet & Hickman. This was a regional brokerage firm where I had been "employed" during the period I was climbing the walls between jobs at Universal and Southwest. I had gone on their payroll for $50 a month and reported to the Houston office every Monday morning for a couple of hours. I would spend the rest of each day studying for the exam to become a stockbroker, which I eventually passed with a grade of 100—but then along came Southwest.

On this particular day, I visited with one of the brokers, whose name I cannot now remember, but who had been kind to me by just recognizing me as a person while I was studying for the exam. I told the kind broker that I was somewhat discouraged. I had run out of people with whom I could arrange an audience, and I still had $750,000 left to place. My friend said that one of his clients was Jim West, known in Houston as "Silver Dollar" West because he liked to drive along in his big, black Lincoln four-door convertible, throwing out handfuls of silver dollars to pedestrians. He maintained a suite at Hermann Hospital, where he went to recuperate from time to time. When the broker mentioned the name West, a light turned on in my head.

Back during my Trans-Texas days, word had leaked out about a group organizing a World's Fair to be held around the San Jacinto Battleground. The president of Trans-Texas' advertising agency, Wendell Hawkins, had solicited my help in raising $100,000 for a group of small-time investors headed by a Dr. Kimmerling, former president of the University of Houston, who had an option to buy a 200-acre tract of land near the San Jacinto Monument. If the deal could be closed before news about the fair became general knowledge, we could flip the property in six months and make a fortune and not worry about the annual payments with interest that were part of the deal. Neither Hawkins nor I had any means, but I told John Connally about it, and he got us an appointment with his distant relative by marriage, Wesley West, Jim West's brother and manager of the family's multimillion-dollar oil holdings. We went to see him at his suburban office near River Oaks, and he wrote us out a check for $20,000 to take a 20 percent interest in the deal. Well, the World's Fair didn't happen, and the first year's payment was drawing nearer and nearer ever so fast. There were some lawsuits, and I was never so embarrassed in my life for being so gullible. We were saved when Bud Adams, owner of the Houston Oilers (now Tennessee Titans) bought the property from our group at a nice profit in order to build a refinery and tank farm. Wendell and I decided to forego any profit in the deal in favor of Wesley West and profusely apologized for so mishandling his trust in us. What did I get out of it? A darn good lesson about (1) investigation and (2) integrity.

Anyway, my friend's mention of Jim "Silver Dollar" West made me wonder if Wesley West would grant me time to make my pitch to him. I picked up the phone on my friend's desk, called West's office, and told his secretary who I was. He came on the line right away. I told him briefly what I was up to. He said, "Come on out!" and I was on my way. After being escorted into his office, I told him that I could give him a ten-minute summary if he was pressed for time, or a thirty-minute full presentation of my ideas and plans. He responded that he had the rest of his life, so go ahead and give him ten minutes, and if it tickled his interest, I could then tell him more.

At the conclusion of my initial presentation, I knew West was hooked when he asked how much of the debenture offering was still available. I told him that the way I figured it, there was $750,000 available. He said, "I'll take it."

I said, "Excuse me?"

He replied, "I said, I'll take it all."

I spent the next two hours detailing all the things that could happen to make his investment completely worthless. His response to that: "If Braniff gives us too much trouble, we will just buy the bastards." This was on a Friday afternoon. We agreed that I should come to his home the following Sunday morning for breakfast with him and Mrs. West, at which time he would have a check in the amount of $750,000 ready for me. To me that represented total forgiveness and redemption for my earlier screwup.

As soon as I left West's office, I called Juanice in Conroe to relate the wonderful news to her. She was, of course, excited but was quick to tell me that Herb Kelleher had been trying to reach me all afternoon and was upset that I had not left the name of a contact. I returned his call, at which time he snapped: "What in the world have you been doing—screwing some woman?" I replied that whether or not I had been screwing was none of his business, but that among other things I had sold the last of the debenture offering and that I was picking up a $750,000 check Sunday morning. He was suddenly unable to remember what it was he had so desperately needed to talk to me about.

I just knew that there would be some slip-up between Friday afternoon and Sunday morning. Somehow, I got through the day on Saturday and weathered a sleepless Saturday night, and I was Johnny-on-the-spot at Wesley West's beautiful home in

River Oaks at 9:00 Sunday morning. We had a very pleasant breakfast, at which the only discussion about the company was what its name should be. Since he was by far the largest investor in the company, he wanted it to be named "Faith Airlines," because he headed up some religious organization called "Faith."

After recovering my aplomb, I said that such a name might be okay for a church or a temple, or maybe even a college or university. But an airline? "I want our customers to fly us because we have the best equipment, best people, and best safety record, and not have to rely on faith," I said. "That could sound like we think we might crash."

He just mumbled something like, "Well, think about it."

"Yes, sir, long and hard," I said.

The other subject of conversation was his desire to buy a Boeing 707, but only if a hole could be cut out of the top of it where they could install a pressurized, clear plastic chamber. It would be big enough for at least two seats that could be hoisted through the opening on some kind of elevator so their occupants could scan Heaven from 40,000 feet up. I told him that this would be a real engineering challenge and that only Boeing could discuss it intelligently with him. The important thing was that I left his home about 11:00 A.M. with a check for $750,000 in my pocket.

The task now was to schedule a closing for the debenture issue as soon as possible so we would have some cash to work with, and I could get on to more important undertakings. I set the closing for 10:00 A.M. Monday, March 10, 1971, at John Walker's office at the Mercantile National Bank in Dallas, which I had chosen as our lead bank because of the good experience I had with them while running Central Airlines. John, a vice president there, had been account executive for Central and now operated in the same capacity for Southwest. This closing date gave me a week to be sure that the full $1,250,000 would be on hand, because we couldn't negotiate any of the checks tendered unless we reached the full subscription of $1,250,000. Either everybody was in by closing day, or nobody was in.

During the week, that shaky $50,000 commitment looked more and more like it would fall through, and I was still leery that the $100,000 from the Leonard brothers would not arrive. I obviously needed some insurance, so at John Walker's urging, I went back to Jack Bradford. John suggested that I just put it to Bradford that he owed me for making him $8 million at Central. Sitting at an empty desk right in the middle of the bank floor, I called Bradford in Midland and told him that I was very close on this debenture deal and that I had set a closing at John Walker's office for the next Monday morning. I said I desperately needed him to be present to pick up any shortfall that might develop at the last minute. I hinted at the Central angle but didn't make a big issue of it. He asked how much money I was talking about. "Hopefully," I said, "the shortfall will be only $50,000, but it might be as much as $150,000. I knew I had him when he said, "Well, Lamar, $50,000 is not enough to fool with."

"Don't talk to me like that," I said. "I have nothing in writing from your friends, the Leonard brothers, and if you want to commit to $150,000 right now, you've got it." He took it. I thanked him profusely, hung up the phone, stood up, and hollered just as loud as I could right in the middle of the banking floor, "Whoooopeeeee!"

The composition of the debenture sale, exactly as it appeared on the deposit slip, was as follows:

M. Lamar Muse–Merc. Nat'l Bank	$ 50,000
Auchincloss, Parker and Redpath, for two clients	100,000
AnLaCo Land Co. (John Murchison)	50,000
Lupe Murchison–1st Nat'l Bank	50,000
Van Ellis–Republic Bank	100,000
Wesley West–1st City, Houston	750,000
Jack Bradford–Merc. Nat'l Bank	150,000
Total	**$1,250,000**

My oldest daughter, Diane Quigley, used the decoupage process to preserve that original deposit slip on a piece of wood that hangs on a wall in my office to this day. In fact, that slip is the only way I knew it was precisely on March 10 that the deal closed and the funds were credited to our account. Southwest was finally solvent. As I think back on it, we accomplished a hell of a lot in less than two months.

At the next directors meeting, we included Messrs. West, Bradford, and Alexander on the Southwest Airlines board, the first two as substantial investors, and Alexander as the senior officer of the co-underwriter of our IPO. With the completion of the interim financing, we were in a position to start taking on some of our midmanagement people and really start moving on the preparation of manuals and procedures necessary for the Federal Aviation Administration to issue an operating certificate. Although the federal government didn't regulate our routes and rates, we still needed its certification as far as technical operations, aircraft, and safety procedures were concerned.

But we couldn't do much in this area until we had identified the aircraft that would be utilized in our flight operations. Southwest's equipment had to be pure jet. Propjets, such as the lumbering four-engine Lockheed Electra L-188 originally proposed by King, were totally unacceptable. The only people who would ride them would be those who couldn't get a seat on the competition's jet aircraft. For our purposes, the options available to us were—in order of general preference—the Boeing 737-200, DC-9-30, BAC-111-400, DC-9-10, Boeing 737-100, and the French Caravelle. Rollin King and I spent a week surveying the operations of the California intrastate airline Pacific Southwest Airlines (PSA) at their headquarters in San Diego and confirmed that the Boeing 737 used by that airline was definitely our first preference.

About the only used Boeing 737-200s then available were three owned by GATX-Boothe and leased to Aloha Airlines, which wanted to switch to DC-9 equipment for some crazy reason. I therefore made a fast trip to San Francisco to talk to GATX-Boothe. The Aloha planes had a moderate number of hours of flight time on their logs, but when I saw the number of rotations (takeoffs and landings) already on the equipment as a result of their very short flights, it was easier to understand why they wanted to let somebody else worry about them. Meanwhile, I learned that Boeing had some "white tail" 737s on hand, built on speculation for PSA, Air California, and Piedmont Airlines, but all three had refused delivery of the aircraft due to the major depression then raging in the airline industry. Boeing had gone so far as to finish off the aircraft using those airlines' interior designs but had yet to paint the exteriors with any livery, thus the term "white-tail." However, they had some pretty fancy ideas about their value, and we got nowhere with Boeing on either price or financing terms.

Though there were plenty of the last four types on our list available, there were no used DC-9-30s — our second preference — on the market. We decided, however, that our best chance was with Douglas, which had expressed strong interest in meeting our requirements with new DC-9-30s, so Rollin and I in late March flew out to LAX, where a Douglas limousine picked us up to take us down to Long Beach to hammer out a deal with them. But the closer I got to Long Beach, the more I realized I really wanted Boeing 737-200s, and because very few other airlines seemed interested in them, this seemed to be the moment to put maximum pressure on Boeing's sales department.

I had Rollin hand me a yellow legal pad from the back seat and started scribbling a set of conditions that I thought we could live with if we could get Boeing to go along with them. I wish I had preserved that piece of paper for posterity, and I'm sure Boeing does as well, because in my view it represented the turning point for the Boeing 737 series of aircraft, from playing second fiddle to the predominant DC-9 series, to becoming the most successful aircraft model ever produced by any manufacturer. This, of course, was exactly what I had predicted a decade earlier when I was with American Airlines and had tried to persuade Boeing's Dan Palmer to speed up the introduction of the 737. Today the Southwest Airlines fleet of Boeing 737 series aircraft is the largest fleet of single-series aircraft in the world, 355 jets as of December 2001.

While I didn't save my scribbled note, I remember almost word for word what I wrote on that sheet of yellow paper back in 1971:

1. Southwest would like to be an operator of Boeing 737-200 aircraft.
2. We would like to commit to three of the white-tail aircraft presently parked in Oklahoma City on which you are incurring interest expense. Delivery to be during May 1971. Additionally, we would appreciate an option on a fourth aircraft.

3. We would be willing to pay $4,000,000 for each aircraft.
4. The form of payment would be nothing down, $50,000 per month per aircraft for 60 months with payments first applied to interest at a reasonable rate above prime and the balance to principal, with a balloon payment of the balance due in 5 years.
5. We would make a 50% down payment on all spare engines, parts, and other equipment required for a scheduled operation with balance due over a 24-month period.

Upon arriving at the Douglas office complex, I went to a pay phone in the lobby and called Dan Palmer, Boeing's director of domestic sales. I told him where I was, what we were fixing to do, as well as what I would prefer to do. Referring to my yellow legal pad, I told him that Boeing had one hour to put us into their equipment—otherwise forget it. Dan said he would be back to us within the hour, whichever way the decision went. He called back within thirty minutes. Boeing had accepted our proposal to the letter with an interest rate of 1.5 percent above prime. Our meeting with the Douglas people was barely underway, and it was a little embarrassing trying to explain to them what had happened, but they were gentlemen enough to give us a ride back to the airport. We caught the next flight back to Dallas, where we could now really get moving on tangible preparation for the commencement of scheduled service.

As an accountant, I had learned early that for every debit there has to be a credit of equal value listed somewhere in the books. (That is, unless you happen to have the name "Enron.") I was beginning to figure out that the same principle applied to just about every endeavor in life to varying degrees. A perfect example of that transpired during the preinaugural period at Southwest. Back in the early days of my tenure at Universal Airlines, after some research on my part, I had recommended to the board of directors that they permit me to cancel our order for five DC-9-30s. I believed that they could not be operated profitably in domestic charter service. However, another supplemental carrier had obviously thought they could do it: Purdue Airlines, headquartered in Lafayette, Indiana, and closely associated with Purdue University. They were most famous for having a contract to maintain and operate Hugh Hefner's coal black DC-9-30 with its white bunny painted on the tail, and Purdue handled the training of the beautiful bunnies (stewardesses) who supplied in-flight services for Mr. Hefner and his guests. But during April 1971, Purdue announced that they were throwing in the towel. Flying gamblers at package rates to Las Vegas just didn't produce enough revenue to pay for the planes, let alone make any money.

While this situation was on the wrong side of the ledger for Purdue's stockholders and employees (debit), it sure presented a great opportunity for Southwest (credit). We needed twenty-two captain-qualified pilots to begin our operation, and there they were, all in one place. As soon as the news of Purdue's demise came out, Don Ogden caught the very next flight to Lafayette, enlisted the cooperation of Purdue's chief pilot, examined the personnel files of all flight crew members, conducted personal interviews, and selected twenty-two cream-of-the-crop captains. Those who were not type-certified to fly the Boeing 737-200 aircraft had to obtain their FAA ticket for it, and we sent them to the United Airlines Flight Training Center at Stapleton Field in Denver, Colorado, at $10,000 a pop.

Don's enlistment of those pilots was great, and we were all very excited to have that major responsibility taken care of, but that coup couldn't hold a candle to the stunt Dick Elliott pulled off. Unbeknownst to the rest of us, he slipped off to Purdue and hired the sweetheart who was in charge of Purdue's stewardesses and personally did all the flight training for Hugh Hefner's bunnies. That jewel of a lady was Jan Arnold. She was very special! Jan had agreed to join Southwest only if her husband, one of Purdue's pilots, also came. Since he was eminently qualified, we had a deal. Unfortunately, approximately a year later, Jan divorced her husband, and because of that, she left the company to become a senior instructor for Continental Airlines in Los Angeles. I tried my best to get her to stay, to no avail.

Like the debits and credits, though, there is always something good for everything that's bad. Jan's departure provided the opportunity for me to bring into the company a man I had worked with at Trans-Texas, and who had been one of my VPs

81

at both Central and Universal. Since Universal's bankruptcy, he had been running Dobbs House catering service for the airlines at the Atlanta airport. Bud Herring and his great family were tickled to death to be back in Texas after he became our VP in charge of all in-flight service, including provisioning as well as handling the purchase, storage, and into-plane service for all our jet fuel requirements.

Additionally, Dick Elliott had brought back several of Purdue's top stewardesses, who were never to be called by that title again. At Southwest they were not stewardesses, not cabin attendants, not flight attendants, not waitresses. They were our passengers' "hostesses." Their job was to make our customers feel welcome and show them a good time — on the airplane only. There were to be no arrangements made for dates with passengers while on duty. I'm sure, though, that there were a few phone numbers passed out.

We decided we would need thirty-eight hostesses for our initial three-aircraft fleet, and the Bloom Agency came up with a great idea to bring in a large selection of beautiful girls for us to interview. We placed a quarter-page ad in the classified sections of the Dallas, Houston, and San Antonio papers, as well as in Los Angeles, San Francisco, Chicago, and New York classifieds. The ad was in the form of "An Open Letter to Raquel Welch," advising her that we were starting a new airline down in Texas and we would sure like for her to come and be one of our beautiful hostesses. We told her we knew she was probably too busy and rich to accept our invitation. However, if she had friends who looked like her, we sure would appreciate it if she would tell them about our new airline and have them send in an application along with a good picture.

We got more than 1,200 applications with pictures and had no difficulty in setting up interviews for the best of the crop. I told everybody that I hand-picked every one of them. Not so! Dick Elliott performed that pleasurable task. They were, as would be expected, all beauties, but what got them hired was, first, their personalities and charm, and, second, their very high scores on the FAA proficiency test.

Our hostesses' orange knit tops and red hot-pants, together with their big white belts and knee-high boots, did not go unnoticed by the public, to say the least. The outfit was designed by a sharp gal at the Bloom Agency named Pat Austin, in concert with and subject to final approval by my wife, Juanice. From the beginning, our airline was known as the one on which male passengers would fight for aisle, rather than window, seats.

Concurrent with the hiring of flight crews, Jack Vidal was selecting his twenty-five mechanics. Doug Lane was hiring an eight-person crew for the purchasing office and the stock room, and Dick Elliott was searching for his eight sales representatives, preferably female. Bill Franklin had already selected his station managers for our three startup cities: George Orr in Dallas, Carl Warrell in San Antonio, and Jim Walters at Houston Intercontinental. Each of them was actively interviewing prospective employees as ticket agents, operations agents, and ramp agents during the weeks prior to our inauguration of service. When hiring was completed, the staff at our three stations consisted of forty-two passenger-handling personnel and nine ramp agents. We bought a fleet of Nash Gremlins, financed by the Mercantile National Bank, painted like our "Love Birds," as moving billboards for our sales reps and officers.

I planned to appoint Rollin King executive VP-operations, thinking he would be pleased that his title included the word "executive." He wasn't. Honor, prestige, and recognition were all important to Rollin King. He wanted the "operations" part of the title removed, for obvious reasons. I told him "no way," since the job he was to do for Southwest had clearly defined duties — overseeing the management of the flight, dispatch, and maintenance operations. Period. He was to have no authority in any other area, nor was I to catch him meddling in ground operations, in-flight cabin service, marketing, public relations, advertising, finance and accounting, or legal. He knew that I meant what I said, and he dropped the subject for the time being.

However, just as important for Rollin King as the executive title was his desire to be a jet pilot and number one on the pilot seniority list. To accomplish this, since he had never flown anything other than small piston-engine planes, he would first have to be type-certified on the Boeing 737. This would mean sending him along with all the ex-Purdue pilots to the United Airlines Training Center at substantial cost to the company. After some thought, I approved this nonessential expenditure, since it would keep him pacified for a while. And if he didn't flunk out, he could serve as a reserve pilot in the event of a pilot shortage. I was happy that he passed and got his ticket, even qualifying to sit in the left seat.

Most of our new officers and top supervisors had brought with them copies of the operating manuals for the functions for which they had responsibility at their previous employers. Additionally, Rollin and I had obtained complete copies of PSA's manuals during our four-day visit to PSA's headquarters in San Diego. The preparation of our operation manuals was therefore primarily a cut-and-paste procedure, taking the best parts from the manuals we had on hand that had already been approved by the FAA. Besides having an outstanding management team, we wound up with the best manuals in the business. As the FAA held Don Ogden in particularly high esteem, we had very little difficulty flying through the certification of our operating manuals, our aircraft evacuation demonstration, and our fifty hours of proving flights.

I was not on the delivery flight of our first Boeing 737-200 from Seattle, but a few minutes after it landed, Don Ogden was in my office asking me if I knew about and approved of the conduct of the hostess crew who had worked it, simulating their first scheduled flight.

"Well, not specifically, but generally, yes," I said. "Why do you ask? Was there something wrong?"

"You're darn right there was something wrong."

Don, who was used to hearing the formal, no-nonsense announcements by flight attendants on American Airlines, was shocked at our girls' humorous freewheeling. At American he had never heard the sort of announcements he heard back in the passenger cabin that day — announcements such as, "Y'all buckle that seat belt because we're fixin' to take off right now. Soon as we get up in the air, we want you to kick off your shoes, loosen your tie, an' let us put a little love in your life on our way to Big D." This had been followed by the laughter and applause of the guest passengers, primarily Southwest mechanics who had been in training at Boeing, and Boeing sales and technical representatives. I pointed out to Don that the hostesses' banter incorporated all of the FAA-required safety instructions, but they had just delivered them with a little "love" thrown in, in accordance with our slogan: "The Somebody Else Up There Who Loves You." Don kind of settled down, and a sly smile came on his face. His only remark was, "Say, this is going to be fun."

I told him that was the central idea. Have fun, enjoy your work, do a good job for the customer, and everybody will be surprised at how short the workday is. The trick was to somehow get that concept across to each and every person on the Southwest Airlines payroll.

When strait-laced Don Ogden remarked that it was "going to be fun," I knew I had made the right selection of advertising agencies. Bloom had done an outstanding job of market research, resulting in the placement of our company as the hip, not-so-formal essence of love, a fun-seeking outfit that would brighten your day while you were being transported from A to B by a group of highly professional and dedicated people. We would ticket you in ten seconds with our love machine (cash register), and ply you with love potions (cocktails or soft drinks) en route, served by lovely hostesses anxious to please, all from our home base at Love Field in Dallas, Texas. We were to be truly "The Somebody Else Up There Who Loves You." Braniff and TI might not love you, but you could count on God and Southwest Airlines.

While we had been hard at work preparing to launch Southwest Airlines, Harding Lawrence, the CEO at Braniff Airways, had been busy as a bee pulling every string he could to make life miserable for us. He even called for a boycott of us by the other carriers. This meant they should not share any terminal facilities under their control or sell us fueling and reservation services. Neither should they provide us with overnight or emergency maintenance contracts, though it was customary in the industry for a new carrier entering a market or a carrier with low-level initial operations to negotiate such relationships with the established carriers — at least on a temporary basis. Despite Braniff's efforts, American Airlines signed an agreement with us to handle our reservation calls. Frontier rented us ten feet of their counter at Love Field, incorporating one baggage well, in return for us signing an agreement for them to handle our passengers' baggage at an exorbitant rate per flight. Delta sub-leased the use of a single gate at both Love Field and Houston Intercontinental. Things were coming together so satisfactorily that in mid-May we felt comfortable in setting our inauguration of service for Monday morning, June 18, 1971.

By this time our "red herring" (registration statement) was being reviewed by the SEC and had been distributed to the un-derwriting group and potential buyers in preparation for our public offering. Then Harding Lawrence's dirty work really started showing up. First, I got a call from our lead underwriter, Todd Alexander, of Auchincloss, Parker & Redpath, saying that it was going to be necessary to delay the public offering for an undefined period of time, which could be forever.

"Why, what's the problem, Todd?" I asked.

It seemed that the largest local brokerage firm in Texas, Rauscher Pierce, had declined to become a member of the un-derwriting group, and my old friends in New York just felt that the offering would not be successful without them.

"Hold everything," I told him. "I'll be in touch. Expect to see me in your office day after tomorrow."

Rauscher Pierce had very close ties to the Mercantile Na-tional Bank, having been spun off from the Mercantile when a change in federal law required the banks' divestiture of broker-age operations. Jack Bradford, one of my directors and in-vestors, was a personal friend of Mr. Pierce, the managing di-rector of Rauscher Pierce. I immediately called Jack, related my problem, and asked him to get me an audience with Pierce early the next morning, which he did. Pierce was quite forthright. He told me that they were scheduled to be an underwriter for all the upcoming Dallas–Fort Worth Airport bonds, worth millions and millions of dollars. He said that Harding Lawrence had made it very clear to them that if their name appeared on our of-fering prospectus, he would see to it that they could forget about having a nickel's worth of the upcoming DFW business. You can't fight something like that, except through a lawsuit, and we would be dead long before we could even get one started.

In the meantime, Todd, knowing I was on my way up there and that I was not going to take no for an answer, had been busy himself. When I showed up in his office the next morning, he advised me that the firm of Model Roland had some interest in participating with them as co–lead underwriter, but that it was up to me to meet with old man Model and convince him that we were for real. Model had strong ties with Italy, and he knew that if the offering was slow in the U.S., he could lay off a sizable portion in Italy, but not if it wasn't a good deal for his customers. Over a period of a couple of hours, I made my pitch and answered all his and his associates' questions, one of whom was an acquaintance of Rollin King and thus was somewhat familiar with our planned operation.

Then the old man—and he was *ancient*—said, "Lamar, we will co-lead this underwriting if you get rid of the provision in your subordinated convertible debentures which permits the holders to get their money back out of the proceeds of any public offering of the company. That smacks of a bailout to me." I told him that this was no small task, since the securities had already been sold, issued, and paid for, but I would be on the next flight to Houston, where I would confront Wesley West with the problem. If he, being the largest holder of the debentures, wouldn't budge, the jig was up.

On the plane back to Houston, I formulated my plan of attack. It was really pretty simple, as most problems are, when properly analyzed. The holders of the debentures either relinquished their right to be made whole out of the upcoming public offering, or there wouldn't be a public offering. And if there were no public offering, there wouldn't be any Southwest Airlines. Even if we cut off all spending, we could only get them back maybe 10 to 20 percent of their investment, but that would be it. On the other hand, if they went along with the change Model demanded, and the public offering was assured, then it would be up to me to make the thing tick. West, being a smart cookie even if he was a little eccentric, went along with me. He only asked, "How come you always change the deal on me in midstream?" All I could do was apologize and thank him profusely for being so understanding. From West's office I went directly to the Vinson & Elkins office and had them draw up a letter for all the other holders to sign, then talked to each of them by phone to let them know the situation. After that I went home to bed, not having been there for some seventy-two hours. The letters were all delivered to Model before the week was out.

There was no rest for the weary, though. The day after my return from New York, I received a call from the head trust officer of the First National Bank in Dallas, advising me that they were not going to be able to serve as registrar and transfer agent for our common stock.

"What do you mean you are not going to be able? You have already accepted the assignment and you are listed as such in our red herring, which has been widely distributed."

This smelled strongly of Harding Lawrence again, and I asked the officer flat out if that was the case. He said he didn't know, that his instructions had come from higher up. I told him that he better get to those higher-uppers right quick and tell them that if they didn't want to get sued, they'd better straighten up. "I have had just about all of Mr. Harding Lawrence [whom I knew to be a director of their bank] that I can take." I got another call a couple of hours later advising that the First National Bank of Dallas would be honored to continue serving as our registrar and transfer agent.

Mr. Lawrence was not through yet. Three days before we were to inaugurate service, I got a call from a reporter wanting to know how I felt about the temporary restraining order that District Judge Betts in Austin had issued against the TAC and Southwest Airlines. This was the same judge who had ruled against Air Southwest receiving a certificate from the TAC back in 1968.

"What's he restraining?"

"Your inauguration of service next Monday."

"On what basis?"

"You guys are planning to begin your operation with brand-new Boeing 737-200 aircraft and you made your case back in 1968 on the basis of American's discarded Lockheed Electra aircraft."

"So?"

"That's Harding's reason for seeking the restraining order."

"Certificates of Public Convenience and Necessity are issued to authorize the most efficient, most comfortable, and safest service management can provide," I told the reporter. "They have absolutely nothing to do with the flight equipment to be utilized. Had Braniff not tried to stop them back in 1968 and let Air Southwest begin service with the aircraft proposed by Rollin King, they probably would have used those old Lockheeds and almost immediately gone flat broke. Then Harding wouldn't have anybody to pick on now. I don't guess Lawrence realizes that when Braniff got their CAB certificate they were probably operating Ford Tri-Motors."

Since our lawyer, Herb Kelleher, and his secretary, Colleen Barrett, had been up in Washington the last few days and were now en route back to Texas, I contacted John Peace, also an attorney, and informed him of the situation. Fortunately, he was going to be in Austin that evening at a party honoring the members of the Texas Supreme Court. He said he would see what he could get accomplished, but he wanted me to find Herb and divert him to Austin for the evening's affair. We caught him as he came through Dallas on his way back to San Antonio, put him on a Southwest Airlines Boeing 737 that was winding up its fifty hours of training flights, and had it deliver him to the Austin airport.

John Peace, in his inimitable way, somehow convinced the members of the court to go into session the next morning (Saturday), bypassing the normal appellate procedure, and hear Herb's arguments asking them to lift the temporary restraining order. By doing so, the court would put the district judge in his place. Herb worked most of the night preparing our pleading. The court did it in spades. With all the obstacles cleared away, and everybody having seen our double-truck introductory advertising in all the Sunday papers, the inauguration of service the following Monday morning was a kind of nonevent.

11. THE LUV YEARS—

First Flight to the #13 War

During the preinaugural period, I had been busier than a cat on a hot tin roof trying to be everywhere at all times and everything to all people. I was very seldom in my office and had absolutely no time to be coddling or romancing our board of directors, which had now grown to ten members with the addition of West, Bradford, and Alexander. With the beginning of operations, however, some semblance of order and regularity started to creep into the picture, and I began attempting to make up for my past neglect.

I initiated a firm policy of composing a letter to the members of the board each month and mailing it to them along with the previous month's internal financial and operations statement. In my letter I would comment on all significant details, variations from budget, and overall results. Additionally, I would comment on important happenings of the past month and try to prepare them for future events that they would either need to know about or approve. Quite often, I sent them letters other than the monthly overall view letter to address specific subject matter that needed immediate attention.

I began to treasure the time spent in preparation of these letters, as it forced me to reflect on all that had happened during the past month and what was anticipated in the immediate future. From the outset, I built a personal file in three-ring binders which contained copies of (1) the monthly internal operating statements, (2) quarterly and annual reports to shareholders, (3) every piece of correspondence to the board as a whole or individual members thereof, (4) every piece of correspondence from members of the board (primarily complaints by Rollin King), and (5) correspondence from or to others having to do with board matters. When on March 28, 1978, I was unceremoniously dumped by my board of directors, I took these accumulated binders with me. They just barely fit into a long file-storage box, which has been stored since then in seven different attics. Some twenty-two years later (March 28, 2000), as I began writing this chapter, I got the box down out of the attic and started leafing through the binders, particularly those from 1971 through 1973, when we were struggling to keep Southwest alive, and the ones from 1977 and 1978, when we were rolling in profits and I was trying to keep Rollin King off my back so as to carry the company to ever greater heights.

I came to the realization that the Southwest story had already been written in these documents. And it had been written as it was happening with all the passion, controversy, mistakes, joy of conquest, and yes, ultimately, hard feelings that make it one of the most dramatic and human stories of the formative and direction-setting years of one of the great companies of all time, bar none. And rest assured, any similarity between this real story and the convoluted tales told in *Hard Landing: The Epic Contest for Power and Profits That Plunged the Airlines into Chaos* (1995) by Thomas Petzinger Jr. and *Nuts! Southwest Airlines' Crazy Recipe for Business and Personal Success* (1996) by Kevin and Jackie Freiberg is purely coincidental. Both of these books were written more than twenty years after the events actually occurred by people who were not only not present but at the time were probably still in diapers.

The next five chapters, therefore, will quote profusely from the storehouse of material just rediscovered in my attic. No re-hashing, sugar-coating, or failure of memory. Just the straight goods as the events were recorded in their chronological order.

The very first Sunday morning of Southwest's life, we narrowly escaped a disaster. The aircraft for the first flight to Houston had been taxied from the maintenance hangar to our gate at the terminal by the mechanics checked out to do that job, then turned over to the flight crew. During the takeoff run, the right thrust-reverser deployed. Only the captain's instantaneous reaction allowed him to recover control and make a tight turn for an emergency landing on one engine.

As part of regular maintenance the night before, that mechanism had been deployed, but when closed manually, it had not been securely locked. A light on the rear panel in the cockpit indicated this, but prior to takeoff, the first officer, Rollin King, had apparently failed to check that panel, and as the aircraft gained rotation speed, the clam shells flew open, putting tremendous drag on the right side. The very next morning, a change was made in operating policy providing that any time an aircraft was taxied from a maintenance facility to a gate, both thrust-reversers would be cycled during the taxi run and the panel checked to make sure there were no warning lights showing.

Up to June 18, 1971, when Southwest began scheduled operations, the fare charged by other airlines for the flight between Dallas and Houston had been $27, and from Dallas to San Antonio it had been $28. With our forecast operating cost and with a nice round $20 fare, including federal transportation taxes, we could break even with a load of slightly fewer than thirty-eight passengers. With nineteen rows in our aircraft's configuration, that meant that all thirty-eight passengers could have an aisle seat and watch the show, or if they chose, a window seat and watch the other kind of scenery. So we began service with that $20 fare, which was immediately met by the competition. Simultaneously, Texas International complemented Braniff's every-hour-on-the-hour service with every-hour-on-the-half-hour flights in the Dallas-Houston market.

Some months earlier, while Rollin King and I had been visiting PSA in San Diego, they had recommended that we set twenty-five-minute turn (ground or gate) times between flights, which is what they used with their Boeing 737s. Since the flight time (gate to gate) from Dallas to both Houston and San Antonio was fifty minutes, that meant we could operate every 1:15 hours. With two of our three aircraft assigned to the Dallas-Houston route, we could only offer service every 1:15 hours in each direction and every 2:30 hours in the San Antonio market. This left us at a disadvantage, but we put our best foot forward with a newspaper ad listing flight times. "How do we love you?" the ad began. "Let us count the ways."

To combat this situation, we decided (erroneously, as it turned out) to take delivery of the fourth aircraft I had arranged for and with it operate flights in the Dallas–Houston market every hour on the hour, even though it represented poor utilization of the fourth aircraft. When our board approved my accepting delivery of the fourth aircraft, there was one dissenting vote: Wesley West. He couldn't understand how we could be taking on an additional aircraft when the three we had were only carrying an average of seventeen passengers per flight. He felt so strongly about it that he resigned from the board. He was right; the rest of us were wrong.

In my letter to the board of directors dated September 27, 1971, which accompanied the horrible August operating statement, I wrote:

> Short of some kind of miracle instantaneous growth of traffic on our flights, we obviously cannot continue very long with our present game plan which includes, effective October 1, hourly and every other hour service to Houston and San Antonio respectively during week-days with a full service pattern on Saturday mornings and Sunday afternoons.
>
> Our financing is great; our PR and advertising have been far beyond expectations; our flight and ground operations have been flawless; and the customers we have attracted unanimously sing our praises. Our single problem has been that there just haven't been anywhere near enough of them (customers). Therefore, a full and frank discussion of the probable total market is in order.
>
> Our original route applications and the prosecution thereof and our final decision to proceed with the inauguration of ser-

93

vices were largely based on market, stimulation, and participation factors supplied us by C. W. Pope of Alexander Grant & Co. I have recently restudied these forecasts and with the facts known today believe them to be grossly overstated.

At the time of Pope's forecast, the latest actual traffic figures available from CAB surveys were for the calendar year 1969, to which he had added annual growth figures of 12.5 percent, and a Southwest service and price stimulation in excess of 30 percent. He had estimated we would take approximately 45 percent of the expanded market, plus a share in some of the connecting business, and come up with an estimate for fiscal year 1972 of 445 average passengers per day in each direction in the Dallas-Houston market and 215 in the Dallas–San Antonio market. But Southwest's actual traffic through August 31 had only averaged 166 and 79 in these two markets, and 194 and 83 during the first twenty-four days of September 1971.

Later CAB figures now available showed that traffic had actually declined in 1970 and even more in the first half of 1971. I now estimated that the actual total market when we began service was 550 passengers in the Dallas-Houston market (versus Pope's 900) and 250 in the Dallas–San Antonio market (versus Pope's 425). That being the case, in September we were carrying 35 percent of the Dallas-Houston market and 33 percent of the Dallas–San Antonio market, while providing about 33 percent of the flights in each market.

The problem for us was that, being an intrastate carrier, the local traffic in the market was all there was, whereas for the interstate carriers (our competitors), the local traffic represented only 41 percent of their onboard passenger load, the remainder being through and on-line connecting passengers (46 percent) and interline connecting passengers (13 percent). We could capture 100 percent of the interstate's local traffic and they would still have 59 percent of their passenger load. With this realization of a much smaller market than originally contemplated, my letter of September 27 continued:

Thoughts or plans of action which should be explored at our October 12 directors' meeting are as follows:

1. Raise the present $20 fare to $25 at the earliest possible moment. Based on premise that market is predominantly business travel, which is not affected by price. Adds $80,000 per month to revenues.

2. Completely cancel all scheduled operations on Saturday and Sunday. Saves $30,000 per month.

3. Temporarily shut down San Antonio operation. Saves about $70,000 per month, assuming we dispose of one aircraft.

4. Consider mid-day cancellations.

5. Reconsider serving Houston on at least part of our flights from Hobby Airport.

6. Get Love Field/Regional Airport question resolved so that long-range plans can be implemented at Love Field.

7. Approve or disapprove purchase of two additional spare engines as discussed in my letter of August 27, 1971.

8. Throw in with TI on some basis, providing them with much needed cash and beautifully financed aircraft, and us with an out.

9. Discontinue operations, dispose of assets, and liquidate.

I hasten to add that I feel there are reasonable solutions short of No. 9, but it should be considered.

Although passenger loads during the past two months have not developed nearly as rapidly as projected, it is still my feeling that the acquisition of the fourth airplane and the resultant schedule improvements will enable us to compete much more effectively with Braniff and Texas International and thus increase our share of the market to an extent which will, over a period of time, justify this purchase.

Some of the plans of action enumerated in that letter had been eliminated from the list of possible alternatives by the time I wrote my next memo to the directors on October 22, 1971. For one thing, none of us would consider number nine. For another, we had secured Southwest's use of Hobby Airport in Houston. I wrote:

We have apparently been able to work out all problems relative to the inauguration of service at Hobby Airport. We have set November 15 as our target date for beginning service at that location, with seven of our 14 round trips to Houston being

95

transferred to Hobby; the inauguration of three round trips between San Antonio and Hobby; the cancellation of four of our seven round trips between San Antonio and Dallas; and the complete cancellation of all operations on Saturday. The Saturday cancellations permit us to rearrange our station personnel so that our present personnel can handle the staffing of the Hobby station as well as take over the reservation function now being conducted by American at a cost of $20,000 per month.

Hobby Airport, located in southeast Houston, no more than six or seven miles from the downtown area, was named for former governor William P. Hobby. It had been a working and busy airport from the dawn of commercial aviation until 1969, when all scheduled service was moved to the new Houston Intercontinental Airport, located some twenty-six miles north of the city. Having been a Houston resident a good part of my life, I hardly gave a thought to service from Hobby Airport at the time we began operations in the Dallas-Houston market, because I knew that most Houston citizens who flew lived in the southwestern and western parts of Houston. With the freeway system, Intercontinental, where all the other carriers were located, was about as convenient for them as Hobby was. Our onboard passenger surveys made it apparent, however, that there were half again as many Dallas-based passengers on our flights as there were Houston-based passengers. Therefore, proximity to downtown Houston, as opposed to its residential areas, took on added significance. This was perfectly logical, since Dallas was a finance and marketing center (supplier) and Houston was more of an industrial center (consumer).

After we decided, based on our passenger surveys, to move half of our flights to Hobby, we literally had to chase the bats out of the terminal. Initially, for our flights we utilized only the ground-level international wing, where there were no bridges to the aircraft: the passengers had to walk across the ramp and climb the aircraft stairway. We had real concerns at first that there might not be an adequate taxi line to serve our passengers because that end of town, when it came to motels and parking facilities, had just died. Anyone familiar with the current-day Hobby, with its multistory parking garage, three active fingers with probably fifty gate lounges, new overpass to the greatly enlarged ticketing and baggage area, and a dozen fine nearby hotels and motels, will have difficulty believing this. But all of these improvements came about because back in 1971, Southwest Airlines was going broke serving Houston Intercontinental Airport rather than Hobby Airport. Some three years later, this lesson became ample reason for our refusal to move our Dallas operations from close-in Love Field to the faraway Dallas–Fort Worth Regional Airport (DFW).

At a meeting in November, the board decided on a plan of action regarding number eight on my list, Texas International, which was now in deep financial trouble. My twelve-year association with TTA, forerunner of TI, had given me, through people still employed there, a steady flow of information on events in their Houston headquarters, and I had watched the company's inevitable decline. It had begun in the mid-1960s when Earl McKaughan, president, CEO, and controlling stockholder of TTA, decided that he wanted to sell his interest in the company and retire. As president of Central at that time, I wasn't interested in acquiring TTA for my company, but I passed this piece of information on to my good friend Clyde Skeen, executive vice president of the aerospace conglomerate Ling-Temco-Vought, Inc. (LTV), of Dallas. Skeen agreed that it would be a good acquisition for LTV and invited me to meet with Jimmy Ling, LTV's CEO, over breakfast the next morning. We agreed that I should arrange a meeting with McKaughan and negotiate the best price I could for his controlling interest. With the valuable assistance of my good friend Jack Ayer, who was still VP-legal at TTA, I met with McKaughan and we agreed on a price of $25 per share, which was acceptable to Ling and Skeen.

However, since transfer of control was subject to the approval of the CAB, we knew there could be stumbling blocks ahead, and we quickly set up a meeting with the CAB to scout them out before proceeding further. Right away we learned that there was a major problem. It happened that LTV's aerospace division had developed a tilt-wing aircraft, a helicopter/airplane hybrid very similar in size and performance to the contentious V-22 Osprey developed for the marine corps in the 1990s. And although LTV's prototype had been designed for military use, the CAB members were convinced that a commercial version of this type of aircraft would wind up being the equipment of choice for the entire local service industry; it would therefore be inappropriate for the manufacturer of such a craft to also be the owner of one of those carriers. It was their unofficial position that an application for approval of LTV's acquisition of TTA would be rejected. As a result, LTV withdrew their offer. Ironically, it was not long after this that both LTV and the military—which was footing the company's bills for the tilt-wing—came to the conclusion that this type of aircraft would never be able to pass the vigorous safety requirements for passenger transportation. (Today's military seems to have no such concern for the marines who are sent up in the V-22 Osprey, in spite of its alarming accident record.)

After LTV dropped out of the running for TTA, McKaughan's controlling share had gone to a group headed up by Carl Pohlad of Minneapolis, which changed its name to Texas International (TI). By 1970 he had worked the company into serious financial problems, strictly from poor management. Attempting to find a way back from the brink, he had retained the consultancy services of Frank Lorenzo's Jet Capital Corporation. A year later, TI was further in debt than ever, and Jet Capital, after collecting cash fees from the company of approximately $1.2 million, offered to buy the whole damn company for an amount approximating the fees they had collected. I guess you would call that sweat capital, only the dapper Frank Lorenzo never sweated. I could see that Southwest's still-abundant cash reserve and beautifully financed aircraft, combined with TI's ready-made interstate certificate, would be a natural. I asked myself, Why just sit there and let Lorenzo steal the company? On December 27, I wrote a memo explaining to the board what had then transpired.

As authorized at our last special directors meeting on Nov. 22, 1971, I signed a letter of intent addressed to the MEI Corporation relative to the acquisition of voting control of Texas International by Southwest Airlines and made a presentation to the TI Board of Directors on the morning of Dec. 1, copies of which are attached.

This proposal provided for Southwest Airlines to invest

$1,500,000 in TI at a first closing for which Southwest would receive 2,400,000 shares of Series B Preferred stock and 1,200,000 ten-year Warrants to purchase shares at $4.00 per share. Our proposal included a relatively firm second closing which would have the effect of providing TI with an additional $1,500,000 to be provided equally by Mr. Bradford, Mr. Murchison, the MEI Corporation, and me.

I was advised by Mr. Pohlad during the late afternoon of Dec. 1 they had tentatively accepted the proposal of Frank Lorenzo's Jet Capital Corporation, who was sitting at the table with all the Texas International Directors at the time of my presentation, primarily due to timing factors and their concern that our proposal would finally not receive CAB approval. At this time, he urged me to make an alternative proposal not involving Southwest Airlines, which he assured me would be acceptable to the Directors, but which I rejected because of my commitments to Southwest Airlines.

To anyone who has read Petzinger's *Hard Landing*, which states that Herb Kelleher was surprised to see Frank Lorenzo at the above-reported meeting when he made his presentation to the TI Board, I can assure you the above account is accurate. I alone made that presentation, staring Frank Lorenzo down. Herb was in his San Antonio office taking care of his law practice, as he was on numerous other occasions enumerated in Petzinger's book.

The day following my presentation to the TI board, a spirited meeting of TI's senior creditors was held. It lasted all day long and broke up with no agreement to support the previous day's decision by the TI board. GATX-Boothe was unwilling to exchange their $5.5 million of 8½ percent subordinated notes for a preferred stock to be issued by the company unless Jet Capital provided at least $4 million of cash equity; at the same time they said they would support the Southwest proposal involving $3 million total equity. Jet Capital was apparently going to try satisfying GATX-Boothe by suggesting a rights offering to TI's other stockholders, without any effect on Jet Capital's voting control. This was designed to bring in an additional $2.5 million cash, but it was only a pipe dream, since such a offering would involve an underwriting and the filing and approval of a registration statement with the SEC.

Meanwhile, back at Southwest, the question of a fare increase, the first item raised in my September 27 memo, was put on the back burner because there was a strong feeling that TI would be cutting back on their Dallas-Houston service, and we stood to gain their customers. And as a matter of fact, that was the one good thing that came out of our attempt to take over TI: they accepted a part of one of our proposals by eliminating two of their midday roundtrips in the Dallas-Houston market. However, two members of our board still believed that Braniff might not go along with our increase, since they felt they had us on the ropes. Further, Kelleher expressed the opinion that any fare increase would now require the prior approval of President Nixon's Price Control Board. As a result, we held firm on our $20 fare at that time. After this series of crises, two of our directors, Messrs. Strauss and Kuhn, resigned from our board—in my opinion, to avoid being connected with what they considered a sinking ship.

One sidelight of interest and significance to future operating results occurred with the deletion of all our Saturday service. Initially, our revised schedule left one aircraft in Houston over the weekend, although it was far preferable for it to be at our base at Love Field for heavy maintenance purposes. A crew would therefore ferry the airplane back late Friday evenings, but it was suggested that instead, we should allow people to fly one-way from Houston to Dallas that one night a week for $10. So we did it. The first flight was almost half full. Then, by word of mouth only, no advertising, every Friday night thereafter, the loads got bigger and bigger. This cheap fare was just available in the one direction, but it was our very first inkling that there might be two distinct markets available to us if the price and timing were right: business travel during the weekday business hours, when fare level was not a significant factor, and personal travel after business hours and during weekends, at prices competitive with the private automobile in these short-haul markets.

Additionally, with no flights on Saturdays, we began soliciting weekend charter flights, primarily to important football games around the country and for excursions to Las Vegas. It was our position that out-of-state operations, when conducted as single-customer charters, did not violate our intrastate authority.

Unfortunately, upon the return of one of these Las Vegas charters, I was advised that Dick Elliott had become intoxicated and abusive and had been an embarrassment to the crew and to the company. I hated to do it, but I kept my word. I fired him.

Having had some experience in the past with associates who were on the verge of being alcoholic, I knew in my bones that if I let this incident go unpunished, it would happen again and again, and Dick, whom I had the greatest respect for, would eventually wind up a confirmed alcoholic. The only solution, in my view, was to administer what I call "tough love," and therefore, as previously stated, I fired him. As it turned out, the Glenn Advertising Agency had been trying to hire Dick from us for some time, for the purpose of assisting them in landing the Philippine Airlines account. Dick spent the next six weeks in the Philippines successfully pursuing that goal. In the process, he became an expert in the development of the passenger charter market and during the remainder of his career was highly successful in arranging vacations via charter aircraft for more than 100,000 passengers to Hawaii, Las Vegas, and foreign destinations. I, as well as Dick's entire family, are happy and proud to say that this was all done by a teetotaler, who even quit smoking in the process. Dick, very kindly, gives me credit for being the catalyst that got the conversion process started. We correspond to this day, and I consider him to be a good friend.

As a result of letting Dick go, I brought in Jess Coker, who had been VP-marketing of a national outdoor advertising company headquartered in Atlanta, Georgia. I had known him for several years through his wife, Judy, and was impressed with his appearance, personality, intelligence, and ability to get things done.

Our charter foray ended abruptly when Braniff took us to court and for the first and only time won their case against Southwest Airlines. A local Dallas judge issued a temporary restraining order that was subsequently made permanent, so our out-of-state charter days were over.

Our fourth aircraft arrived and was included in our schedule on October 1, 1971, but we quickly discovered our mistake.

Wesley West had been right. Fortunately, we found a profitable way out, as I explained in my letter to the directors dated April 21, 1972:

As discussed personally with each of you by telephone, we have contracted to sell one of our four aircraft to Frontier Airlines for a consideration of $4,090,000 plus the return to us of all passenger cabin material (seats, galleys, passenger service units, carpets, fittings, etc.), as well as many of the black boxes making up the avionics system. The material being returned has an estimated value of $156,000. A book gain in excess of $500,000 is being realized from this transaction. Additionally, we have received a commitment from Boeing that the principal reduction of our debt to them as a result of the payment we make to them to obtain release of title will be held in abeyance for our future use in connection with the purchase of a new fourth aircraft through July 1973. All we have to do to hold on to this favorable financing is to place a firm order no later than that date, and certainly by then we will know what our Dallas airport situation is going to be.

In our first-quarter 1972 report to shareholders, I explained this move by writing:

With experience we have gained during our initial operating period we have determined that all of the important transportation services which we presently perform in our three markets can be accomplished with three Boeing 737-200 aircraft. Therefore we have arranged to dispose of one of our four Boeing 737-200 aircraft with delivery to be made on May 13, 1972, under terms which are most satisfactory to Southwest. Immediately thereafter, our daily weekday schedule pattern will consist of 36 flights, as opposed to the current 42 flights per day, with flights eliminated being certain mid-day departures that have not produced satisfactory results. At the same time, we plan to consolidate all of our Houston operations at Hobby Airport, thus eliminating the very high cost of operation, which we previously have incurred at Houston's Intercontinental Airport. We expect the elimination of the owner-

102

ship costs of the 4th aircraft, the terminal costs at Intercontinental, and the direct flight costs of the trips being eliminated
to provide further substantial improvements in our financial
results in future periods.

One very important meeting, along with the determination
of a bunch of dedicated pilots, hostesses, mechanics, and, most
of all, station personnel, was left unmentioned in the above
paragraphs. I had called a staff meeting to inform our supervisors that Southwest was bleeding to death with the burden of
the fourth aircraft, that I could accept a very fine deal I had
worked out with my friend Al Feldman, president of Frontier
Airlines—Lou Diamond having long since been disposed of—
but that we were still dead in the water unless we could continue our every-hour flights in the Dallas-Houston market with
only a three-aircraft fleet. I explained that the only way we
could do that was to fly the airplanes fifty minutes and turn
them in ten minutes, as opposed to the twenty-five minutes we
were currently scheduling. Their response? We can, and we
will! Would you believe that our flight completion and on-time
performance factors actually improved after instituting the ten-
minute turns into our schedule on May 15, 1972? It was a team
effort led by Bill Franklin.

About this time, our In-flight Service Department was recruiting hostess applicants for our third class in training. We
were now a year old, and still our hostesses were 100 percent
white, and I wanted the instructors to include at least three black
women in this class, which they did. However, by the end of the
first week two of them had flunked out, and three days before
graduation, the two instructors came to me for permission to
drop the last one. I told them that since she had made it this far,
she was going to go all the way, and I expected them to devote
whatever time was necessary in extra training to see to it that she
was at the upcoming graduation ceremonies, at which I planned
to pass out the diplomas. The new hostess graduated with my
comment that we were proud to have one graduate who had an
extra-nice suntan. Her name was C. J. Bostic, and the last I heard,
she was one of Southwest's more senior hostesses.

Shortly after C. J. started flying the line, one nontypical Southwest passenger called her over and asked, "When did Southwest start letting n-----s on their airplanes?"

C. J., with no change of expression, looked all around the aircraft and said in a voice loud enough for several rows of passengers to hear, "Where is that son of a bitch? I'll throw his ass off this airplane."

I understand the smart-ass passenger had not another word to say, and when the door opened in Houston, he was the first one off and disappeared in the crowd. Later on, when another black woman joined the team, they always bid the same line of time. And since that crew of three hostesses included two black ladies and one white one, C. J. always introduced them as the "Oreo Crew."

On the same day we moved 100 percent of our Houston operations to Hobby Airport, May 15, 1972, Braniff leased an old Boeing 720 that United Airlines had retired and started running it back and forth between Love Field in Dallas and Hobby Airport in Houston. It was nice for a change to see somebody else coming in second. With their outmoded, inefficient long-haul airplanes, they were carrying less than half the load we were carrying, and most of their passengers were either connecting or interline, or nonrevenue TI employees who still had their headquarters at Hobby. We were by this time carrying an estimated 90 percent of the local traffic in that market, in spite of Braniff.

Meanwhile, we had petitioned the DFW Regional Airport Board to grant Southwest an exemption to continue utilizing Love Field after the planned opening of DFW in early 1973. We were sure that our petition would be eventually rejected, but it put all parties on notice that we had no intention of moving our service to the new airport when it officially opened. After they finished selling to the public all the revenue bonds they planned to issue, the airport board issued on June 6, 1972, Resolution No. 72-96 denying our petition and simultaneously filing with the federal district court in Dallas (Judge Taylor's court) a Complaint for Declaratory Relief naming the Cities of Dallas and Fort Worth and the Regional Airport Board as plaintiffs, with Southwest Airlines Co. as defendant.

Because of the fight we were waging to stay at Love Field after the opening of DFW, our name was mud at Dallas City Hall and in the eyes of most of the city fathers. It seemed that only the people who put them in office loved us. For instance, the City required us to pay almost three times as much property tax on our small fleet of aircraft as Braniff paid on their fleet of eighty aircraft, though we were headquartered at the same airport. Like treatment was being handed out to all individuals who dared to have an association with Southwest. This placed John Murchison in a bad spot, because he was the only one of our directors who lived in Dallas and also had substantial property holdings within the city. As a result, he reluctantly sent me a personal letter dated June 8, 1972, stating that it was necessary for him to resign his board membership that day, gratuitously adding, "Please let me assure you that this action does not in any way diminish the high personal regard which I have for you."

Even though we were still losing big money, after our May 15 changes in operation and the success we were experiencing with our still-minimum effort for that other market (still unnamed) with its $10 fare, I was beginning to see the glimmer of just a little light at the end of the tunnel. An opportunity arose to give some encouragement to our employees, which I did with the following June 1972 memo:

> In a recent issue of the Aviation Daily there was a short article attributing Continental Airlines' success to employee motivation. There is no question whatsoever that Continental Airlines is generally regarded by both other airlines and airline passengers as being the best of the CAB certificated carriers from the standpoint of service to the passenger and productivity of its employees. Therefore, I am sure you will be pleased to know that during Southwest Airlines' first year of operation, we provided our customers with a substantially more reliable service than Continental, and the productivity of each of our employees was, practically speaking, 100% better than that of Continental's as set forth in the following tabulation.

	Continental	Southwest	Southwest Superiority
Service Features:			
Flights on-time or within 15 minutes	86.4%	96.0%	9.6 pts.
Schedule completion factor	99.0	99.0	–

	Continental	Southwest	Southwest Superiority
Units of production per employee:			
Passengers carried	639	1,297	103%
Aircraft departures performed	18	59	228%
Available seat-miles flown (000)	1,000	1,532	53%

Even though our passenger loads are not yet sufficient to produce a profit from our operation, our 195 employees have performed much better than any other airline in the world, and it is for this reason you will receive substantial increases in take-home pay effective July 1, 1972.

If each of you continues to perform in our second year the way you have in our first, and I know you will, no one including "Brand X" will be able to stop us, and you may be assured that you will share in the rewards!

With sincere congratulations and thanks to each of you, I am

Cordially yours,
M. Lamar Muse

My September 27, 1972, letter to the board cites a clear example of the marvelous effect, or conversely, the disastrous effect that leverage can and does have on airline operations (and on many other industries). I copy one paragraph from that letter.

The leverage inherent in airline economics is dramatically shown in our results of operations for the months of July and August 1972. As will be seen on Schedule G, our passengers carried were 1.4% less than forecast. The yield was 2.3% less than forecast, producing operating revenues of 4.1% less than forecast. Our operating and non-operating costs were 0.7% more than forecast producing a net loss of 14.7% more than forecast and a *negative* cash flow from operations of *$61,200*, as compared to a forecast negative cash flow from operations of $5,000. If the variance in passengers carried, yield, and costs had all been positive rather than negative, our net loss would have been 13.6% less than forecast, and we would have enjoyed a *positive* cash flow from operation of $40,400, a swing of

106

$101,600 in cash flow. The difference is strictly *luck*. *Nobody* can *manage* results any closer than that.

Those minor variations from budget, had they been positive rather than negative, would have swung the actual negative cash flow of $61,200 to a positive cash flow of $40,400, and that is just with our small three-aircraft operation. Magnify that a hundred times and you have today's Southwest situation.

On several occasions, questions had arisen as to whether our late-night $10 flights were carrying their weight and also if we should just abandon the Dallas–San Antonio (DAL-SAT) market to Braniff. Initially, the only $10 flights had been the one flight a week on Friday night from Houston and San Antonio to Dallas. Due to those flights' popularity, we had added a full pattern in each market (eighteen flights per week), effective May 14, 1972. Then, to find out their true effect on break-even need, I prepared a tabulation for the months of April through July 1972, breaking down our total operation. The study covered all $10 flights operated in all markets (added direct costs only), our Dallas–San Antonio full-fare flights (added direct costs, plus San Antonio station costs, plus all ownership costs of third aircraft), with all remaining costs assigned to the full-fare flights operating out of Hobby to Dallas and San Antonio (admittedly overburdening that operation). The results of this study were as summarized below:

	DAL-SAT Flights				$10 Night Flights			
	April	*May*	*June*	*July*	*April*	*May*	*June*	*July*
No. of trips operated	315	317	310	293	8	49	78	78
Passengers carried	6,633	6,007	6,451	5,368	573	2,190	4,636	5,720
Avg. passenger load	21.1	18.9	20.8	18.3	71.6	44.7	59.4	73.3
Yield per psgr. carried	$18.75	$18.86	$19.05	$21.70	$9.44	$9.54	$9.27	$9.65
Operating rev. (000)	$124.4	$113.3	$122.9	$116.5	$5.4	$20.9	$43.0	$55.2
Operating cost (000)	$162.4	$158.6	$164.1	$179.6	2.0	12.0	18.9	20.1
Net inc. (loss) (000)	$(38.0)	$(45.3)	$(41.2)	$(63.1)	$3.4	$8.9	$24.1	$35.1

Short of some miraculous improvement in passenger loads — an unlikely event — it was perfectly obvious to me that the Dallas–San Antonio market had to go. Conversely, we were sitting there starving to death with a ham on our shoulder in the form of many more potential low-fare (not necessarily $10) evening and weekend flights. Jess Coker and I went to the Bloom Agency for a work conference with Ray Trapp, our account executive, and their creative group. I told them that I wanted to present the public with a new airline, and I wanted to do it effective October 30 for the winter schedules. First I wanted our full-fare flights to be called Executive Class and our low-fare flights to be called Pleasure Class. I wanted to move the hour of weekday transition to 7:00 P.M. from 8:00 P.M., and I wanted to resume a good Saturday operation. Executive Class flights would be those that departed after 6:30 A.M. and before 7:00 P.M. on Monday through Friday. All flights that operated from 7:00 P.M. weekdays, and on Saturday and Sunday, would be Pleasure Class flights. Incidentally, it was Bill Franklin who finally convinced me to make all weekend flights Pleasure Class. He was so right.

We told the Bloom group we had to have more than the present $10 for the Pleasure Class flights when they became an integrated part of our marketing plan, but I didn't want it to sound like an increase. So the way we were going to do it was to increase our present single $20 fare to a new Executive Class fare of $26 one-way and $50 roundtrip, which fare would now include free cocktails. That way our customers' afternoon libations would for the most part be paid for by their employers, a tax-free benefit and further encouragement for them to fly Southwest. We would then offer our Pleasure Class flights at *half-price*, $13 one-way and $25 roundtrip—but with no free cocktails. To accentuate the half-price feature, I wanted them to get to work on a campaign that we could break one week before the new schedule became effective.

I was perfectly willing to sink or swim on this concept. And President Nixon's Price Control Board could do whatever they damn well pleased. As it turned out, we never heard a peep from them. I further told the agency to be forewarned that I was probably going to abandon the Dallas–San Antonio route at the end of the year and to be thinking of the way to announce that setback with the least possible damage.

While we reorganized fares, I was pursuing a course of action to lighten the financial burden we would soon face when the $1.25 million debentures came due. Ever since Wesley West had resigned from our board, he had been bugging me to pay off the debenture he held. Under the circumstances, I wanted to

108

accommodate him, but not at the expense or peril of our share-holders. With the much brighter light that I now saw at the end of the tunnel, I persuaded the board to make an offer to all the debenture holders to select one of three options, as follows:

1. Convert their debentures at face value into common shares at a one-time reduced price of $2 per share as of November 1, 1972.

2. Accept as full payment for the debenture its face value less all the interest which had been paid on the debenture to date (thus making them whole, but with no income).

3. Do nothing, and we will see what happens come March 10, 1973, when the debentures will otherwise be due.

As it turned out, that was about as fair an offer as could possibly be conceived.

I spent at least two hours in West's office trying to convince him to leave the cash and take the stock, not only because I felt indebted to him for being the one person in the world who made Southwest Airlines possible with his $750,000 investment at a critical moment, but also because it was a lot of money that I didn't want to have to pay out at that particular time. He wouldn't budge. He wanted the money.

Jack Bradford had split his holdings among his three grand-children, and he thus felt a fiduciary responsibility to take the cash and not gamble it on Southwest. Van Calvin Ellis had donated his debenture to the Dallas YMCA, and, of course, they couldn't see beyond the found cash. John Murchison took 25,000 shares of stock for his $50,000 debenture, but he felt it was too risky for his wife, Lupe. (She never forgave him.) The two New York clients of Auchincloss, Parker and Redpath also took the cash. I took another 25,000 shares of stock for my $50,000 debenture. All the holders still had their warrants, which were exercisable for three-plus more years.

It's hard to believe, but had West taken 375,000 shares of stock for his debenture, rather than the approximately $675,000 cash he needed like he needed another hole in his head, he not only would have been Southwest's largest stockholder, but in today's market, after fourteen stock splits, those 375,000 shares would represent 112,500,000 shares at approximately $22 per share, or $2,475,000,000. Ain't that a pistol? Just in case you can't read a figure that big, that's two billion, 475 million U.S dollars. That one investment equals the net worth of Robert Bass, the 157th richest person in the country according to Forbes' current rankings. Wesley is dead and gone, so it makes little difference to him, but his heirs and his Faith Foundation would sure be different now. They might even be able to build that airplane he wanted and observe old Wesley up in Heaven, 'cause I'm absolutely sure if there really is a Heaven, he is there. He was a good man.

The other cushion we had built into the Southwest picture was a promise by Boeing in the fall of 1971 that if the cheese got to be too binding, they would make some scheduled payment deferrals, rather than take back their airplanes, which was the last thing they ever wanted to do. That time came in November 1972. Our October 31 payment of $150,000 on our three aircraft was the last regular payment made for a period of twelve months, with the understanding that we would pay to Boeing 50 percent of all positive cash flows during that twelve-month period. In other words, if we had the funds to pay them, we did, and if we didn't, we paid nothing. It was a great help, particularly after paying out $1,009,125 to retire $1,150,000 of debentures on November 1.

After Braniff and TI had failed to have the CAB exert jurisdiction over our operations earlier that year, the question of possible jurisdiction over our intrastate air carrier operations was finally put to bed on December 11, 1972, when the Federal Circuit Court of Appeals for the District of Columbia favorably and decisively ruled against the joint Braniff-TI appeal of the earlier CAB decision. In Judge Miller's concurring opinion, he said: "It is now five years since Air Southwest applied to the Texas Aeronautics Commission for a Certificate of Public Convenience and Necessity. This litigation should have been terminated long ago; its undue prolongation approaches harassment." Approaches? Probably the understatement of the year.

While by the end of 1972 we were doing somewhat better systemwide, the Dallas–San Antonio (DAL-SAT) market was still a drag. Braniff had hourly service throughout the day, whereas we were operating just four roundtrips in the market. I had threatened to abandon the route at midyear but decided to give it another six months. Now the six months were up, and I needed to either fish or cut bait. I decided to fish. On January 22, 1973, we reduced the fare on every DAL-SAT seat on every flight on every day of the week to half-price, or $13 each way. We advertised this heavily on both TV and radio, as well as newspaper and billboards, as a sixty-day half-price sale, and our loads took off. Even though we planned to leave the fare effective for an indefinite period of time, we called it sixty days in the hope that Braniff would slough off our price action. They did for a while, but when our average loads got up to the seventy to eighty passengers-per-flight level, they reacted by meeting the fare on their four flights nearest the time of our four flights. That action hardly affected our loads at all. Since that hadn't worked, Harding Lawrence put his devious mind to work again.

12. THE LUV YEARS —

Those Bastards

About 6:30 A.M. on Thursday, the first day of February 1973, I was munching away on my half grapefruit, cold cereal, peanut butter toast, and coffee while reading the *Dallas Morning News*. After digesting the headlines and the secondary stories on page two, I turned the next page, and there staring at me was a full-page Braniff Airways ad in heavy block print announcing a "Get Acquainted Sale" in the Dallas-Houston market at half-price to last till April Fools' Day.

My immediate reaction was, "Those bastards!" Having begun air service between Dallas's Love Field and Houston's Hobby Airport in the early 1930s, Braniff had balls to call their response to our sixty-day half-price sale in the Dallas–San Antonio market a "Get Acquainted Sale." I immediately called Carole Ann, my secretary, and told her to call every officer of the company plus Camille Keith, our PR director, and have them and herself in my office at 8:00 A.M. sharp. Next I called Herb Kelleher and told him to get the hell out of bed and catch the first Southwest flight from San Antonio to Dallas. Then I called Ray Trapp at home to be there, too; he had already seen the Braniff ad.

It happened that I had an appointment that morning with a

realtor to execute the purchase agreement for a beautiful new condominium on Preston Road in the block just south of the Cooper Clinic in Dallas. My wife Juanice was very unhappy that I had been putting Southwest Airlines ahead of her, and I had been hoping that a new home would keep her occupied till such time as it was not absolutely necessary for me to spend every waking moment either physically or mentally at Southwest— which was admittedly my primary love. Of course, my appointment with that realtor had to go by the wayside.

I opened the staff meeting by pointing out that at least we now knew for sure what Braniff's response was to the highly successful sixty-day half-price sale we were conducting against them in the Dallas–San Antonio market. It was to hit us hard in our only profitable market: Dallas-Houston. But I pointed out that every action Braniff had ever taken against us had turned out to be to our advantage. So how could we take this one and turn it in our favor?

I have found over the years that staff meetings never accomplish a whole lot. There was general agreement that we had to face the problem presented by Braniff's action, but I was not at all sure that just matching their new fare was the complete answer. We agreed that the Bloom Agency had to have a significant ad for the Monday edition of the Dallas and Houston morning and afternoon newspapers, but there were muddled suggestions about what the ads should say. After two hours of talk, I told everyone to go about their business and I would work on a newspaper ad.

About that time the real estate agent telephoned, and in a weak moment I took the call. He said he fully understood my failure to keep the appointment and that he had a suggestion for my problem: savings and loan organizations had been very successful over the years in getting new accounts by giving away some kind of gift to new customers, like a toaster or a waffle iron or something of that nature. "Just think about it," he said, "and I will see you in sixty days."

I did think about it, and in a matter of minutes I formulated what I wanted to say in a double-page spread for Monday morning's papers. I considered Southwest to be a class outfit, and I believed our customers felt the same way. So anything we gave away had to be of value, useful, and desired by our predominantly male, business-oriented passengers. No, definitely not any of our hostesses. But since they served so much free liquor on board our flights, our passengers obviously enjoyed a cool one. So-o-o, why not maintain our regular fare of $26 and give away a bottle of booze that cost no more than $13, hopefully less. All those guys and gals on expense accounts would jump at the chance to stock their home bars at company expense. Naturally, since we were a class outfit, it had to be good stuff. So over the weekend we stocked the Dallas and Houston stations with cases of Chivas Regal, Crown Royal, and Jack Daniels. (Herb, I know we should have included Wild Turkey.) For the Baptists who professed not to drink, Jess Coker bought a thousand leather-lined ice buckets from Tuesday Morning, all items negotiated at prices less than $13.

On the left page of my proposed double-page spread, I wrote in big, bold print: "Nobody is going to shoot Southwest Airlines out of the sky for a lousy $13." On the right side I listed numerous reasons why if people knew what was good for them, they would never fly Braniff again but always fly Southwest where available. I started with: "We think our $26 fare is a fair fare, and if you will continue to pay that price, we've got a nice gift for you. If your comptroller finally catches on and instructs you to fly Braniff at $13, don't! Come to us and we will take you for $13 and leave off the gift. If you think you have great service between Dallas and Houston, you know damn well that it is because of Southwest's competition. If you want to lose that great service, fly Braniff during this critical period. I promise you, you will find out right quick how bad service can get and how high fares can climb."

Herb got to Dallas about noon, and he, Jess Coker, VP-sales, and I headed for a knockdown-dragout meeting at the Bloom Agency. They had by that time summoned their lawyers, and in an unusually cooperative manner we hammered out a double-page spread that we all thought the papers would accept and which would avoid suits for libel. The actual ad was more of a compromise than I thought necessary, but I agreed to it, provided we printed a handout brochure over the weekend that was more in line with my original concept. Old man Sam Bloom did a yeoman's job of hand-delivering the ad copy to the four news-papers over the weekend, obtaining assurances that they would print it and getting highly desirable space in each edition.

Over the weekend, we had 50,000 four-color brochures printed that were much closer to what I had originally com-posed, particularly my signed pronouncement. They were physically delivered on Monday morning to every office in every office building in downtown Houston and Dallas. Addi-tionally, they were handed out to the Monday and Tuesday noontime crowds on major downtown street corners by off-duty Southwest pilots and hostesses in full uniform, assisted by tem-porary help. And they did it on their own time. What an outfit! How could we possibly lose?

Here's what happened traffic-wise for Southwest as a result of the two big sales going on—Southwest's half-price sale in the San Antonio market, which had begun January 22, 1973, and Braniff's "Get Acquainted" sale in the Houston Hobby market.

Week Ended	No. of Passengers	Avg. Psgrs. Per Flight
Jan. 19, 1973	7,525	36.9
Jan. 26, 1973	8,512	41.9
Feb. 2, 1973	9,122	45.2
Feb. 9, 1973	10,246	57.6
Feb. 16, 1973	12,500	63.1

With growth like this—number of passengers up 66 percent and average load by 71 percent in a matter of four weeks—I forecast in a note to our directors that we would make our first net profit in February 1973. As it turned out, I missed by one month: March 1973 was to be our first profitable month. In my enthusiasm, I had forgotten that airlines get killed in February because their fixed costs get spread over fewer days. Also, a lot more people than expected paid the $13 fare rather than opt for the $26 and a bottle of booze. Those sharp-eyed corporate comp-trollers caught on quicker than I thought they would. At the time, I considered that fact to be a minus. But twenty-nine years later, I realize that it was a big plus. Why? Because those people who were paying $13 could have ridden Braniff for the same price, and on their own they chose Southwest, even though they would probably be sitting next to someone who was cradling a bottle of Chivas Regal in his lap. Incidentally, during the months of February and March 1973, Southwest Airlines gave away more Chivas Regal than Chivas Regal sold in the state of Texas. And we never even got a thank-you letter from the distributor.

Even though we still lost money in February, we had a positive cash flow before debt service of $148,000, and compared to the previous February (which had twenty-nine days), we carried 117 percent more passengers with fewer flights—three aircraft now versus four then—for a 152 percent higher average load. Average cost per passenger was down 56 percent, with the spread between average yield (fare) and average cost per passenger declining from $17.51 to $1.81. That's 90 percent, man! The most common remark among all Southwest employees was, "All we need now is for Braniff to make just one more stupid mistake."

I knew we were doing the right things when one afternoon in late February I got a call from my friend Fayez Sarifim in Houston, who said in his own peculiar accent, "Lamar, I flew your airline up to Dallas this morning and they gave me a bottle of Chivas Regal. And when I came back this afternoon they gave me another bottle of Chivas Regal. That's class, Lamar! Besides that, both flights were full. I smell money, Lamar, and I'm going to start buying your stock." Within a couple of months, Fayez was our second-largest shareholder. Who is Fayez Sarifim? Just one of the world's most famous portfolio managers for the rich and famous.

The March net profit was small, only $18,173, but the important thing was that it was black, not red. We reported a first-quarter loss of $176,268 as compared to $843,697 in 1972, but that was the very last quarterly loss that Southwest has ever had to report. Thus began the journey to greatness. We had the tiger in our tanks (Exxon) and we were ready to fly high with both feet on the ground!

On April Fools' Day, Braniff was more than glad that their disastrous sixty days were up. There were no more $13 fares during the weekday business hours in the Dallas-Houston market, but our San Antonio sale had been extended for an indefinite period — that is, for as long as we could operate such a relatively low frequency of flights in that market. We would have to wait and see what happened to the traffic volumes in April and succeeding months.

Meanwhile, our Love Field trial had begun, and I covered the initial phases of it in my memo to the board of April 5, 1973, this way:

> Our Love Field trial before Judge Taylor in Federal District Court began on Monday, March 26. The cities of Dallas and Fort Worth and the Regional Airport Board consumed the entire first week plus Monday of the second week in presenting the plaintiff's case. We began presenting our case late Monday afternoon. I was on the stand all day Tuesday and John Eichner, our economic consultant, was on the stand all day Wednesday. Judge Taylor recessed the trial last evening until Monday, April 16, at which time we will complete our case to be followed by argument for both sides. I feel the trial has gone very well up to this point and that our representatives have done everything humanly possible to present properly our arguments. Only time will tell whether or not that was enough.

I didn't tell the directors about the first morning of the trial. Herb had just purchased his first Mercedes and was so proud of it that he drove it to Dallas from San Antonio for the hearing. Naturally, he wanted to drive it to the courthouse from our office that first morning. I assumed he knew exactly where the federal courthouse was; I only had a general idea of its location. We drove up and down main and cross streets for a good ten minutes before finding where we were supposed to park that beautiful new thing and got to the courtroom just before Judge Taylor appeared. Going up in the elevator, I told Herb that here I was in one of the most important business trials of the century and I had a damn lawyer who couldn't even find the courthouse!

13. THE LUV YEARS —

Our First Route Expansion

At the first sign of positive cash flows in late 1972, I had begun thinking about which market we would tackle next. There seemed to be no question in the minds of Messrs. Kelleher and King as to where that expansion would take place: "Austin, our state capital, of course, dummy." They had favored Austin because the Texas Aeronautics Commission, the Texas legislature, and the Texas Supreme Court were all located there, and all of them had been instrumental in enabling Southwest to take to the air. I was not at all enthusiastic about that choice, for the simple reason that it was less than 100 miles from our San Antonio market and less than 200 miles from both our Dallas and Houston markets. If we had learned anything in our first year and a half of operation, it was that the private automobile was our foremost competitor, not the interstate airlines. Therefore, distances were critical. In the normal market, distances of under 200 miles, which could be completed on the interstates in less than three hours, were tough to compete with. When you figure on one hour getting to the airport, checking in and waiting for the actual loading of the flight and departing, fifty minutes of flight time, plus whatever time it takes to get to the baggage claim, claim luggage, and hail a taxi for an ultimate destination, the individual could have been there in his own car and enjoyed the convenience that the car provided.

I put together the statistics from the CAB's Origination and Destination surveys, plus the current schedules of the CAB carriers to and from the following midsize Texas markets: Amarillo, Austin, Beaumont–Port Arthur, Corpus Christi, El Paso, Lubbock, Midland-Odessa, and Rio Grande Valley (which includes Brownsville, Harlingen, and Mission–McAllen–Edinburg, through the McAllen airport).

Deciding which market we would first apply for was similar to the problem of choosing advertising agencies prior to commencement of our operations: we would not have the luxury of changing horses in midstream. Our selection had to be right the first time. I was reasonably sure that whichever market we selected, but particularly if it was Austin, we would receive the enthusiastic approval of the Texas Aeronautics Commission, but that was not the question. Past experience showed that any favorable decision by the TAC would immediately be taken to court by whoever the opposing carrier or carriers were. Therefore, our proposed service had to fill a definite public need and be found necessary for the area's economy. In other words, the "Public Convenience and Necessity" test had to be adequately met. While it was clear that the competitive spur of Southwest's style of service would be good for almost any market, I did not consider that factor sufficient to blindly select Austin. We would get our brains beaten out on appeal.

With the exception of the Rio Grande Valley, my analysis indicated that the scheduled flights of the carriers serving each of the markets were matching fairly well the amount of traffic currently generated. I further found that each of these midsized cities was extremely proud of the "trunkline" service they had (American, Braniff, Continental, and/or Eastern) and were not at all enthusiastic about supporting a new intrastate-only carrier, which might cause the discontinuation of their trunkline service.

However, while Braniff served Brownsville in the Rio Grande Valley, only Texas International served Harlingen, located in the very center of the Valley, and Mission–McAllen–Edinburg in the upper Valley. I could not envision either Brownsville or Braniff trying to make a case against our serving the Harlingen or McAllen airports, and none of the remaining towns could care less whether Texas International stayed or not, provided they could have service by Southwest. As long as there was some question about which airport or airports Southwest would serve, chambers of commerce and city and county officials would support our service. When we subsequently narrowed it down to Harlingen, we lost the support of the Mission–McAllen–Edinburg group.

Another major reason for selecting the Rio Grande Valley (RGV) market over the Austin market was that the Austin market would provide absolutely no continuing traffic for Southwest's present system, whereas the RGV market would initially produce traffic on our Houston–Dallas and the light Houston–San Antonio trips. As the market developed and we added nonstop service to San Antonio, those trips would add traffic on our present San Antonio–Dallas flights, and I could envision nonstop flights between the two extremes of our system (RGV-DAL) during peak traffic periods like Friday and Sunday afternoons and evenings to serve the ever-more-popular South Padre Island resort area.

Additionally, in this dog-eat-dog world of ours, the strong attack the weak. Seven of the eight markets being considered were presently served by trunk carriers, while the RGV market was served only by the weak sister, Frank Lorenzo's Texas International. Sure, Braniff served Brownsville, but with limited flights to fulfill certificate requirements. Both Braniff and Eastern had been originally certificated into Brownsville, not to serve Brownsville, but to deliver continuing traffic to Pan American World Airways' northern terminus for its Central and South American routes. When the CAB moved Pan Am's northern terminus from Brownsville to Houston, they just forgot to also amend the other two carriers' domestic authority. Eastern's subsequent abandonment of Brownsville had left enough local traffic for Braniff to stick around, but I couldn't imagine them putting up a fight for it.

Since Kelleher still favored Austin, he dragged his feet in the preparation of an application to serve the Rio Grande Valley. When I knew that we were in our first profitable month, I sent him an interoffice memo dated March 5, 1973, telling him that we planned to operate initially 147 flights per month from Houston to Harlingen at a total added cost of $66,882, or only $455 per flight, which would require only 3,028 passengers, equal to 12.6 percent of the current market—forget about growth—to break even. If we could average fifty passengers on these Valley flights—which promised to be a breeze with the growth in market we would be assured of—our net income from the new service per month would be $143,864, far above any other extension of service we might consider within the confines of the state we were restricted to. I wound up the memo with this admonition: "The purpose of this letter is to convince you to get our application prepared at the earliest possible moment so that we can start reaping those very substantial profits. Something like that gives us a lot more strength to really be competitive with Braniff in the Dallas-Houston/Dallas–San Antonio markets. GO, MAN, GO!" To Herb's credit, once he realized that the decision had been made to pursue that route extension, he was behind it 100 percent.

Meanwhile, my private life had undergone a change. Toward the end of the $13 War, Juanice, my wife of thirty-two years, decided she had put up with competing with Southwest Airlines long enough and asked me to move out, which I did. Rather than rent an apartment, I bought a Winnebago motor home and parked it at a trailer park a couple of blocks from our office. I owned a piece of lakefront property, over on Lake Palestine near Tyler, on which I had wanted to build a home for some time. Now that the company was in the black, I figured I could take the weekends off to get the house started and meanwhile would live in the Winnebago at the lake property; that way I could move the house along much faster.

Southwest had begun producing profits. The big test once the $13 War was over was what was going to happen to traffic. During April 1973 we carried 47,154 passengers and had net income of $51,562, and in May we carried 45,629 passengers, with our net income climbing to $82,863. For the second quarter as a

121

whole, as compared to the same quarter in 1972, our passenger count was up 77 percent and transportation revenues were up 72 percent, but total costs were up only 12 percent, resulting in net income of $183,000 versus a loss of $589,000 before special items in the same period of the previous year. The average passenger load was 51.4 versus 28.7. How wonderful leverage is when it is in the right direction!

The second quarter of 1973 also brought a favorable ruling by Federal District Judge Taylor in the Love Field case, confirming our right to stay at the close-in Love Field for our short-haul commuter flights rather than being required to move our operation to the distant DFW Airport when it opened the following year. Of course, the three complainants took it to the Fifth Circuit Court of Appeals in New Orleans, but we felt that this was nothing more than a nuisance factor.

Just as important, in early June 1973, the Universal Air Travel Plan (UATP) finally accepted our application to become a member. The rules of this plan permitted any carrier member to blackball the application of any proposed new member. Braniff had kept Southwest on the blackball list since our inaugural flight, thus forcing UATP card holders to pay their airline charges for travel on Southwest directly to us rather than through the central billing facilities of the plan. This was a big nuisance to our customers, and it created a material overhead cost as well as larger-than-necessary bad debt expense for Southwest. When the Anti-Trust Division of the Justice Department had started an investigation of the practice at Kelleher's suggestion, we refiled our application, and lo and behold, we got unanimous approval to become a full member the following month. So very thoughtful of Harding Lawrence to permit it. We told our customers about the development with a jubilant newspaper ad: "At last, Southwest can say, 'Pick a Card.'"

About the same time, our application for extension of our route system to the Rio Grande Valley, served through the Harlingen International Airport, was duly filed, and Kelleher did a first-class job of preparing our case to be heard by an examiner of the TAC. Still, we fully anticipated that any favorable decision ultimately handed down by the commission would be appealed by Texas International to accomplish as much delay in the inauguration of service by Southwest as possible.

By now we were doing so well on our four $13 flights in the Dallas–San Antonio market that we figured out a way to squeeze in a fifth flight. Braniff retaliated by instituting a heavy advertising program about their "select and save" flights in that market, these being the five of their fourteen flights in each direction that were the closest in time to our five flights. We responded with an ad that revealed Braniff's tactics. It appeared a week late because the newspapers rejected our original ad for being too critical of our beloved competitor. It began, "Read this and you may never again want to fly Braniff between Dallas and San Antonio."

One more major decision had to be made during this time period. I had put it off, knowing that there would be strong opposition from both Kelleher and King at the time of board action, but since we were now entering a profit mode, it had to be faced. That decision was the establishment of a meaningful profit-sharing plan for all of our eligible employees. My plan would require SWA, after deducting a calculated 8 percent after-tax return on the shareholders' investment, to put aside 15 percent of all remaining pretax operating profits in a profit-sharing trust, to be administered by the Mercantile National Bank of Dallas. All funds deposited in this trust fund would be invested in the common stock of Southwest Airlines. (This was before the days of ERISA, and it was legal to do so.) I wanted this provision because it was to be a profit-sharing plan, not a pension plan. I wanted all SWA employees to become eligible to share in these profits on the January 1st after their date of employment (no long waiting period), and I wanted them to vest in 50 percent of their share of the accumulated fund after five years, with an additional 10 percent vested each year thereafter until fully vested. My rationale was that if the employees did their jobs well, there were surely going to be profits made, and if there were profits, the company's stock would most certainly at some time or other increase in value. Therefore, the plan I proposed would give the employees what I called a double-whammy. And that's good.

If we didn't put in a meaningful plan — and by meaningful I meant 15 percent, no 5 percent or 10 percent compromises —

then eventually, whether the company was highly profitable or not, it would be forced to establish pension plans for each of its various employee groups. I didn't want to go that route, since pension-plan payments must be made whether the company is profitable or not, but a company only pays into a profit-sharing plan out of profits made. Also, employees look upon profit-sharing contributions as something coming voluntarily from the employer, whereas pension-plan contributions are something the employees have worked for and thus feel entitled to. A properly executed and administered profit-sharing plan builds employee morale. Pension plans are dead weight.

During the last couple of decades, much has been written about the quality, enthusiasm, and esprit de corps of the Southwest Airlines group of employees, with 100 percent of the credit invariably going to the company's longtime CEO. I venture to say, however, that Herb Kelleher would be the first to admit that the number-one factor is actually the Southwest Airlines Employees' Profit-Sharing Plan, established back in the second quarter of 1973, the company's very first profitable quarter. The only thing that has damaged the plan was the passage by Congress (for the benefit of employees) of ERISA, whereby it became no longer legal for the company to mandate that funds would go into its own stock. This change permitted employees in many cases to make far less favorable investments. Even so, last year Southwest's profit-sharing contribution totaled $149 million, and there is not a twenty-year employee of Southwest who is not a millionaire. I'm not just talking about the officers, supervisors, and pilots. I'm talking about that porter at the curb checking your bag and the ramp agent emptying the honey bucket. This is, of course, true only if he or she chose to stay with the original Southwest stock plan.

With the likes of Enron and Global Crossing, ERISA would be good legislation only if there was some way to make it applicable just to companies whose top management are a bunch of crooks looking out only for themselves.

One other action the board had to take at this time was to authorize me to salvage the suspended credit we had coming from Boeing for the payment we had made them to release title on our previous fourth aircraft when we sold it to Frontier Airlines.

We were certainly in dire need of a fourth aircraft now, not only for the expanded traffic volumes we were enjoying, but for the new route to the RGV, which we hoped to be operating sometime in the not-too-distant future. Even though this aircraft was largely prefinanced by our Boeing credits, it was like pulling eyeteeth to get the board members' approval in time to exercise the option Boeing had granted us. I simply could never get across to the Southwest board, particularly my troublemaker, Rollin King, that you had to spend money to make money, and if you were going to make major strides, you occasionally had to take major risks.

By late 1973 a new factor was entering the airline equation. Richard Nixon had been in office long enough to get his Energy Policy Office into business, and now, between the Energy Office and the Arab oil embargo, it began to look as if we just might not get large enough fuel allotments to run our current schedule, let alone added service. Additionally, after January 13, 1974, all other carriers' scheduled flights that had been using Love Field at Dallas would be operated from the new Dallas/Fort Worth Regional Airport located in Irving, Texas. The only exceptions were Southwest's flights, so it was hoped that the move would substantially increase the amount of traffic we were carrying. My anticipation of these conflicting situations caused me to write a three-page, extremely confidential memo with attachments to all my officers and members of the board on December 6, 1973. The subject was "Southwest's Financial Metabolism." There is too much detail in that memo to include it here in its entirety, but I will summarize it to illustrate from a financial standpoint what makes an airline tick, and the leverage inherent therein.

Basing my memo on the June through October 1973 experience of Southwest's operations in its three markets, I pointed out that $491,000 of the company's monthly costs were relatively fixed; they consisted of long-term ownership costs; other long-term fixed costs, including general and administrative, sales representatives, and advertising; and what we called long-term variables, including all maintenance management, overhead and labor costs, terminal (ground) operations, and undistributed payroll burden. There were direct costs associated with

(1) the number of trips operated (at $176 per trip), including flight crews and hostesses payroll, fuel and oil plus "into-plane" service, and landing fees; (2) the air-time hours flown (at $111 each), including outside repairs, maintenance materials, and provisions for future maintenance; and (3) the number of passengers carried (at $1.12 per passenger), including beverages and supplies, agency commissions and discounts, and liability insurance.

During this sample five-month period, we had been operating approximately 900 flights per month, and at the above cost levels, we would have had to average 41,185 passengers per month (45.8 per flight) to break even at that period's average revenue per passenger of $18.50. Fixed costs at that 900-flights-per-month level amounted to 64 percent of our total costs; trip and air-time-hour costs were 30 percent; and passenger costs were only 6 percent. If because of fuel shortages we had to cut back to 800 flights, we would still require 39,745 passengers (49.7 per flight) to break even. This is only 3 percent fewer passengers, with 11 percent fewer flights. On the other hand, by adding 100 flights to bring us up to the 1,000 level, we would only require 42,625 passengers (42.6 per flight) to break even. This is the same 3-to-11-percent ratio, but in reverse.

If, because of fuel shortages for automobile drivers, Southwest carried 50,000 passengers, only 7,375 more than break-even (17.3 percent), the pretax profit would be $128,300 per month. And if we dreamed a little and carried 60,000 (60 per flight), the profit would jump to $302,100 per month, that being the total average revenue of the last 17,375 passengers at $18.50 each, less the direct cost of $1.12 per passenger. To prove it, divide $302,100 profit by 17,375 passengers and see if you don't get $17.38 ($18.50 less $1.12). In total, these result in very minor changes — fixed costs drop from 64 percent of total operating costs to 60 percent, direct-flight costs of the additional 100 monthly flights raise those costs one point to 31 percent, and per-passenger costs go from 6 percent to 9 percent. But these minor changes take profits from break-even to more than $300,000 per month.

The lesson to be learned is that leverage is hell in the wrong direction and heaven in the right direction. This axiom is especially apt in the airline business but is true to varying degrees in millions of other businesses, as well as in government. The figures I cited are worth reading over and over for anyone really interested in making fortunes. It is a damned important lesson.

As early as October 1973, it had become obvious that due to the rapid inflation resulting from the manufactured oil shortage, the CAB was going to approve a major fare increase for the airline industry, probably in December. At Southwest, we decided we would piggyback on that increase to the extent of a $2 increase in our fares from $26 to $28 for Executive Class and $13 to $15 for Pleasure Class, at the same time eliminating the $1 roundtrip discount we had previously offered. This gave us an extra $5 per roundtrip passenger (including federal tax), and it simplified our ticketing.

With passenger traffic growing by leaps and bounds, partially because of drivers' fear that they might get stranded for lack of available fuel, the year 1974 started off with a bang, and our employees' performance caused me to write the following letter to each of them, dated March 11, 1974:

Southwest Airlines Excellent February 1974 Results

If anybody ever needed additional proof that Southwest Airlines' employees and the equipment it utilizes have it all together, February should have provided that proof in spades!

Of the 852 trips scheduled during the month of February, we completed 848, for a completion factor of 99.5%. Of the 848 flights completed, 837 of them arrived at their destination within 15 minutes of scheduled arrival time, for an on-time performance factor of 98.7%. Additionally, 88.2% of our flights departed the gate within 5 minutes of scheduled departure time and 99.2% departed the gate within 15 minutes of scheduled departure time.

These fine on-time performance statistics were accomplished during the month that we carried the largest passenger loads in the history of the Company. The Dallas-Houston flights averaged 72.8 passengers. The Dallas–San Antonio flights averaged 66.9 passengers. The system average load was 66.7 passengers per flight operated.

127

As a result of this fine performance, the Company made its largest monthly net profit to date. Our operating revenues totaled $1,099,103; our total cost of operation before provision for employees' profit sharing was $853,092, producing a net profit before profit sharing of $245,616. During February, we created our first Provision for Employees' Profit Sharing in the amount of $22,270. This represents 15% of all profits in excess of $95,833 (1/12th of the $1,150,000 minimum annual profit referred to in the Southwest Airlines Employees Profit Sharing Plan).

That amount of money will buy at the current price of Southwest common stock 4,454 shares for the Trust Fund, of which 8.7 shares would be allotted to the lowest paid employee on Southwest's payroll and 65.3 shares would be allotted to the highest paid employee of Southwest's payroll — me, and everyone else would fit in at the appropriate spot on a pro-rata basis.

If we can "keep it all together" like that, we can all retire early, rich, and buy our own Cadillac ... or Mark IV ... as the case may be.

MLM/cab

That "/cab" after my initials above reminds me that I have been horribly negligent in not bringing into this story that wonderful lady who had been my right hand from early on in this Southwest adventure. Carole Ann Brown came to me from a top stenographic job at Arthur Young & Co., CPAs, against the advice of her bosses, whom I had fired when I became president of Central Airlines back in 1965. She ignored their pleadings, took the gamble, and I am sure never regretted it.

The Love Field legal situation continued to rumble in both Dallas and Fort Worth city halls and in several courtrooms. In State District Court on March 11, 1974, TI was granted the right to lease space at Love Field so long as Braniff continued to do so. Immediately, the two cities plus the Regional Airport Board sued Braniff and TI in Federal Judge Mahon's District Court in Fort Worth to force the two carriers' removal from Love Field. Meanwhile, oral argument was being held before the Fifth Circuit Court of Appeals in New Orleans on the plaintiff's appeal of Judge Taylor's decision in the Love Field case. As though that were not enough, Dallas City Council passed an ordinance on April 15, 1974, to bar all commercial air service from Love Field effective May 1 and providing penalties totaling some $6,400 per day thereafter if Southwest continued its Love Field operations. On April 17, at our request, Federal District Judge Taylor issued a temporary order restraining the City of Dallas from enforcing its new ordinance and setting a hearing for a preliminary injunction against the City of Dallas for May 17, which injunction was subsequently granted.

Shortly after DFW Airport opened and all the other carriers moved their operations from Love Field to DFW (with the exception of Braniff's flights to Hobby Airport), I had lunch one day with Ron Chapman, king of Dallas radio, and our discussion led to the numerous charges passengers were finding at the new DFW terminal. Even the dollar change machine only returned 95 cents. Ron suggested in a kidding manner that we ought to install change machines at Love Field and return $1.05 for each dollar. "That's a great idea," I said, and before the day was over, we had change machines at each gate spitting out $1.05 for each dollar bill inserted. This gimmick got us thirty seconds on both national and local news programs, and we were featured in newspaper articles throughout the country. It easily amounted to $100,000 worth of advertising and publicity—for less than $1,000 worth of nickels.

Up through June 17, 1974, we had been taking deliveries of our jet fuel requirements from Exxon at a cost of 11 cents per gallon, but on June 18, 1974, we not only celebrated our third successful year of scheduled operation but kissed goodbye the three-year fuel contract we had enjoyed with that company. Beginning on that date, we took deliveries under a new one-year contract at 38 cents per gallon, a 245 percent increase. While that was quite a blow, fuel being our second-largest expense behind payroll, it was offset by the fact that we were enjoying substantially higher passenger loads diverted from the interstate highways by fear of not being able to get enough of the higher-priced fuel to get back home.

During this same time period, we were getting a lot of tongue-in-cheek complaints from businessmen who had been using their own private single-engine Beechcraft Bonanzas or

Navions for business flights. They said that our low fares and frequent flights had ended their justification for using their personal aircraft for business, but that our beautiful hostesses and free cocktails at least partially made up for it.

My personal life was in transition. My estranged wife, Juanice, was diagnosed with a fast-growing lung cancer, no doubt from the two packs of Camel cigarettes she had been smoking daily for the past thirty-plus years. For over a year, Juanice suffered mightily until her merciful death on July 5, 1974. The lady I now kept company with, Barbara Vaughn, had been an employee of mine at Trans-Texas Airways years earlier. She was now divorced and had rejoined Texas International as manager of their accounts payable department. We liked the same things, particularly the water, boating, and building something tangible, like a house. We spent many weekends together with her daughter, Lisa, at Lake Palestine. Barbara and I were married in a private ceremony on July 27, 1974, by my pastor, Leighton Farrell, at Highland Park United Methodist Church and, with our darling Lisa, went on a weeklong honeymoon in the Winnebago to Beaver Lake up in northwestern Arkansas.

Although Southwest took delivery of a fourth aircraft on September 14, 1974, we delayed expanding our schedule till October 1 so that we could make another equipment adjustment. The original fourth aircraft, which we had put into service back in October 1971, was equipped with a cargo door. The door had added a couple of thousand pounds of empty weight to the aircraft, cutting our payload capability and burning more fuel. But there was an airline down in Central America named VASP that owned a freshly overhauled Boeing 737 and wished to trade it for a similar aircraft with a cargo door. That was right down our alley. During the seventeen-day interval, between delivery of our fourth new aircraft and instituting our new four-aircraft schedule on October 1, we and VASP flew the two subject aircraft to Seattle and made a switch of all the cabin furnishings and many of the black boxes, while both aircraft underwent thorough inspections by Boeing. Then we brought the VASP airplane back to Texas, along with VASP's check for the $700,000 difference we had negotiated, although we had only paid Boeing an extra $200,000 back in 1971 for the unwanted cargo door. Not a bad deal! Our pilots immediately dubbed the VASP aircraft "The Banana Boat."

At the time of our October 1 schedule expansion, which added several more flights in the Dallas–San Antonio market, we reduced our $28 Executive Class fare to $25 and began charging this new $25 fare on the weekday daytime flights in the Dallas–San Antonio market, which since January 22, 1973, had been going first for $13 and later $15. Frankly, we were making so damn much money by this time that we were ashamed of ourselves. Anyway, the loss of revenue in the Dallas-Houston market would be largely offset by the $10 increase we were instituting in the Dallas–San Antonio market. Wasn't that magnanimous of us?

A picture sometimes tells more than a thousand words. The graph on the following page shows what happened to the Dallas-Houston and Dallas–San Antonio markets as a result of the service provided by Southwest. For the four-year period from 1967 to 1971, immediately preceding inauguration of service by Southwest, passengers per day had maintained a flat average of 1,458. In both 1973 and 1974, the CAB carriers continued to carry approximately the same numbers, but the total number of passengers carried rose to 2,888 in 1973 and 3,307 in 1974. Obviously, we hadn't just skimmed the cream and stolen the CAB carriers' traffic, as they often alleged, but rather we had doubled the total market in 1973, and in 1974 we generated 60 percent of a total market that was 127 percent larger than the base-period markets.

In February 1975 we discovered once again that it is sometimes preferable to be just plain lucky than smart. In the fall of 1974 we had won a favorable decision from a TAC examiner for our Harlingen route expansion, but we had still anticipated a long delay in inaugurating service to the Rio Grande Valley even if we received a favorable opinion from the TAC, because we knew TI would take any award to court. Therefore, we had placed no orders for the RGV terminal office, ticket counter, or ground or ramp equipment, nor had we planned any training programs for new employees. As luck would have it, in early February, just a few days prior to the oral arguments before the

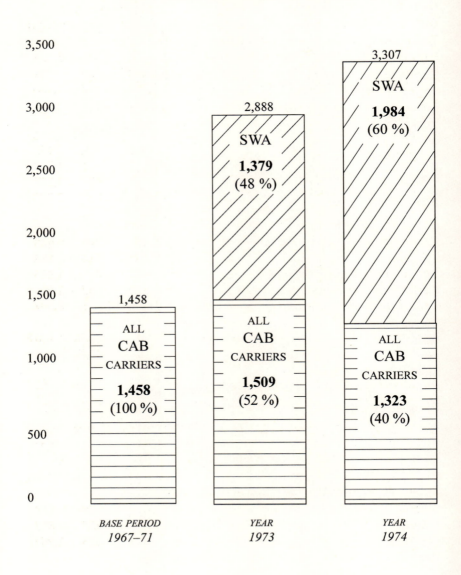

Passengers
per day

4,000

DALLAS-HOUSTON AND DALLAS–SAN ANTONIO LOCAL MARKETS: AVERAGE DAILY PASSENGERS

3,500

3,307

3,000

2,888

SWA
1,984
(60 %)

SWA
1,379
(48 %)

2,500

2,000

1,500

1,458

ALL
CAB
CARRIERS
1,458
(100 %)

ALL
CAB
CARRIERS
1,509
(52 %)

ALL
CAB
CARRIERS
1,323
(40 %)

1,000

500

0

BASE PERIOD
1967–71

YEAR
1973

YEAR
1974

SOUTHWEST AIRLINES CO.

DEVELOPMENT OF SOUTHWEST AIRLINES MARKETS AND EFFECT ON CAB CARRIERS

	DAL TO		
	HOU	SAT	TOTAL
Base period – 1967–71			
Braniff	803	371	1,174
Other	245	39	284
Total – CAB carriers	1,048	410	1,458
Year 1973			
Braniff	847	469	1,316
Other	181	12	193
Total – CAB carriers	1,028	481	1,509
Southwest	902	477	1,379
Total market	1,930	958	2,888
Year 1974			
Braniff*	810	395	1,205
Other	102	16	118
Total CAB carriers (Jan.–June 1974 avg.)	912	411	1,323
Southwest (Jan.–Nov. 1974 avg.)	1,317	667	1,984
Total market	2,229	1,078	3,307
CAB carriers traffic as % of base period–1973	98%	117%	103%
–1974	87	100	91
Southwest traffic as % of base period–1973	86%	116%	95%
–1974	126	163	136
All carriers traffic as % of base period–1973	184%	234%	198%
–1974	213	263	227

Breakdown of Braniff 1974 traffic between airports

Love	444	240	684
Regional	366	155	521
Total	810	395	1,205

commission were to take place, the pilots at Texas International went on strike, and TI's attorney, Jim Wilson, stated during oral argument that since TI was not currently operating in the markets, they would not seek court action until service was resumed.

At that point, I slipped out of the hearing room and called Bill Franklin, my VP–ground operations, from a pay phone (no cell phones back then) and told him the situation. Would it be humanly possible, I asked, for him to borrow people and ground equipment from our three stations to use at the Harlingen airport on a temporary basis, then prevail upon the FAA to make their required station inspection over the weekend? If he could do this, we could begin service Monday or Tuesday morning before TI had a chance to get some district judge to grant a restraining order. Exactly as when we went from twenty-five-minute turns to ten-minute turns, Bill's response was, "We can and we will." The commission issued its favorable decision from the bench before noon on that same day, Thursday, February 7, 1975.

Talk about a wild weekend, that was one. We did in three days what other carriers would take three months to do with all of their chains of command and stifling rules and regulations. While Bill and his folks were busy setting up the ground operation, Harold Riley, our chief dispatcher—who incidentally had become a damn good schedule man—and I were rearranging our schedule to accommodate the new market. By that time, we were operating 300 trips per week with our four-aircraft fleet. We wound up deleting 41 of those trips and adding 50 trips to the Valley, for a net increase of nine trips per week: one per weekday, and two on Saturday and Sunday. As the 41 trips we deleted had been the lowest load-factor trips on the system, if we could come anywhere near our forecasts for Valley traffic, our profits should skyrocket. On Saturday and Sunday, the flight department and in-flight service department rescheduled all their crew routings and assignments and got word to all the crew members.

Had Bill Franklin and I not moved the way we did that weekend, it is entirely likely that service to the RGV by Southwest could have been delayed a year or more by court action. Several days after service was inaugurated, Texas International

134

finally found a judge who would accept a petition for review of the TAC unanimous decision in the RGV case, but since we had already begun our flights and they were being patronized so enthusiastically by the citizens of the Valley, it was too late to issue any kind of restraining order. But TI's action meant that we had to gear up for still another court battle.

In February 2000 the Harlingen Chamber of Commerce and the airport board threw a big invitation-only party celebrating the twenty-fifth anniversary of service to the RGV by Southwest Airlines. They asked Southwest to provide them with a list of people to invite who had been factors in bringing the service to the Valley at the outset. The list, prepared by Colleen Barrett of Southwest, excluded the names of Bill Franklin and Lamar Muse.

Cookie Cutting (Five New Markets)

The big question in my mind in February 1975 was whether the operating practices and fare policies we had evolved over the past three-plus years of operations in our relatively large markets would be applicable in the Rio Grande Valley market. I shouldn't have been concerned; in short order, the introduction of the Southwest style of service made a big market out of what had been a small one. From the very first day, we experienced profitable loads on all flights. In fact, by mid-March we had to add roundtrip, nonstop, late-night flights from Dallas to the RGV on Fridays and Sundays and a roundtrip flight from San Antonio to the RGV at midday on Saturdays just to handle the weekend traffic destined for South Padre Island, a popular weekend getaway. People could now afford to fly there rather than buck the two-lane highway that served the area.

In January 1975, immediately prior to inaugurating service to the RGV, we had handled 70,000 passengers (a record) and realized pretax income of $112,000. In March 1975, the first full month after beginning RGV service, we handled 91,000 passengers and reported net pretax income of $363,000, that is, 30 percent more passengers and 224 percent more income. The results I had predicted and explained to Herb Kelleher in my memo of March 5, 1973, urging him to file an application for the Rio Grande Valley authority, had come true in spades. It was a very low-cost extension of our route with plenty of passengers anxiously waiting at the gate to patronize our flights. Southwest's second-quarter 1975 earnings were up 48 percent from the $673,000 earned in the first quarter but were purposely held slightly below $1 million, because I wanted to save crossing that benchmark till the next quarter.

In March 1975 the *Dallas Times Herald* published a feature story on a study they had done showing that air service through Love Field and Hobby Airport during 1974 had saved Texans $24 million and 368,000 travel hours. With Dallas City Hall experiencing defeat at every turn in their crusade to destroy Southwest, there was only one thing left that they could get away with: taxing us to death! They were already doing a pretty good job of it on our property taxes, but now they went after landing fees. The old rate that all carriers had paid was 5.9 cents per thousand pounds; from April 1, 1975, we had to pay 55 cents per thousand pounds of aircraft weight per landing. This had the effect of immediately increasing our annual cost by $300,000. About the same time, Houston raised our Hobby landing fee rate by 150 percent without changing the rate charged all the carriers using Intercontinental. It was totally unfair, but there was no way to fight it.

In a general-news letter dated April 3, 1975, I told our directors that, with our passenger traffic at its present levels and with the avalanche of traffic we would have on the RGV routes come summer, we could use our fifth aircraft right then. We had planned to accept delivery of this fifth aircraft in late August but held off adding it to our schedule until October 1, so that we could send each of our original three aircraft back to Boeing for a ten-day visit to be refurbished and updated. When Boeing advised me that, with slight schedule revisions, they could move delivery of number five forward from late August to July 1, I told the board that I had decided that day to accept the earlier delivery. We would now go to a five-plane schedule on July 2, then return to a four-aircraft schedule during the low-traffic period between Thanksgiving and New Year's to allow for refurbishing each aircraft at the Boeing factory, and resume the five-aircraft schedule on January 3, 1976. While I recognized this as a calculated risk, unquestionably we were presently forcing substantial traffic to DFW in Dallas and Intercontinental in Houston because of our inability to handle it all, as indicated by our average passenger load in the Dallas-Houston market of 81.8 passengers during March, with over half the flights being blocked out. When our system average load reached 79.1 passengers during August 1975, it was obvious the calculated risk had paid off.

Meanwhile, in anticipation of having to make a delivery payment on our fifth aircraft sooner than we had planned, E. F. Hutton & Co. recommended that we consider a long-term debt proposal from an insurance company. Because of the very restrictive covenants generally included in insurance company loans, I wanted an alternative arrangement with a bank, preferably the Mercantile in Dallas, and I presented a proposal to them for a $16 million loan with which to prepay the Boeing debt and make the final payment on our fifth aircraft. I was sure their credit committee would approve the loan. In a letter addressed to our account representative, John Walker, I summarized the deal I had informally discussed and now wanted. The letter was dated March 21, 1975:

> During the first quarter of 1975 Southwest Airlines expects to have operating revenues of approximately $4,650,000 with total costs of some $4 million and net income before federal income taxes of $650,000. Included in the $4 million operating costs are depreciation of $410,000 and interest payments to Boeing Financial Corporation of $335,000. The total available cash flow for debt service, therefore, will be approximately $1,400,000 during this quarter.
>
> Effective sometime this summer I expect to begin utilizing $500,000 of these funds to retire over 32 quarterly payments a $16 million loan to Southwest Airlines by Mercantile. Additionally, I expect to use up to $320,000 each quarter for the

payment of interest at no more than 8% per annum on the balances due on such debt. The total maximum quarterly payment to the Mercantile of $820,000 represents 58.5% of the current quarter's available cash flow. With the remaining 41.5% of this cash flow we would anticipate making income tax payments beginning in 1978 or 1979 at an effective rate of some 25% of taxable income. Additionally, available cash flow would be used for making progress payments to Boeing for additional Boeing 737 aircraft at such times as we see the need for same.

With the $16 million we would prepay our debt to Boeing Financial Corporation in the approximate amount of $12.5 million, thus enabling us to deliver to you first mortgages on four Boeing 737 aircraft and $2.7 million worth of spare engines, APU's and other support equipment. With the remaining $3.5 million we would make a final payment on our fifth Boeing 737 aircraft to be delivered this summer and provide you with the first mortgage on that $6 million airplane. This equipment will have a current book value of some $21 million and a current market value of some $25 million.

If for any reason I am not on the same wave length as you and the other senior officers of the bank, I need to be advised promptly of that fact.

Cordially yours,
M. Lamar Muse

Since a loan of $16 million would require Mercantile to lay off a portion to another institution, they suggested leaving the Boeing debt in place for the time being and providing us with a loan of $3.4 million repayable in five quarterly payments beginning December 1, 1975. This was accompanied by an informal understanding that a new loan of $4 million would be granted in December 1976 to provide the delivery payment on the sixth aircraft. Since the bank debt could be prepaid, this gave us the alternative we wanted when considering a long-term insurance company arrangement.

In early July 1975, after considerable pressure, the assigned judge finally disqualified himself from presiding over the suit filed by Texas International in their efforts to reverse the favorable decision by the TAC in the RGV case, after which the case was assigned to Judge James M. Meyers of the 200th District Court of Travis County, Texas. He set the hearings to begin on August 17, 1975, and for months it was necessary for Herb, his secretary Colleen Barrett, our economic expert John Eichner, and myself to practically move to Austin, where the case was being heard. From the very first day of hearings, there was absolutely no way Judge Meyers could have entered any decision but one favorable to us. Had he issued an adverse decision, requiring Southwest to discontinue service to the Rio Grande Valley, the state would have been faced with such a mutiny it would have had to call out the National Guard. At the close of the hearings, Judge Meyers reserved his decision, and in the end, the only thing the case accomplished was to keep one judge busy for fourteen months and to make a half a dozen lawyers filthy rich. Forget about my wasted time.

With the monster increases in landing fees and jet fuel we were experiencing, we were darn lucky to have all these new passengers flocking to our flights. For the year 1975 we carried 1,136,000 passengers, up 50 percent from 1974. We totaled 298 million revenue passenger miles, up 63 percent; $23 million in transportation revenues, up 54 percent; and $3.4 million in income after providing $467,000 for employees' profit-sharing and $271,000 for Uncle Sam, having used up all our earlier loss carry-forwards. Naturally, the investment community was beginning to take a look at Southwest, and I was invited to make a presentation during November 1975 to the New York Society of Security Analysts. There was a lively question-and-answer session that lasted forty minutes after the presentation. In reporting this occasion to my directors, I sent them a copy of my remarks and a transcript of the questions and answers — but didn't keep one for my own file. I do recall pointing out that we were currently enjoying after-tax earnings at the rate of $3 per year per share, or a price-earnings ratio of three to one.

In January 1976 the husband of my administrative assistant, Carole Ann Brown, was transferred to Austin, necessitating her resignation. At the going-away dinner that I gave for her, she presented me with a brass plaque with a poem inscribed on it that says it all. It hangs in a place of honor in my office to this day.

ODE TO A BOSS

A resignation letter is the proper way to say,
"Farewell to all; it's been a ball; I'll miss you every day."

But since I don't consider you an "ordinary" boss;
I hope you won't consider me an "ordinary" loss!

I came to you from Arthur Young not quite five years ago:
I had no airline knowledge . . . just some skills and my ego.

I figured I could handle you, though many told me then
About the personality with which I would contend.

"He's hard to please, can't stand mistakes, and very much con-
ceited."
"In fact," they said, "he really is an (expletive deleted)!"

So, scared to death of what I'd done, I took a chance on you.
And found a man who's nothing like the one they said they
knew.

A soft warm voice, a pleasant smile, a gentle man who's shy,
But one who has high standards . . . that's a fact I can't deny.

I guess you'd say we're much alike—we both have a short fuse;
So, that's the guy I came to know and love whose name is Muse.

We'll soon be five, and man alive, have we come a long way . . .
There positively is no doubt, Southwest is here to stay!

I could never imagine how much fun this thing would be,
And now I have to leave what has become a part of me.

I've had the fun of seeing you and Barbara be in love
And marriage which developed that has fit you like a glove.

I can't forget dear Lisa with the twinkle in her eye,
And know the years are few before she's smitten with some guy.

I'll cherish all these memories and friendships left behind
And look to future challenges which hopefully I'll find.

Just one thing is for certain though...they won't be like
   Southwest;
There is no place to go, you see, 'cause I have left the best!

Your Devoted Former Secretary
(signed) Carole Ann Brown
January 30, 1976

Carole and Dick have now moved back to Dallas, and Carol is
not only an interior designer and a member of the ASID, but
also is one of the top producers in Dallas for Coldwell Banker
Residential Brokerage. Quite a gal!

Carole Ann was replaced by Sherry Phelps, whom I stole
from Jess Coker, our VP-marketing. Sherry was very reluctant
to make the switch because she was unsure of her qualifications,
but I finally prevailed on her to give it a try. I consider myself to
be a good judge of people, and I just knew she would be great.
She was, and she is now an official in the Human Resources Department at Southwest and, along with Camille Keith, is one of
the very few old-timers left.

Meanwhile, the relationship between Rollin King and myself had become more and more strained as each month went
by. I think our incompatibility was due to the fact that he considered himself to be high-brow and me as low-brow. He had
come from a wealthy and prominent Cleveland family and had
a graduate degree from the Harvard Business School; I, on the
other hand, came from a Palestine, Texas, workingman's family
and didn't even have an undergraduate degree. He knew he
could do a lot better job of running Southwest than I was doing
and made his opinion known to everyone. In early 1976 our dif-
ferences got to the point that I just could not afford to have him
in the management lineup any longer, and I so informed the
board. I included this synopsis in my memo to the board dated
January 9, 1976:

I have had several discussions with Mr. King concerning
his future with Southwest and have proposed three alternatives. The one which he and I seem to prefer involves him taking the assignment of thoroughly investigating and perfecting

142

the feasibility of Southwest, through a subsidiary company, inaugurate intrastate airline operations within the state of New York between LaGuardia airport on the one hand and Buffalo, Rochester, and Syracuse on the other hand. Mr. King and I will be prepared to discuss this proposal more fully at the upcoming directors meeting.

However, the day before the January 22 board meeting, I decided that the New York proposal was nothing more than a make-work project and would not solve the basic problem. On March 1, 1976, Rollin was permitted to resign his position of executive VP-operations and exercise his seniority to become a flight captain on the line. King, of course, continued his position on the board of directors and, I am quite confident, began making it his top priority to get my job by hook or by crook. From that point forward, he took exception to everything I said or did, although he dispatched the following memo to all employees under the heading "Change of Status":

> The purpose of this memo is to inform you that I have decided to resign as Executive Vice President–Operations and exercise my seniority as Captain effective March 1, 1976.
> The last ten years of my life have been devoted to Southwest to the almost total exclusion of any outside activities. Now that the Company is past the initial start-up period and very healthy and profitable, I would like more free time to do other things, including one of my true loves, flying.
> While I plan to remain on the Board of Directors, my decision to remove myself from any active management role was facilitated by one fact—that fact is that Lamar Muse and the other officers of Southwest are the best management team in the business. I have every confidence that if we all continue to pull together as we have the past five years, they will lead us on to bigger and better profit sharing checks!

What King was saying was, now that he had steered the company safely through its startup period, it was okay to leave the daily routine up to management, since he would still be calling the shots as a member of the board!

For some time I had admired the rapid growth I had observed in another Texas company, The La Quinta Inns, and the similarities in their business philosophy to what I was trying to accomplish at Southwest. Therefore, back in 1975, I had made it my business to become acquainted with Mr. Sam Barshop, La Quinta's San Antonio–based chairman and president. I discovered that we thought a lot alike, and when I had invited him to become a candidate for membership on our board, he accepted and become a member at our 1975 annual meeting. Subsequently, we talked about the early days of La Quinta and its problem of always being short of capital. He told me that to furnish his inns he had gone to the Furniture Mart in Dallas and found that Mexican-style furniture was the least expensive. To match the furnishings, his inns had to have a Mexican-sounding name, and he came up with La Quinta, just because it sounded cute, not because it meant "the fifth." Barshop then developed a strategy that he called "cookie cutting," a name that I thought was most fitting. He said that once he got the right formula for growth and expansion, each new venture was as simple as cutting out cookies from rolled dough, and he could see from our experience at Harlingen that we obviously had the right formula. We agreed that further expansion of our service with ever-growing profits should be a piece of cake—or cookie—as long as we stuck to our formula.

Since we had mastered the RGV addition practically over a weekend but had to spend almost two years in hearings and court cases, I decided that our next route application to the Texas Aeronautics Commission would incorporate everything we thought we could handle, both financially and operationally, at one time. I didn't figure it would cost any more time or money to prosecute an application for five new markets than it had for the one market in the Valley. Therefore, on March 24, 1976, Herb Kelleher filed our application with the TAC, requesting authority to extend our service to five additional metropolitan areas within the state of Texas, including Austin, Corpus Christi, El Paso, Lubbock, and Midland-Odessa. The TAC set a prehearing conference concerning the application for April 29, 1976, and established a date of June 21, 1976, as the beginning date for hearings before an examiner. We did not anticipate a final decision in the route matter before year-end, and without the luck we had in the RGV case when TI's pilots went on strike right at the perfect moment, we figured we would probably have to sit out another extended delaying tactic in the Travis County Courthouse before any favorable decision could be activated.

Until the fall of 1975, I had personally handled all of our banking relations and Boeing financing, but with our rapid growth and expansion and ever-pressing need for more aircraft and more capital, those negotiations had gradually taken up entirely too much of my time. Meanwhile, my son, Michael Lamar Muse, after taking a degree from Vanderbilt University with an economics major, had graduated from the University of Texas School of Law and passed both the bar exam as well as all four parts of the Certified Public Accountant's exam during January 1972. He then garnered three years' experience as a tax accountant with Price Waterhouse, in their Dallas office. He was the obvious choice to give me a hand, and he had come to work for Southwest at that time as manager–contracts and administration.

During the second quarter of 1976, Mike proved his worth by finalizing an agreement with the Mercantile National Bank as the lead bank and First City National Bank in Houston as a participant for a loan of $14.5 million, with principal payments beginning March 31, 1977, at the rate of $725,000 per quarter through December 31, 1981. With this development, we prepaid all of our Boeing debt, and with the funds from our planned public offering we would be able to manage the delivery of the four aircraft on order. (Subsequently, at our January 1977 meeting, the board elected Mike to the newly created position of VP–finance and administration, though not without remarks about nepotism and some jealousy on the part of a couple of our directors who had sons still living off Papa.)

As we anticipated spending a goodly part of the summer of 1976 in Austin at the hearings for the five new markets, Barbara and I loaded up our seventeen-foot, inboard-outboard ski-towing runabout and hauled it down to Lake Austin the weekend before the hearings were to start, planning to spend some enjoyable evenings and weekends in the cool waters there.

145

Much to our surprise, we were able to present our case without interruptions and objections from either Braniff or Texas International, and when we were through, they presented their flimsy case about the markets already being adequately served. Apparently, they had learned their lesson in the RGV case and were ready to accept the inevitable fact that we were going to be right on their asses in these five additional markets and it was just not worth the effort to put up a fight. The only real fly in the ointment was John Johndroe, city attorney for Fort Worth, who had appeared in every case we were ever involved in to object to the fact that we operated out of Love Field in Dallas rather than the distant DFW Airport. But since there were no serious objections to our rebuttals, the case was soon over. As a result, Herb, Colleen, Barbara, and I had only one real opportunity to explore Lake Austin and get in a little skiing before it was time to get back to work, in San Antonio for them, and in Dallas for Barbara and me.

Believe it or not, this failure of Braniff and TI to fight our application created a serious problem for us, because we did not have new aircraft coming onstream in time to inaugurate service promptly after the expedited award that might be granted by the TAC. Due to my mistake of taking delivery of our original fourth aircraft back in 1971, even though we made a half-million dollars on its disposition, it was like pulling eyeteeth to get the board's approval for the timely ordering of additional equipment. We needed an absolute minimum of four new aircraft to begin service to the five new markets—six to do the job really right—but doubling our six-aircraft fleet was too risky for our board members to even contemplate without the route award in hand. As a result, we had placed an order in June 1976 with Boeing for four aircraft, to be delivered one each month in June, October, November, and December of 1977.

Meanwhile, as weeks and months passed after the conclusion of the hearings before Judge Meyers in the reopened RGV case, all of us at Southwest began to worry that he must be considering a reversal of the TAC's decision. It would have been so easy to issue a favorable decision—in fact, he could have done that from the bench—but it would have been much more difficult and time-consuming to come up with any logical reasons for a reversal. Having anticipated an early favorable decision in the matter, we had filed, on April 30, 1976, a Registration Statement with the SEC to distribute 366,242 shares and thus increase our outstanding shares to an even 2,000,000. Because of the delay, E. F. Hutton, the lead underwriting company for this offering, was dragging its collective feet on taking the issue to market. We needed this money for (1) progress payments on the four aircraft, (2) finalizing a new loan agreement with the banks to make the delivery payments on the four new aircraft, and (3) dealing with the six-month extension we had negotiated on the exercise of the five-year warrants issued with the original debenture offering. We had planned to piggyback the shares to be issued as a result of the exercise of the warrants with our own offering of 366,242 shares. The six-month extension we had negotiated would expire on September 10, 1976.

We were also anxious to get the offering closed, since the five-points hearings before the TAC examiner had gone so well. After their rebuttal testimony, Texas International had announced that they would not participate further in the case, leaving only Braniff and the City of Fort Worth to oppose an award. As Braniff had hardly participated in the case, we knew they were not likely to try for a reversal. The City of Fort Worth certainly would contest the decision but, not being a carrier, they had nothing to lose and would surely have any case they presented thrown out of court. It therefore appeared that we would have authority to operate many months before the equipment for the new service was scheduled to arrive.

Boeing came through for us one more time, however, by making available two aircraft ordered by a foreign carrier for 1977 delivery. That order had become unstuck, and therefore we would now receive our four 1977 aircraft, one each in May, June, July, and September. Boeing further advised that we could retain our November and December position for our eleventh and twelfth aircraft if we so desired. And I certainly desired, but whether I could ever get our board to go for it was questionable.

Our public offering finally went to market on September 30, 1976. Earlier in the trading day before the issue went to market, the shares had been trading at $19.50, but for some strange reason there was a 100-share trade one minute before the market

147

closed at $17.50. I could never shake the feeling that something fishy was going on, but need for the funds made us decide to proceed with the offering at that price with an underwriters' discount of $1.20. On October 7 we received checks from E. F. Hutton in the amount of $5,969,744.60 for the 366,242 shares the company sold and $574,750 for the exercise of the 95,000 warrants included in the offering. A sizable portion of the proceeds were utilized to pay off the short-term debt we had incurred in anticipation of the delayed public offering.

Some two and a half years before the Congress finally got around to passing the airline deregulation bill, extensive hearings were held before the Senate Aviation Subcommittee and the House Public Works and Transportation Subcommittee. Just about every airline president testified before those committees, generally citing "the Texas intrastate airline experience" as the showcase reason why there should be no deregulation of their industry. On April 21, 1976, Bob Ginther of Senator Howard Cannon's committee called to say that the chairman would like very much to have me testify before his committee, since most of the testimony to that time had covered only the CAB carriers' side of the so-called "Texas Experiment." He asked that I testify on June 17, immediately after Harding Lawrence of Braniff. I couldn't imagine anything more exciting and I accepted immediately. My written testimony covered seventeen pages plus two exhibits, and it was designed to totally destroy the four principal myths that the prior witnesses had planted in the committee members' minds. Those myths were:

1. Southwest only operates in high-density markets and skims the cream from such markets, thus making those markets no longer profitable to the CAB carriers but highly profitable to Southwest.
2. Southwest offers lower fares than the CAB carriers only because of lower payroll costs as a result of having low-seniority employees and no unions representing those employees.
3. Southwest's $25 Executive Class fare is diversionary and is used to cross-subsidize Southwest's Pleasure Class passengers, whose fares do not even meet Southwest's variable costs of operating its Pleasure Class flights, and

4. Southwest will institute substantial fare increases after mo-
nopolizing the markets it serves, as it has done in the Dallas/
Houston market.

Exhibit One, attached to my written testimony, refuted myth
number one. It showed the CAB carriers' traffic in each of the
four markets we then served as it had been during the calendar
year immediately preceding inauguration of service by Southwest. For comparative purposes, it then showed just the passenger traffic carried by Southwest during the year ended May
31, 1976, in each of those markets and the percentage that traffic
was of the CAB carriers' earlier monopoly market. In total, the
base-period traffic generated by the CAB carriers was 696,390
passengers, while the traffic Southwest alone handled was 187
percent of the base period, at 1,301,035. However, during
the same period, the CAB carriers had still carried 480,280
passengers at their substantially higher CAB fare. The total
market of 1,781,315 thus represented an increase in size of 156
percent. I pointed out that rather than cream-skimming major
markets, we were actually developing major markets out of
small markets and then dipping the milk therefrom. As an example, the Dallas-Houston market was the thirtieth-largest market in the United States when only the CAB carriers provided
service, and already we had moved it up to number nine, along
the way passing such well-known markets as New York–
Detroit, –Pittsburgh, and –Atlanta; Los Angeles–Las Vegas; and
Washington-Boston.

Alleging that our low unit costs were solely due to mistreat-
ment of our employees with low pay scales and nonrepresenta-
tion by unions particularly pained all of us at Southwest. In the
first place, 53 percent of our employees were represented at that
time by international unions, but we made sure that those who
weren't made more money than those who were. The real secret
to Southwest's low unit costs were (1) no complicated, expensive, and stifling CAB regulation; (2) very high productivity of
our employees with equipment specifically designed for our
routes; (3) our low competitive fare structure with the resultant
higher load factors it produced, which in turn produced low
unit costs; and (4) a smile and warm welcome for our passen-

gers, rather than a scowl. Concerning employee productivity, here was the picture during 1975.

	Southwest's Performance	Per Employee	
		Next Best Carrier's Performance	
		Amount	Carrier
Revenue generated	$64,128	$57,200	Northwest
Aircraft hours	32.6	21.9	Braniff
Aircraft departures	47.9	19.1	Braniff
Enplaned passengers	3,195	930	Delta
Total operating expense	$48,534	$51,568	Ind. avg.

In summary, I stated that we just did a better job than our competitors, not only in cost control but in market development, which is really the name of the game. You can be the most efficient operator in the world and go broke if you don't develop the markets you serve. We had done that and, as a result, were extremely profitable. I pointed out that other carriers could do the same if their hands were not tied by the CAB.

My second exhibit destroyed the claim that our low Pleasure Class fares were predatory in that they did not even cover Southwest's variable costs of operating its Pleasure Class flights. The figures I presented covered the year 1975 and broke down our operation into Executive Class flights and Pleasure Class flights. The following summary of that exhibit tells the story:

Statistics:	Executive	Pleasure	System
Trips operated	11,486	6,066	17,552
Passengers carried	643,823	492,495	1,136,318
Average load	56.1	81.2	64.7
Total dollars (000 omitted):			
Revenues	$15,019	$7,809	$22,828
Operating expenses—			
Variable	7,505	4,445	11,950
Ownership costs, excl. interest	1,528	807	2,335
All other fixed costs (% of rev.)	**2,059**	**1,071**	**3,130**
Total operating expenses	**11,092**	**6,323**	**17,415**
Income:			
After variable expenses	$7,514	$3,364	$10,878
After all operating expense	3,927	1,486	5,413
As % of revenues	26.1%	19.0%	23.7%

I told the committees that this exhibit had been presented to the court in connection with TI's appeal in the RGV case. Therefore, Frank Lorenzo, president of Texas International, had been in possession of this information when he had testified the previous month to the contrary. Most CAB carriers dream of enjoying operating ratios of 4 to 5 percent but seldom realize their dream. Southwest enjoyed a 19 percent operating ratio on the very Pleasure Class flights that the CAB carriers were alleging could not possibly be covering even their variable costs.

I professed ignorance as to what fares would be charged in the future by Southwest but pointed out that, in the Dallas-Houston market where Lorenzo alleged we had already raised our fares, during our first year of operation our average net fare had been $17.83, and in the most recent year it had averaged $18.80, an increase over the nearly five-year period of 5 percent, or 1 percent per year. This compared to the 85 percent increase by the CAB carriers from $20 to $37 in that market. I pointed out that when and if deregulation came about, Southwest would immediately inaugurate service between Tulsa, Kansas City, St. Louis, and New Orleans. After receiving service for more than thirty-eight years by the CAB carriers, those markets, as well as hundreds of other short-haul markets across our land, remained smaller than the air market Southwest had developed in one year from the very small city of Harlingen, Texas. If that didn't prove that all those markets had a crying need for the type of service that Southwest Airlines was dedicated to providing — short hauls, frequent flights, low fares, and service to all the people and not just the expense-account crowd — then I was a monkey's uncle.

To the complete satisfaction of the members of the two subcommittees, I categorically refuted all four myths, though they had all been testified to as fact by the previous witnesses. If I do say so myself, it was an absolutely superb presentation, and it garnered a letter of commendation from John W. Snow, deputy undersecretary of the Department of Transportation.

Now that the deregulation movement for the industry had stirred up substantial controversy in Congress and the Washington bureaucracy, the American Enterprise Institute (AEI) sponsored a televised panel discussion or debate conducted by my favorite TV newscaster in earlier days, John Daly. The mem-

151

OFFICE OF THE SECRETARY OF TRANSPORTATION
WASHINGTON, D.C. 20590

DEPUTY
UNDER SECRETARY

June 23, 1976

Mr. M. Lamar Muse
President, Southwest Airlines
1820 Regal Row
Dallas, Texas 75235

Dear Mr. Muse:

I would like to take this opportunity to commend you for your testimony and appearances before the Senate Aviation Subcommittee and the House Public Works and Transportation Subcommittee.

Both your written testimony and the question and answer sessions before both Committees were very helpful in clarifying the past and current situation with the Texas intrastate airline experience. As you know, during the process of both hearings a lot had been said about Southwest Airlines, its operations, and its employees. Your convincing appearance on behalf of Southwest should set the record straight across a variety of topics.

It may interest you to know that in contrast to your appearances before the Subcommittees, on many other occasions, witnesses were received by a mere handful of spectators -- sometimes as few as three or four in the large hearing rooms. The attendance during your appearance speaks for itself in terms of interest here in your company's service to the traveling public in Texas.

I would also like to thank you for your prompt reply to our wage rate survey. We will shortly supply that information to the Senate Aviation Subcommittee along with similar data from several certificated carriers and other intrastate airlines.

Sincerely,

John W. Snow

152

bers of the panel, as they were seated from left to right, were John Robson, chairman of the CAB, who surprisingly was a strong advocate for deregulation of the industry; Senator Ted Kennedy, the most effective deregulation proponent within the Congress; myself, as the president and CEO of the company that supporters of deregulation wanted the rest of the industry to emulate; Al Casey, chairman and CEO of American Airlines, who bitterly opposed deregulation; and Ed Colodny, president and CEO of Allegheny Airlines, a local service airline and another misinformed opponent of deregulation. It is interesting to note that after deregulation came about, Colodny's company changed its name to USAir and enjoyed unbelievable growth through merger and acquisition of other carriers — with a new boss at the helm, of course — only to wind up in bankruptcy court.

The audience for the debate was composed principally of CAB members and staff, congressional staff members, and a large contingent of aviation news and security analysts headed up by Wayne Parrish, publisher of the *Aviation Daily*, who sided with his bread and butter, the scheduled CAB carriers which, with the exception of United Airlines, all opposed deregulation.

At one time I owned a VCR tape of that entire two-hour panel discussion, but it has mysteriously disappeared after being played for every guest I could coerce into sitting still for that long. Obviously, I was proud of it. The reason? At the conclusion of the program, Al Casey, with Ed Colodny in tow, came over to me and publicly announced, "Congratulations, Lamar. You killed us tonight!"

Although I can't, of course, quote actual exchanges from that lost tape, I do clearly remember two that had the audience rolling in the aisles. The first was when John Daly asked me if Southwest was not regulated to some extent by the Texas Aeronautics Commission (TAC), just as the major carriers were regulated by the CAB. I replied in the affirmative that yes, we had to have a Certificate of Public Convenience and Necessity issued by the commission, and we had to file our tariffs with them.

"Then Mr. Muse," asked Daly, what is the difference between regulation by the TAC and the CAB?"

"Well, sir, the major difference is that the TAC figures that

153

we know more about running an airline than they do, and they let us do it."

John Robson agreed that this was true. And he continued by saying that after the CAB got through telling its carriers where and when to fly, how much to charge, and what to serve the different classes of passengers en route, there wasn't very much left for old Al and Ed to do during the day.

The second memorable exchange came after Daly mentioned in passing that the question of deregulation did not concern passenger safety, since all air carriers would still have to operate under the rules and regulations of the FAA. Al Casey violently disagreed with this assumption. He felt that the cut-throat competition that would be the norm with deregulation would cause great financial difficulties for many carriers, who would then cut corners on aircraft maintenance and safe flying procedures. He thus inferred that only a profitable carrier would be consistently safe. I asked him if that meant that Southwest, with its 20-plus percent of revenue brought down to the bottom line, was ten times as safe as American, which was lucky to bring 2-plus percent of their revenues to the bottom line. Old Al just sputtered something like "Don't be ridiculous!" But the audience got the point, loud and clear.

On October 27, 1976, the TAC examiner, John G. Soule, issued his favorable decision in the five-points case. It now appeared that it had been a piece of cake for him to rule favorably and the matter would therefore probably be finalized by the full commission sometime between Thanksgiving and Christmas 1976. Now, even with the accelerated delivery of equipment, we were going to have a four- or five-month waiting period, but as very few of the affected cities had supported our application, due to their fear of losing their trunkline service, there was no big clamor. As it turned out, both Braniff and the City of Fort Worth did file petitions for reconsideration, which were denied by the TAC on December 29, 1976, but the parties were given thirty days to take it to the courthouse. Neither did, so on January 28, 1977, Southwest was free to phase in the new service.

Coincidentally, just one day after Examiner Soule's decision recommending even more new routes for Southwest, Judge Meyers finally issued his favorable decision on TI's appeal of the RGV case. I quote the first three sentences of the letter he dispatched to Herb Kelleher suggesting Herb prepare a judgment in the case. "Gentlemen: I have, at last, finished my work on the above styled and numbered cause. I have concluded that the order of the Texas Aeronautics Commission should be sustained. I did not reach this conclusion easily or lightly, but I did reach it after what I believed to be a thorough examination of the briefs, the Examiner's report and the record." Since we had been operating the route for over a year and a half very successfully and had gotten through the public offering of our stock without his decision, it was kind of a non-event when it finally did happen.

With six aircraft now in our fleet and the prospect of doubling that within less than a year, we needed to make plans for more adequate maintenance facilities than our present arrangement—the one-bay hangar with minimum shop and stores space with which we had begun operations back in 1971. Mike Muse negotiated a twenty-year lease on an eight-acre construction site at Love Field. Then, serving as the contracting officer, he and Jack Vidal, VP-maintenance, designed a four-bay hangar with ample space for all spare parts, accessory shops, and maintenance offices. With completion planned for March 1978, the project's estimated cost was $1.7 million, and it came in at $1.8 million.

During this period, Mike had also been busy as a beaver lining up financing for our rapid growth. He first put together a $30 million package with Mercantile and First City of Houston. Then he managed to get the Texas Commerce Bank of Houston and the Republic National Bank of Dallas to join the group for a $40 million bank loan with a $10 million subordinated loan from Boeing. The bank group then decided they would prefer to take the entire $50 million, and a loan agreement incorporating that amount was executed on December 22, 1976. The only problem was that the group insisted on a payback schedule of no more than five years, and this was not in the best interest of the company. It was important, though, that four of the five largest banks in Texas were now committed to Southwest, with the fifth, First National of Dallas, acting as our registrar and transfer agent.

Top priority in 1977 was therefore to find longer-term money in order to increase our financial flexibility. John Stanton, of E. F. Hutton, and Walter Lubanko, of Lehman Brothers, were both anxious to secure such financing for us by various means, but the proposal that fit our circumstances the best was one brought to us by Lubanko from Citicorp Leasing (New York). Their proposal was to loan Southwest $50 million, with payback beginning in 1979 at a low figure and extending through 1986. Mike and I spent the entire day of May 4, 1976, in our offices with four representatives of Citicorp Leasing and Lubanko of Lehman Brothers, hammering out the very best rates and covenants we could. I had told them all along that we were prepared to accept a proposal that day that carried an interest rate of no more than 9 percent, but the best they could offer was a fixed rate of 9.33 percent.

After they departed our office to catch the flight back to New York, Mike and I went to work designing a proposal to present to our banks the next morning for their consideration as an alternative to the Citicorp loan. It was a maximum credit of $60 million drawn down during the remainder of 1977 and 1978 with a payback of $5 million beginning in 1979, increasing $1 million each year until it hit $9 million in 1983, continuing at that rate through 1985, with the balance of $7 million paid in 1986. It would thus be a ten-year payback, as opposed to the five years in our present loan agreement, and would encompass a $10 million larger draw-down. The interest rate was to stay tied to the prime rate, as in the current agreement, but had to incorporate an interest cap of 9.5 percent.

The next morning, May 5, 1977, Mike took the proposal to George Clarke, executive VP at Mercantile, and they jointly had a conference call with the other three banks. I stayed at my office to compose a letter to our directors filling them in on our negotiations. That letter incorporated the principal pluses of the two proposals. If we stayed with the local banks, we would have lower net interest costs as long as the prime rate stayed below 8 percent (it was currently 6¼ percent), retain our fine relationship with the banks, avoid the necessity of two separate credit agreements, and save a quarter-million-dollar placement fee to Lehman Brothers. The pluses for the Citicorp loan were a slower payback from 1983 and beyond, and the opening of a new source of financing down the road. I quote one paragraph from my memo to the board:

156

Mr. Lubanko of Lehman Brothers has done a yeoman's job in bringing to us the fine offer made by Citicorp Leasing after having spent substantial effort in trying to interest insurance companies in our credit. Clearly, our group of banks would not have stretched to the point that they have were it not for this valid competitive offer. Therefore, with your permission, I plan to advise Mr. Lubanko that we would be more than happy to pay up to, say, $50,000 for financial services rendered in connection with this transaction.

The next day, May 6, 1977, I sent another memo to our board. It read:

You just wouldn't believe the chain of events which has occurred this morning. After numerous calls to and from New York and the Mercantile, during which it was determined that the Citicorp loan was going up for final approval at 2:00 pm New York time and a firm commitment by us was needed before such event, Mr. George Clarke of Mercantile got all his folks into agreement to accept our proposal and so advised me at 12:05 pm, whereupon I called Mr. Lubanko to advise him that we had accepted the bank deal and would, therefore, not be accepting the Citicorp proposal.

Within 30 minutes, he called back saying that Citicorp would still like to do the deal and was now offering the 9% rate which I had been saying for the last eight months that I would accept for long-term financing and wanted a firm answer on that proposal. I told him that there was no way I could give him such an answer today, and that, at best, I would have to re-circulate my Directors which could not be done until next week, and if they could not proceed to final approval with that, then just forget it. After hanging up and reflecting on the offer for a few minutes, I called back Mr. Lubanko and told him that if Citicorp had made the 9% proposal to us on Wednesday when they were in Dallas, we no doubt would have accepted it, but that since I had since made a definite proposal to the banks which they had accepted, and I had accepted their acceptance, I would no longer consider any outside proposal, no matter what the rate was. Mr. Lubanko requested that I call Mr. Elliott Conway at Citicorp Leasing and advise him of our position directly, which I have just completed doing. Mr. Conway understood my position and I think, in fact, respects us more for it. He stated that they had been in and out of this deal very promptly and that there were certainly no hard feelings, and he offered their services to us anytime in the future that we might have need thereof.

It is only 1:25 now, so things have been moving rather quickly. We will start preparing the new agreements with the banks next Monday.

P.S. If the actions of today don't speak well for the free enterprise competitive system, I don't know what does!

On that very day I wrote a letter addressed to the loan officers at each of the four banks, personally thanking them for the fine cooperation and consideration evidenced during the last forty-eight hours in connection with our long-term financing, and advising them that our board was unanimously in favor of the decision made. Late that afternoon of May 6, Sherry placed this memo on my desk:

MLM—

Rollin came by this afternoon and I gave him his copy of the memo of today. He asked me to tell you that he agrees with everything you did except he doesn't think we should pay Lubanko $50,000 for bringing in the second-best deal.

slp—Friday—3:45 pm

None of the records I possess give any indication as to whether we made a voluntary payment to Lubanko's Lehman Brothers firm or not, but if we didn't, it just shows the absolute pettiness surrounding everything about King. My apologies to Lubanko and Lehman Brothers.

Since Gene Bishop, chairman of the board of Mercantile National Bank, had now become such an important factor in our future, I invited him to join our board; he accepted and became a member at our April 1977 annual stockholders meeting, and I became a member of the Mercantile's advisory board.

The story of Southwest's continuing success began with cost

control, about which management must be continually vigilant. Low costs, with good equipment that is operated efficiently, permit low fares, which in turn produce high passenger load factors, which in turn produce unit costs that cannot be matched by ordinary competitors. Two good examples occurred at Southwest in 1977, both related to insurance, a major cost factor for airlines. At the renewal of our group life, health, and accident insurance, Provident Mutual raised our premium rates 35 percent, even though our claim experience had been exceptional. Mike Muse began looking around for a better solution to this problem, and effective March 1, 1977, he canceled the Provident Mutual policy and signed a contract with Republic Life of Dallas. We now bought life insurance at a 10 percent discount from what we had been paying and arranged for Republic to pay, for a 7 percent fee, whatever claims against the health and accident plan were incurred. Additionally, Mike purchased catastrophe insurance for any single claim exceeding $25,000 during any twelve-month period. The first year's experience was as follows:

	Republic Life Actual	Provident Mutual Rates	Savings Amount	Savings Percent
Life insurance	$51,593	$57,311	$5,718	10%
Health and accident premiums (computed)		347,585		
Claims paid	129,415			
Claims handling fee	9,060			
Catastrophe fee	7,231			
	145,706	347,585	201,879	58
Total program cost	$197,299	$404,896	$207,597	51%

Had we stayed with Provident Mutual, in all probability there would have been another boost in rates at the next renewal.

The next hurdle was our aircraft hull and passenger liability insurance, which was coming up for renewal on August 1, 1977. I can best describe the series of events that led up to this date by inserting my memo to our directors dated July 21, 1977:

Over the last two weeks, I have experienced a most interesting series of negotiations relative to the renewal of our major hull and liability insurance premiums for the 18-month period beginning August 1, 1977.

As you may know, our major insurance coverage has from the beginning of operations been placed directly with Lloyd's of London, since back in 1971 they were the only insurance group who would consider insuring a brand new company. Each year since then we have enjoyed what I consider to be fair reductions in the various hull and liability rates as our stature has improved and our covered volumes increased.

Because of the tremendous losses that Lloyd's incurred as a result of the two 747s running together on the ground in Europe this spring, the insurance market has been in a state of flux, and Lloyd's had adopted a policy of increasing the premium rates 20% on all renewals. This is what we faced when our brokers, Humphrys, Sims, and Cline of Houston, together with Cravens, Dargan in Houston, approached the London market recently. We pleaded the special circumstances of Southwest and the tremendous increase in insurable values which are occurring as a result of this year's expansion program. As a result, the first offer of Lloyd's was to renew for an additional 18 months at our current rates with no increase. I explained again to our agents that with the tremendous increase in hull valuations and revenue passenger miles on which liability insurance is computed, we deserved a substantial reduction in rates and advised them that if they could come up with a 10% reduction in hull rates and a 15% reduction in liability rates, I would give them the order to place the business.

They went back to London with this proposal and were successful in obtaining these rate reductions, but offsetting this was a reduction in the profit sharing formula for good experience from 25% of 75% of the gross premiums, less claims paid, to 20% of 65% of the gross premiums, less claims paid. This had the effect of making the net reduction in premiums overall of only about 9%. Indications were that this was the very best that could be done.

I recently learned that Delta Airlines, who had been insured through Lloyd's, switched to the domestic markets with their renewal on July 1, and assumed that they had experienced the same problems that we were experiencing. I therefore contacted Johnson & Higgins, who had placed this insurance domestically for Delta, and authorized them to canvas the domestic market, which market is currently very hungry for business, and gave them some parameters of what it would take for them to become our insurance broker. They came through yesterday with a tentative offer (not yet fully placed) based on a package which would produce net premiums during the next 18 months, totaling $1,660,000. I advised our Houston agency of this fact and told them if overnight they could come within shooting distance of that figure, we would place the order this morning.

This action apparently really shook Lloyd's, who considers Southwest Airlines to be their premier account, and they came through this morning with rates which will produce net premiums during the next 18 months, net of the profit sharing during the previous 18 months which we would not have gotten had we not renewed with Lloyd's, of $1,657,000. We therefore placed the order with Lloyd's about an hour ago.

This insurance cost for the next 18 months is $405,000 better than their last best offer, and approximately $1 million better than their initial offer.

That is just one of the many exciting things about being president of Southwest Airlines!

(signed) M. L. Muse

Just those two extra efforts on our part produced savings that paid the total employment cost for our cadre of company officers and directors for at least one full year. It is that kind of dedication that produces superior results.

While on the subject of cost control, top management must always be vigilant of every organization's most prevalent illness — creeping bureaucracy. As long as I ran the company, there were never more than two layers of management between the newest employee of a department or function and the CEO, me. A new first officer reported to Don Ogden, VP–flight operations, who reported directly to me — that is, after I eliminated Rollin King. Same with the chief dispatcher. A mechanic or cleaner re-

161

ported to his crew chief, who reported to Jack Vidal, VP-maintenance, who reported directly to me. A flight hostess reported to the chief hostess, who reported directly to Bud Herring, VP-in-flight service, who reported directly to me. All customer service and ramp personnel reported through their respective supervisors to the station manager, who reported to Bill Franklin, VP-ground operations. Every department had a clearly defined function to perform and had the responsibility — as well as the authority — to make things hum. Up until 1977, when we doubled the size of our fleet, we only had one service department, that being finance and accounting. In that year we added Ed Lang as VP-personnel to assist the other operating departments with recruiting and hiring, our only concession to creeping bureaucracy.

During the month of May 1977, Southwest's common stock was admitted for trading on the New York Stock Exchange. A few days before trading was to begin, the exchange called Mike to select the symbol our stock was to go by, all three of the preferences we had named having been previously taken—SWA, SW, and S. When he called me to see what we wanted to do, I told him to ask if we could have L-U-V. We could, and that's the way Southwest's shares have been listed ever since. I thought it most appropriate, since our original slogan at startup back in 1971 had been "The someone else up there who loves you" — meaning, of course, that Braniff *didn't* love their passengers. Then, with the inauguration of our five new markets, we had adopted as the central theme of our advertising program the slogan "Spreading love all over Texas."

Although our first new aircraft—number seven—had yet to arrive, by reshuffling schedules of our six-aircraft fleet, we were able to inaugurate service to Corpus Christi with four roundtrips to Houston and on to Dallas effective March 1, 1977. In February we had carried 133,000 passengers, an average of 73.2 per flight, and had a pretax net of $414,000. In March, with Corpus Christi added to the system, we carried 161,000 passengers with average loads of 76.2 and pretax net of $614,000. This service was a very low-cost addition to our system due to continuing traffic beyond Houston on trips already operating between Houston and Dallas.

The seventh aircraft finally arrived on May 17 and was put to good use three days later: four roundtrips between Dallas and Lubbock, and another four between Dallas and Midland-Odessa. The Lubbock flights averaged 77.1 passengers during the last twelve days of May, and the Midland-Odessa flights 57.6, both well above break-even. During the month of June, the first full month with those two cities in the system, we carried 195,000 passengers, with average loads of 80.8, and cashed in with pretax income of $755,000, which again reflected a lot of continuing traffic beyond Dallas to Houston.

At the time we began service to Lubbock, which had opposed our application, their fine new airport terminal, a total plant that was supposed to take care of their traffic needs to the year 2000, had been open for under thirty days. Only ninety days after the inauguration of our flights, the city fathers were scratching their heads, trying to figure out a way to double the size of the terminal parking lot without looking like fools.

Our eighth aircraft was put into service on June 30, 1977, with a total of six flight arrivals and departures from El Paso. There were two nonstops to Dallas, two extensions of Dallas-Midland flights on to El Paso, and two extensions of Dallas-Lubbock flights on to El Paso. We utilized the ninth aircraft first to beef up our Dallas-Houston market, which was turning away local passengers because of the seats being occupied by over-and-beyond traffic from the four new cities on our system, and then to add additional flights covering Dallas-Lubbock and Houston–Corpus Christi, to relieve the pressure on those markets. Our pretax income climbed even further, to $920,000.

Finally, on September 15, with delivery of the tenth aircraft and no more excuses to delay service to Austin, we inaugurated six roundtrips from Dallas to Austin, with two of them continuing on to Corpus Christi. As a result, the September average load dropped from 80.4 passengers to 69.4 and profits to $459,000, just one-half those of August. The average temporarily climbed back to 74.2 passengers per flight in October but never attained that level again for as long as I was running the company, which turned out to be not very long at all. The Austin gambit was what I had said it would be when Rollin King and Herb Kelleher had been unable to understand why I chose the

Rio Grande Valley through the Harlingen airport over—in their minds—the obvious choice: Austin, the state capital of Texas.

But I knew that the private automobile over interstate highways driven at 75 to 80 miles per hour is just too much competition for distances under 200 miles. Admittedly, this disadvantage was partially offset by the proximity of the Austin airport to downtown Austin, the state capital, and surrounding government offices, just five minutes away. Eventually, we did make a profitable market out of Austin by operating flights from Houston to Austin, where there was no interstate highway, and beyond Austin to either Midland-Odessa, Lubbock, or El Paso, thus providing Houston with a better one-stop through-service to those three destinations and at the same time giving nonstop service to the state capital from those far-west Texas cities.

The initial "cookie cutting" period lasted from calendar year 1975, when service to the RGV was inaugurated, through calendar year 1977, when service to the five new cities began, to calendar 1978, the first full year of the total intrastate Texas operation. The growth of the company during these years may be summarized as follows:

	Calendar Year			Annual Percentage Increase
	1975	1977	1978	
Trips flown	17,552	35,415	54,816	70.7
Originating passengers (000)	1,136	2,340	3,528	70.2
Average passenger load	70	75	76	2.8
Operating revenues (000)	$21,726	$49,113	$81,065	91.0
All costs, net (000)	18,055	41,568	64,061	84.9
Net income (000)	3,671	7,545	17,004	121.1
Net inc. as % of operating revenue	16.9	15.4	21.0	8.1
Operating revenue per passenger	$19.12	$20.99	$22.98	6.7
Total cost per trip flown	$1,071	$1,174	$1,169	3.0

A 70 percent larger operation each year produced 91 percent more revenues versus 85 percent more costs, resulting in 121 percent more net income per year. Sweet leverage. Operating revenue per originating passenger increased because every new market but Austin was generating multisegment passengers at

$40 Executive Class and $25 Pleasure Class, the new fare for those passengers traveling over more than one segment, plus the general fare increase instituted effective at midyear 1978. Unit costs per trip flown were only up a net 3 percent per year, much less than that period's inflation rate.

Overall from 1972, the first full year of operations, through 1977—a period of five years—there was a compound annual growth rate approximating 50 percent, as shown in the 1977 Annual Report. This report, incidentally, should be required reading for all students of business.

	Compound Annual Growth Rate, 1972–77
Passengers carried	49.9%
Passenger miles flown	56.0%
Average revenue per passenger	2.0%
Average revenue per passenger mile	(2.0)%
Operating revenues	52.3%
Total costs of operation	38.6%
Pretax income (000 omitted)	From ($2,124) to $7,545

Although our passenger fare philosophy changed from 1971's initial $20 single fare for all flights throughout the week—which came darn close to bankrupting the company—to a two-class Executive and Pleasure class fare of $25 and $15, the overall revenue yield per passenger and passenger mile stayed constant during those years (1972–77), while the CAB certificated carriers' fare increases approached 100 percent.

The opportunities for Southwest were now totally unlimited. And things would only get better when and if the Congress ever got around to passing the airline deregulation bill, for which I and many others had worked so hard. Dedicated supporters included Senators Edward Kennedy and Howard Cannon, John Robson (past chairman of the CAB), Presidents Ford and Carter, staff people such as Phil Bakes, Stephen Breyer, and Mary Schuman, plus the one other airline besides Southwest which was in favor of deregulation—United Airlines.

165

15. THE LUV YEARS —

The Demise of Muse

Throughout 1976 and 1977, the SWA board was obsessed with management strengthening. The board members kept asking me the same old question: "What would happen to Southwest if you got run over by a truck?" Well, in the first place, I was not going to get run over by a truck, unless it might be one driven by Rollin King. In the second place, I was in excellent health and in my prime at only fifty-seven years of age, which at my current age of eighty-two sounds awfully young. I had a good eight years left before the usual retirement age, and if I happened to be like one of our directors, I was fit enough to remain in the CEO's chair till they carried me out feet first. However, in the unlikely event that a calamity did occur, we already had on staff two officers who could very nicely fill my shoes temporarily while a search was being performed: Bill Franklin, VP–ground operations, or Mike Muse, VP–finance and administration.

Besides, the board could rest assured, there would be hundreds of guys slobbering all over themselves to get my job, since from that point forward it involved nothing more than keeping the cookie-cutting machine well greased and oiled. Furthermore, John Eichner was a prime prospect. A partner in the firm of Simat, Helliesen & Eichner, he had acted as my economic consultant right back to my days at Universal Airlines in the late 1960s, and we now paid him from $60,000 to $80,000 a year in consultant fees. He could hardly afford to come to Southwest as my number-two man, not only for financial reasons, but status as well. If I were out of the way, though, he would be champing at the bit for my job, as he proved to be when he interviewed for my job at Southwest after my demise finally occurred. At that time, several of the Southwest officers signed a letter to Herb Kelleher, the new chairman of the board, recommending John Eichner as my replacement, but since Kelleher and Eichner had never had a lot of respect for each other, nothing ever came of it. While Kelleher now disagrees that such an interview ever took place, company officers met with John both immediately before and after his session with Mr. Kelleher.

In an effort to comply with the board's wishes for management-strengthening, I spent a lot more time during 1976–77 interviewing prospects than I wanted to and passing those possibilities on to our board committee on organization and compensation. There were zero results, because no really qualified number-one man is going to be satisfied sitting in a number-two spot for an indefinite period.

Meanwhile, Rollin King continued his policy of harassment, and he wrote a July 15, 1976, letter addressed to me but really written to the other board members. In order to set the record straight and show how this and subsequent letters influenced future events, the third and fourth paragraphs of his letter are included below:

> Since joining the ranks of outside Directors, I have become acutely aware of how little outside Directors know about what is going on. It is only through your fine memos and the quarterly meetings that we have even the most rudimentary idea of the decisions being made and actions being taken which, according to some of the articles in Forbes, we can be held accountable for.
>
> I would like to suggest that perhaps we have reached a stage in which the responsibilities of the Board could be better fulfilled by monthly rather than quarterly meetings. I would

further like to suggest that regardless of how often the Board meets, it is vital to its proper functioning that the Board have a full and complete agenda for the items to be considered by it, along with recommendations and justification, at least a week before each meeting. I know that preparing and documenting an agenda as I suggest places a burden on management; however, I believe it places a greater burden on Directors to come into a meeting cold not aware of all the decisions it will be asked to make or prepared at the beginning of the meeting to intelligently discuss them.

Additionally, he inquired about directors liability insurance. I received and answered his letter the same day it was written, so apparently it had been hand-delivered to Sherry, my secretary. My entire response appears below.

In this day and age when directors' liability is at the forefront and so many stockholders suits are being filed, I am most reluctant to be writing memos on the subject. But your letter alleging dereliction of duty in this very area makes it mandatory. I would sincerely appreciate your being more explicit about the charges made in the third paragraph of your letter in which you state how little outside Directors know about what is going on and that even with the information supplied, you have only the most rudimentary idea of the decisions being made and actions being taken.

Since first becoming a chief executive officer some 11 years ago, I have always taken what I consider to be justifiable pride in the efforts I extend to keep my bosses (the Board of Directors) fully advised of not only what I am doing, but also what I am even thinking. After reading your letter, I have searched my mind for any relevant matter which the Southwest Board has been asked to act upon which has not been thoroughly briefed through correspondence well prior to any Directors meeting at which such action was required. The only instance that I can recall was when I changed my mind the day before a Directors meeting about the advisability of establishing a subsidiary company of which you would be the president. If there are any other such instances, I would appreciate your advising me specifically what and when they were so that corrective action can be instituted.

As to the subject of monthly meetings vs. quarterly meetings, according to my recollection, there have been only three times during the past five years that it has been necessary for the Executive Committee to meet and act for the Board. While even monthly meetings might not have eliminated the need for these Executive Committee meetings, that certainly indicates that the Board is well able to handle its business on the present quarterly meeting schedule. Frankly, neither Mr. Kelleher nor myself have the time to devote to monthly Directors meetings, and I feel that several of our Directors would probably be forced to resign our Board if we established such a schedule. Nevertheless, if at the next Board meeting, it is the consensus that monthly Board meetings would be appropriate and desirable, I will, of course, do the best I can with that type of schedule.

As to complete agendas, along with recommendations and justification for all actions to be considered, supplied to each Director at least a week before each meeting, that might be possible with a hum-drum company who does the same thing month in and month out with no material growth. In our company, an agenda prepared a week before the meeting would be an antique by the time of the meeting. I reiterate, however, that in my opinion, our Directors have never been asked to take an action that they have not previously had the opportunity to be fully briefed on. In other words, the information has been made available to them, and if they haven't chosen to digest it, then that is their fault, not management's.

Concerning Directors insurance, I will attempt to have sample policies and quotes available at the next Directors meeting for consideration by the Directors as to whether or not they wish for the Company to purchase same.

I never heard another word from either King or any of the other directors concerning board agendas, more adequate briefing, or more frequent meetings, as discussed in the above-quoted letters, although the directors did vote for insurance, which the company provided as expeditiously as possible. But as a result of King's letter, my memo to the board of August 5, 1976, contained the following two paragraphs:

> Also at next week's meeting, I would like to have a general discussion on the duties and responsibilities of our Board of Directors and the proper relationship between our Board and Management of the Company.
>
> Additionally, I will discuss with you at the meeting some tentative thoughts I have regarding expansion of our operation outside of our present area.

The first paragraph referred, of course, to King's July 15 recommendations, and the second paragraph to my thoughts about capitalizing on the apparent desire of the members and staff of the CAB to experiment with some new low-fare services around the nation. Even before inaugurating our services in the five new Texas markets during 1977, I had been looking down the road to the day in 1979 or 1980 when—after extending service to the Texas Panhandle through Amarillo and possibly far East Texas through the Beaumont–Port Arthur airport—Southwest would have no place to go as an intrastate carrier, turning it very quickly into a cash cow. To me, anyway, this was a very dull prospect, to say the least.

I had made many trips to Washington during the previous two years to walk the halls of Congress, testifying before Senate and House committees on transportation, working very closely with the office of Senator Kennedy, who was by far the most effective person in advancing the cause of airline deregulation, and making speeches to anybody and everybody who would listen. When President Ford lost his reelection bid, however, and President Carter took over, I was afraid that the powerful certificated airline lobby, in concert with all the unions representing airline employees—both groups being illogically opposed to deregulation—would bring enough pressure to keep the matter bottled up in committee until it died a natural death.

However, some of the CAB members and staff officials had begun to make noises about low-fare experiments, though they would be tightly controlled by them with designated markets and fares discounted no more than 35 percent. In the same breath

170

that they put forward these ideas, they generally referred to the outstanding success of Southwest Airlines in Texas, never mentioning that Southwest's fares were generally more that 50 percent below established CAB fare levels. The CAB staff's report to their board even suggested that Southwest should be permitted to operate one of these suggested trial markets, from Dallas to New Orleans, Louisiana. I decided to take this concept a major step further. If the folks at the CAB, primarily due to pressure from Senator Kennedy, were thinking of experimenting with a few discounted fares in selected markets scattered around the nation, I had a much better idea for a real experiment.

Midway Airport is a close-in facility near downtown Chicago, Illinois, in the same relationship to the city as Love Field and Hobby Airport are to downtown Dallas and Houston. From Midway Airport there were at that time two flights per day by Delta Airlines to St. Louis, Missouri. That was all! But checking the distance to surrounding cities, I had determined that there were fourteen cities of logical size (100,000 airline passengers per year or more) that were more than 200 miles and less than 500 miles distant from Chicago Midway. Who could possibly dream up a more perfect cookie-cutting exercise than that? If we could convince the CAB to award such authority with no limitation on fare levels to the preeminent low-fare, high-frequency carrier in the entire airline industry, such an award could take care of our growth requirements well into the 1980s. Surely, with the success of an experiment such as this, covering the entire midwestern part of the country, there could be no lobbying effort strong enough to stop total deregulation of the airline industry, no matter which party was in control. And when the inevitable deregulation of the airline industry did come, we would have the entire nation to conquer, rather than just our intrastate operation in Texas plus the area around Chicago's Midway Airport.

My big mistake was discussing my idea one evening in Washington with two employees of John Eichner's Washington office. They took my idea to the former president of West Coast Airlines, Irv Teague, and together they formed a $1,000 paper-shell corporation called Midway Airlines and filed an application for the five largest of my fourteen markets, giving them the big advantage of being first. This meant that if Southwest was not going to get left in the dust, I was going to have to get my board in action and form a subsidiary company to file an application, then operate any authority granted. This action would insulate our intrastate Texas operation from the interstate services out of Midway Airport, as well as from the clutches of the CAB.

The pressure I had to put on our board to get authority to accomplish this was the beginning of the end for me at Southwest. Rollin King was vitally opposed to everything about the plan and was more than happy to allow the company to turn into a cash cow in another year or two. I guess he figured that even he could be president of something as simple as that. My concept of the proposed Midway operation was set forth in some detail in an interoffice memo dated August 19, 1976, to Herb Kelleher; Paul Seligson, our Washington counsel; and John Eichner, our economic expert. In this document I listed the fourteen airports, their distance from Midway Airport, their traffic growth over the last five years, which averaged only about 1 percent per year, present CAB fares, probable Southwest fares, and initial roundtrip frequency in each market. I determined that we would require four gates at Midway, providing departures every ten minutes during peak hours, and one gate at each of the fourteen markets. It would take fourteen Boeing 737-200s, at $7.5 million each, for a total capitalization—including walking-around and working-capital funds—of $125 million. With 50,750 flights annually and, say, seventy passengers per flight, this operation would produce revenue of $85 million against costs of $61 million, leaving $24 million for missed forecasts, interest, profit-sharing, taxes, and, last but not least, profits.

Due to the filing of the application by Midway Airlines and the ensuing publicity it received, it became absolutely necessary, in the opinions of Messrs. Kelleher and Fleming, of Vinson & Elkins, and Seligson and Stanton, of E. F. Hutton, that we immediately file a press release to protect our position. Unfortunately, this would be a full ten days before our board was due to meet, at which time I would have the opportunity to solicit their approval. Although we had informally discussed my thoughts on a Midway project at our August 1976 meeting, with enthusiasm expressed by those smart enough to grasp the opportunities, no hard figures had been produced and, of course, no action taken. However, on Friday, October 15, 1976, I prepared the press release to be issued Monday morning, October 18, at 10:00 A.M. and sent copies to all directors that same day, advising them that the matter should be acted upon at our upcoming meeting.

On the afternoon of October 25, 1976, after our directors meeting broke up—I won't say that it adjourned—I wrote a letter to the members of the board. This letter is so important in establishing the tone of my relationship with the board that I am taking the liberty of inserting it in its entirety at this point. It carried the subject heading "Midway."

> While no resolution was presented, seconded, or voted upon at this morning's Directors meeting concerning Midway, the discussion held during the last few minutes of the Directors meeting clearly indicates that at this time our Board is opposed to doing anything in furtherance of the Midway project. The discussion that did transpire consisted principally of statements of concern for the demands on our management team in expanding our route system to five additional cities during 1977 and concern about present management's ability to even do that, let alone be involved in possible Civil Aeronautics Board proceedings covering Midway. Additionally, some concern was expressed about expending any of Southwest Airlines' funds in the pursuit of this objective, with one Director expressing the view that any such funds could be better utilized for additional current dividends to shareholders.
>
> When you consider that this very management team, with five years less experience than they now have, put Southwest Airlines together from scratch and began flying between March 10, 1971, and June 18, 1971 (a total of 100 days), and that, with no advance notice, Harlingen service was installed over a period of five days, it would seem that expanding service of a well-established carrier to additional points over a period of six months would be a piece of cake, and I certainly expect it to be just that. The principals and operating policies have already been established; the equipment is already ordered and payment arranged for; the marketing program has been delineated and is already in the production stage; draw-

ing from experience, our fares will be the right fares from the very first day; and the managers for each of the five new cities are already tagged for promotion. All that is left is just waiting for the calendar to roll around to the time for execution, which I cannot believe you seriously doubt our ability to perform.

The hiatus your action of this morning left me in is untenable, and must be resolved promptly. As an example, this afternoon I started preparing the President's letter for the third-quarter report to the shareholders. What do I say about Midway? My choices are to (1) say nothing; (2) finesse it as though I didn't hear what you said this morning; or (3) flat out state that Southwest's Board is no longer interested in the previously announced Midway proposal. Using hindsight, quite obviously I should have brought the Midway subject up as the first item of business this morning and ignored the other subjects covered, but I didn't.

Therefore, because this subject is of such importance to the future development of Southwest Airlines, I feel that it is absolutely necessary that we hold a special meeting of the Board to discuss this item, and I hereby call such meeting to convene at 9 AM, Wednesday, November 3, in my office. I will hold up issuance of the third-quarter report pending the conclusion to be reached at that meeting.

Since I was given no opportunity this morning to say anything about Midway, I would like to do so at this time. If Southwest is to be an active applicant in any Midway service case set down by the CAB, the next few weeks are critical. The way you win cases before the Civil Aeronautics Board is to, at the outset, get those cases set up in such a manner that only you can win. That is the activity that needs to be accomplished promptly, and merely involves the filing by the company of a very simple, barebones application with the CAB, setting forth the routes which we propose to serve and the manner in which we propose to serve those routes. That document, together with a subsequently filed petition for expedited hearing which would incorporate more detailed exhibits about our proposed Midway service, are prerequisites to getting a proper order from the Civil Aeronautics Board setting down a pre-hearing conference at which the rules of the game will be delineated. With such actions by Southwest, a pre-hearing conference could be set for late 1976 or early 1977.

If we are successful in those initial steps, then we can decide on a much more intelligent basis whether to commit additional resources and time to the prosecution of our certificate application through the hearing process.

The cost to Southwest of the initial application should be substantially less than $5,000. The cost of the petition for expedited hearing and the supplemental data attached thereto should not cost more than another $45,000. According to our attorney, Mr. Seligson, the hearing process should involve no more than $100,000 - $150,000. These three steps, together with other miscellaneous expenses, should be "do-able" for an outside figure of $250,000 and carry us at least through 1977 year-end.

A final decision by the CAB, even on an expedited basis, could not possibly be rendered by the Board before 1978, since it quite obviously will be a contested case. Beyond that point, there would, no doubt, be court action which we would only be involved in if we were the successful applicant. Only after all that is accomplished sometime in 1979 would we be faced with major financing and equipment purchasing programs, with operations planned to commence in late 1980, after delivery of the initial aircraft.

Even evaluating maximum downside risk, it seems to me that the expenditure of $250,000 in an effort to obtain a Certificate of Public Convenience and Necessity which would permit operations realizing upward of $20 million per year pre-tax profits is an excellent investment in the future.

You can rest assured that by late 1980, no matter how efficient and effective Southwest's management may be, our growth within the borders of Texas will be largely completed, and without another project on the front burner at that time, we will be facing the same problems that PSA has been facing for the last three years. I think each of you owe it to the Southwest shareholders and employees to give much more serious consideration to the Midway proposal than you have to this date, and I hope that you will between now and November 3.

When Al Norling of Kidder, Peabody & Co. published a

175

bullish report on October 26 about our application, I forwarded copies of it to our directors, together with a very positive story which had appeared in *BusinessWeek* on October 29. I don't have copies of the minutes of our board meetings, as they were always prepared by Herb Kelleher, who in addition to being our general counsel was also secretary of the company, but apparently of the five members present at our November 3 board meeting, at least three voted against any further involvement by Southwest in the Midway case. While I can't remember positively, I can surmise who the five members were. It had to be Kelleher and me for continuation of our involvement in the Midway case, and King, Bradford, and Adger voting negatively. Mr. Bradford had always been a conservative soul (witness him taking the discounted cash rather than discounted stock for his debentures back in 1972), and Sid Adger would always vote whichever way the last person to talk to him wanted him to vote, and in this case that last person was obviously King.

In my memo to the board dated November 10, 1976, again under the subject "Midway," I wrote:

> Attachment No. 1 is the press release prepared after our Directors meeting last Wednesday reflecting the majority decision of the five Board members present for that meeting. Upon the recommendation of Messrs. Seligson, Eichner, Kelleher, Fleming, and Murchison, the press release was never sent.
>
> The second attachment is the wording which is being included in the third-quarter report to be mailed over the weekend and has been approved by Messrs. Kelleher, Fleming, and Murchison. While the wording being used in the quarterly report is not in concert with the resolution passed last Wednesday, it is my understanding that presently six of our eight Directors now favor pursuing the Midway project with various limitations and stipulations.

The next memo to the board of directors was dated November 16, 1976, under the heading "Special Meeting Called Monday, Nov. 22, 9:00 A.M." Below are the first and third paragraphs of that letter:

In circulating the Board, it appears that all members can be present for another special Board of Directors meeting next Monday morning in my office. The principal purpose of the meeting is to reconsider the Board's action at its special meeting of November 3 relative to the Midway project. If the full Board elects to amend the position previously taken, then we will want to discuss and take action on the desirability of forming a subsidiary company to actually file our application with the Civil Aeronautics Board and decide the amount of funds which we were willing to initially commit to the program.

Additionally, if you so choose, we can discuss at this meeting any adjustments you deem appropriate in the employment status of myself and Mike Muse.

Why did I gratuitously include that short paragraph about the employment status of my son, Mike, and myself? The truth is I had taken just about all I could of Mr. Rollin W. King, and if he could in some way talk the board into firing my ass—which would also mean Mike's departure—I would (1) collect on my employment contract; (2) file my own application for the Midway project; (3) form a beautifully financed company, of which my associates and I would be the controlling stockholders, to activate the "for certain" route award I would receive from the CAB; and (4) take Mike Muse, Don Ogden, Bill Franklin, Bud Herring, and Jess Coker with me.

I have to presume that the members of the board sensed what was about to happen, as everything was love and kisses at the November 22 meeting. They approved the formation of the wholly owned Midway (Southwest) Airlines Co., with the exact amount I had previously recommended as initial capital, $250,000, and authorized the filing of all necessary documentation with the Civil Aeronautics Board. I got great pleasure in sending the following memo to the board on November 30, 1976:

Yesterday, Monday, Nov. 29, 21,900 shares of Southwest Common traded on the American Exchange and closed at $20-1/8, a new record high. This morning, Southwest common opened at $20-3/8 and traded 5,600 shares during the first 30 minutes in a down market. Unquestionably, this substantial interest in Southwest in the marketplace is a direct result of the very fine story in the December 1 issue of Forbes magazine, relative to our planned Midway application, copy attached.

It was during my interview with Hal Watkins of Forbes some three days after the Midway Airlines filing with the Civil Aeronautics Board that I decided that there would be big pluses for Southwest if we announced our Midway intentions at that time. Forbes had intended to write a short personality sketch on me personally: the Midway story changed that to a very excellent story on Southwest Airlines, with the resulting market interest in our stock subsequent to the release of that story by Forbes.

Admittedly, I handled it poorly with my Directors, but the end result is what is important to Southwest Airlines. P. S. Our stock closed today at $20-3/4 with 16,000 shares traded, with a high of $20-7/8.

That was up 1,000 percent over what it had been in the 1972–74 period. This stock movement was subsequently recognized in *D Magazine's* "Best in Dallas Award" to Southwest Airlines as "Best 1976 Dallas–Fort Worth Stock," certainly helped along by our expressed interest in the Midway project.

We finalized our Midway application in John Eichner's New York office on December 8–9 and filed it with the CAB in Washington on the morning of December 10, 1976. That same day, I sent copies of our exhibits and my planned oral testimony to members of our board and to Todd Alexander, recently resigned from the board for health reasons. I'm quite sure that Herb Kelleher, John Murchison (who had rejoined our board after the favorable decision in the Love Field case), Sam Barshop, and even Jack Bradford were impressed and perused it in a positive manner. Sid Adger probably never looked beyond the front cover, but it was Rollin King's response that was to influence subsequent events.

Paul Seligson was ecstatic when he reported to us via phone on December 29 that the Civil Aeronautics Board had just issued an order establishing a new docket, number 30277, for an expeditious case, to be styled "The Chicago Midway Low-Fare Route Proceeding," and made both Midway Airlines and Midway

(Southwest) parties thereto. Seligson was more than pleased with the manner in which the order was written, which largely accomplished the flexibility that we desired in the case, as well as the expeditious manner in which the board was apparently going to handle our application.

In May 1977 the CAB put out an order limiting the case to the six largest cities included in our original application: Cleveland, Pittsburgh, St. Louis, Kansas City, and Minneapolis/St. Paul from Chicago's Midway Airport. We could perform this service with nine airplanes operating 108 flights per day, generating annual revenues of approximately $51 million and operating profits of $13 million. While this cutback was not particularly good news to me, I'm sure it was pleasing to the more conservative members of our board.

Meanwhile, on October 3, 1977, the U.S. Supreme Court refused to grant the CAB carriers' petition appealing the previous favorable decision of the U.S. Fifth Circuit Court in the Love Field case. While this result had been anticipated by Southwest, its significance was that for the very first time since the inception of Air Southwest back in 1967, the company was totally out of the courthouse. Oh, what in the world would Herb Kelleher do now? I'm sure that brain of his was twirling.

During the jolly Christmas season of 1977, things really began to boil between Rollin and me. I quote his December 22 letter in full here to show how it influenced subsequent events.

I have just begun my review of the Exhibits to the Civil Aeronautics Board in the Midway (Southwest) Airway Co. case. It is certainly very comprehensive and will take a good deal of time to complete. However, I do think that it is extremely significant that John Eichner, who initially was skeptical about the project, is now very enthusiastic and recently told me that he considers the Midway project at least twice as good a bet as the original Southwest Airlines at the same stage in its development.

As I told you, John Eichner also told me that the reason he did not agree to join the Southwest management team when the opportunity was presented to him earlier was because of complications involved in his present partnership. However, he also recently told me that if the offer were made in 1978 that he might very well be in a position to accept. You told me that you had heard about this comment made to other people, but he had never made it to you and that you had no intention of doing anything about it until he made it to you. With John having been everybody's first choice and considering that we made a substantially better offer to the second choice (Dan Reid) than we did to John, the timing might be right to go back to John one more time. I would certainly hate to see it fall between the cracks. Perhaps if you do not feel comfortable bringing up the subject, one of the other members of the Committee on Corporate Organization and Compensation could contact him and determine whether further discussion would, in fact, be fruitful.

I noted that in Exhibit SW – 611, a statement is made that no charge is being made to Midway (Southwest) for consulting and advisory services by Southwest Airlines personnel. I also note that in the September 30, Midway (Southwest) Statement of Financial Position, there are no expenses shown for travel, postage, or anything else being expended by Southwest Airlines Co. in behalf of Midway (Southwest). I wonder if it would be possible prior to the January board meeting to have a new Statement of Financial Position for Midway (Southwest) showing the various categories of expenses other than salary that have been expended on behalf of Midway (Southwest) since its formation of November 1976.

I also wonder if the Board might have, prior to the January board meeting, more details of the $150,000 deposit to Boeing you plan to ask us to approve, to insure delivery to Southwest of six new aircraft in 1979. In particular, I would be interested in knowing when the deposit must be made, for what period, if any it is refundable, when a definitive contract must be executed committing us to the full purchase price of the six aircraft, what the schedule of progress payments would be, and what, if anything, would be Southwest Airlines Co.'s out if the Midway (Southwest) project did not go through or was substantially delayed past the end of 1979.

Best personal regards,

Cordially,
(signed) Rollin

180

I answered Rollin King's letter the very next day, December 23, in a letter to the board with the heading "Various Matters":

In my memo of December 8, 1977, in which I set forth a scenario that could develop in this case, I stated that an award would probably be made by the CAB to *either* Midway Airlines or Midway (Southwest). Both Messrs. Seligson and Eichner feel very strongly that in this time period, the CAB is not going to turn down any innovative applicant and is of a mind to let the marketplace decide who shall serve each market. Under this thinking, probably both Midway Airlines and Midway (Southwest) would receive permissive authority, in which event I do not believe Midway Airlines would ever get into operation, because financing in the face of competition by Southwest would undoubtedly be impossible.

Concerning Mr. King's letter to me of December 22, with copies to other members of the Board, individual Board members have the right to do anything they want to concerning reopening negotiations with Mr. Eichner. I would point out, however, that we are currently conducting very sensitive negotiations with an excellent prospect who lives right here in Dallas. Hopefully, we will have something more tangible on this by the time of our January Board meeting, but at this stage of the game, I think the less said about it, the better.

As concerns Dan Reid, we have put him on the back burner pending a resolution of our present negotiations. Mr. Reid has just not been straightforward with us throughout our negotiations with him, and if we have troubles in that area before he comes with us, I fear the troubles we would have after he came with us. In this connection, he is out of TWA effective December 31, and he is most anxious to make almost any kind of arrangement with Southwest.

The only expenses incurred by Southwest to date not charged to Midway (Southwest) are (1) travel expenses incurred by me in connection with Midway (Southwest) business, (2) a five-day trip I sent Bill Franklin and Bud Herring on surveying the airport situations at each of the seven cities, and (3) the approximately $1,000 postage expense for mailing out our exhibits, which is being charged to Midway (Southwest).

Of course, substantial time has been spent by numerous Southwest employees, but frankly, I don't know how you would place a value on that, since no individual time records have been maintained.

As concerns the request contained in the final paragraph of Mr. King's letter, I am attaching copies of (1) the two proposals received from Boeing, the first being for two aircraft to be delivered during the months of May and June 1979, and the second for six aircraft to be delivered, two each, during the months of October, November and December, 1979; (2) a telegram from Boeing dated December 5, 1977 authorizing amendments to their proposal; and (3) our letter to Boeing dated December 9 accepting their proposal. I am sure this is a lot more detail that most of you want, but in summary, what it does is provide for deposits of $200,000 which were made on December 19, of which $50,000 is applicable to the two aircraft and $150,000 is applicable to the six aircraft. The Board authorized purchase of the two aircraft at our last meeting, and the $150,000 deposit is subject to the approval of our Board at our January meeting and is fully refundable if, at that time, you decide not to tie up these six aircraft.

We wish you and your families a very Merry Christmas and most prosperous New Year.

King was obviously busy as a bee spreading Christmas cheer all around, because the same day I wrote the letter just quoted, December 23, 1977, he wrote me yet another two-page letter, which apparently did not arrive in our office until Tuesday, December 26, when I was away. I quote it in full to show its relationship to subsequent events.

In the memorandum to the Board of Directors dated December 8, 1977 concerning the Chicago Midway Project, you mentioned that you planned to ask the Board, at our January meeting, to approve a $150,000 deposit to Boeing to ensure delivery during the final quarter of 1979 of six Boeing 737 aircraft. Since this subject had never been mentioned to the Board previously, I asked some questions about this transaction in my earlier letter assuming that we would have a complete discussion of the

182

subject at the Board meeting at which time the Board could either decide to approve /disapprove or delay a decision on this matter. However, I have just read the second paragraph on page five (5) of your testimony submitted to the CAB in which you stated that Southwest Airlines Co. has already committed this $150,000 to be paid to the Boeing Company.

Lamar, it strikes me that you are putting the Board in a position which will make it difficult, if not impossible, for the Board to make an objective decision since you have already stated in writing that the action which you are asking the Board to consider has already taken place. This seems to me to be almost completely identical to the situation where you released to the press a statement to the effect that we were establishing a subsidiary and making application for Midway authority prior to the time you consulted or gained approval from the Board. I recall clearly that during that Board meeting of November 21, 1976 you stated to the Board that you understood their displeasure with being committed prior to being consulted and that this would not happen in the future. It appears that it has happened again.

I am also concerned that if the Board agrees to this $150,000 deposit that it may, in effect, be committing itself to a $60 million odd investment which would be the full purchase price of the aircraft.

Although I do not know how any of the other Board members feel on this subject, I personally feel that perhaps it might be wise to try to resolve this issue prior to our next regular scheduled Board meeting on January 24. If I recall my dates correctly, January 24 is only a matter of a few days prior to the time that you will be going to Washington to testify in person.

Very truly yours,
Rollin W. King

cc: Board of Directors

I have to admit that when I saw the letter on January 2, 1978, it infuriated me. I shouldn't have let the man get my goat that way, but that did it. Shown on the following page is the draft of my response as edited in my handwriting, including the note at

INTEROFFICE MEMO

TO: BOARD OF DIRECTORS

FROM: M. Lamar Muse

DATE: January 6, 1978

SUBJECT: MR. KING'S SECOND LETTER OF DECEMBER 23, 1977

Since I took a four-day vacation in Seattle between Christmas and New Year's, I did not know about Mr. King's second letter until I started going through the mail Tuesday, January 2. I have refrained from answering it until this time in the hope that I would cool off a little bit during the interim.

Obviously, Mr. King will not believe anything I say, so I have read this letter to Paul Seligson, our CAB counsel, and by copy of this letter am sending him a copy of Mr. King's letter and have requested that he try to explain to Mr. King and our other Directors about CAB procedures and policies.

During the time period in which we were putting together our proposed equipment and financing plans for presentation in our exhibits and direct testimony, I frankly did not have the time to devote to calling and attending special Directors meetings. Had the slightest thought crossed my mind that any Director, including Mr. King, would be opposed to tying up these six 1979 delivery positions for a nominal $150,000 deposit, fully refundable through February 27, 1978, ~~more than a month after our scheduled January meeting,~~ I would obviously have called a special meeting. At this stage in time, I considered this to be a normal everyday business decision involving interest costs for the $150,000 deposit of ~~less~~ approximately ~~than~~ $1,000, as compared to the $3,500 cash cost plus my ~~valuable~~ time to hold a special Directors meeting for nothing.

If this kind of reasoning is in conflict with the opinion of a majority of the Southwest Board of Directors, I strongly suggest that you have the wrong man in the Chief Executive's ~~position~~ chair. If, on the other hand, ~~a majority~~ feel that my actions have been proper, then I think it is incumbent upon you to see that a Board is elected at the annual meeting which will work with me and not against me. ~~It is your choice,~~

MLM/slp

SOUTHWEST AIRLINES

184

the top: "Not mailed—MLM." On reflection, I firmly believe that had I mailed that letter to the board, as finally edited, they would have either corralled Rollin King or, as I suggested in the unsent letter, kicked him off the Southwest board. Note that I subsequently deleted the last sentence —"It's your choice and frankly at this stage I don't really give a damn which one of us goes"—because it was the only misstatement in the document. I most certainly did give a damn which one of us left. Southwest was the embodiment of everything I ever stood for. I wanted it to be the very best airline in the world, and I did not feel that could be accomplished with the likes of Rollin King as a board member.

The next missive from Mr. King was dated January 12, 1978, and in it he complained that I had said back in 1976 that we would bring other investors into the Midway Project, and here we were committing funds as 100 percent owners. Then again on February 3, 1978, he recommended the establishment of a board committee to plan and institute all future financing of the company. I responded to both letters with my letter of February 14, 1978.

Dear Rollin:

Your fourth letter relative to future financing of Southwest Airlines' activities, dated February 3, was read today after my return from two weeks of Midway hearings in Washington. The letter does not indicate that copies were sent to our Directors, so copies of this letter, as well as your letter of February 3, are being circulated to the other Southwest Directors.

Quite obviously, you and I were clearly adversaries at the last Board meeting, and seemingly, I was at odds with several other Directors. Only time will tell whether, in fact, I was. As I stated at the meeting, my mistake was in ever supplying the Directors with copies of the detailed presentation which management made to the CAB in an effort to obtain for Southwest the valuable rights applied for in the Chicago Midway Low-Fare Route Proceeding. I stated at least six times during the meeting that all I was asking for at this meeting was approval to tie up six additional Boeing 737 aircraft for a period of some six months for a cost to Southwest Airlines of $150,000.

The additional material supplied was for the sole purpose of showing that if we elected to actually purchase the six aircraft at the end of the six-month period, plans could be formulated to pay for such aircraft, with or without Midway authority.

Your suggestion that Southwest's Directors, or a committee thereof, formulate currently a detailed financing plan for a future period involving numerous imponderables would seem to me to be an exercise in futility and would not be worth the paper it was written on when the actual time came to raise specific financing for a specific project.

Except for the approximately half million dollars raised back in 1967 principally by Mr. Peace, every dollar of financing provided for Southwest Airlines to this date has been raised personally by me, with the approval of the Southwest Board. Your suggestion that this responsibility be transferred in the future to a three-man committee of the Board seems to me to be an action whereby you are trying to fix something that already works very well. I am, therefore, opposed to your suggestion.

As concerns your disagreement with 100% ownership of Midway by Southwest, I may well agree wholly with you at such time as this matter properly comes before the Board for a decision. My decision relative thereto will be related wholly to the value and the risk/reward ratios inherent in whatever decision the CAB makes this summer. If we actually receive from the CAB the authority we have requested, quite obviously, the risk/reward ratios are such that we would be negligent in our responsibilities to Southwest's shareholders to sell off for a pittance any portion of the gains which had been made as a result of our past successful operations.

Cordially,
M. Lamar Muse
President

Just before entering our regular quarterly directors meeting on the morning of January 24, 1978, I received a letter from our recently resigned board member Todd Alexander, praising our exhibits presented to the CAB in the Midway Case, with particular reference to the financing plan included therein. He pointed out that while I had used the word "dilution" several times, he did not consider the 30 percent extra stock which would be issued as dilutive at all, since it made possible additional earnings of $14 per new share and would almost double the per-share earnings for all outstanding shares. Copies of this letter were distributed to each director, and I am sure they were most helpful in taking some of the wind out of King's sails.

I advised the board that it appeared very likely that for the first time in years our first-quarter earnings report would show lower earnings than the previous year. In the 1977 first quarter, we had been running a very tight six-aircraft schedule, with very high load factors. In the 1978 first quarter, we were taking delivery of our eleventh and twelfth aircraft with attendant training costs and substantially lower load factors. While it was a strictly temporary situation, it would definitely affect the market price of our stock adversely. Upon the advice of Mr. Fleming of Vinson & Elkins, I therefore informed the directors that no stock sales should be made by any director until forty-eight hours after the public release of the first-quarter results in late April. Mr. King then requested that we buy 7,500 shares from him as treasury stock for our employees' profit-sharing contribution, but we had already acquired all the shares we needed for that purpose.

On March 3, 1978, we received notice from Goldman, Sachs & Co. that King had sold 5,000 shares of Southwest common stock on the open market. While it was Fleming's feeling that King obviously had "larceny in his heart," there was really nothing we could do about it. I said to myself, "The hell there ain't!" The end was drawing ever nearer.

A *Forbes* editorial, which had appeared in their March 6, 1978, edition and mailed to subscribers in February, had taken exception to a speech by SEC Chairman Harold Williams on "corporate accountability" and had specifically addressed the problems I was incurring with my board. Williams had apparently told his audience that there should be only one member from management on a board, as well as no outside counsel nor investment bankers nor commercial bankers or others who might be inclined to take management's side. But *Forbes'* editor pointed out that the ultimate "vehicle" for corporate accountability is the bottom line, and he asked if Williams really thought that a board with little or no firsthand knowledge about a business would be a benefit to that business. "Does ignorance lead to sound judgements?" he asked. I highlighted several paragraphs of this editorial and forwarded copies of it to the board with the one-word comment "Amen!" Those paragraphs are duplicated below:

> If a board is "independent" in Williams' sense of the word, then its members will inevitably be second-guessing management. How else does one prove one's independence? Under those circumstances, the imagination and foresightedness needed from top management would be stifled. Decision-making by committee leads to mediocrity.
>
> Williams appears to have forgotten that, inevitably, boards must be made up of people, and people will make mistakes. What happens if a board overrules the CEO and events prove the CEO right? Who makes the board accountable? Or what if management and the board agree on policy and the policy was a mistake? Who blows the whistle then?
>
> A board can offer advice and ask questions, but, fundamentally, the running of the company must be left to management. A board's job is to pick top management and to fire 'em if they don't perform.

I say again, twenty-five years later, Amen! Obviously, Southwest's board was not on the same wavelength as *Forbes* and I were. At least Rollin King wasn't, and the board had not the guts to corral him.

By this time, we had twelve Boeing 737-200 aircraft in the fleet, with arrangements already set for the arrival during late 1978 for three new aircraft to replace our original three Boeing 737-200s acquired back in 1971. We had paid $4 million for each of them in 1971 with 100 percent financing, realized the 7 percent investment tax credit, utilized them more than ten hours per day since then, and now held a firm offer to purchase them for $4.1 million each. Not bad! However, if desirable when the time came, these three could instead be the seventh through the ninth aircraft required for the scaled-down markets in the Midway case.

Being a CPA, I always practiced conservative accounting. In my opinion, when you took delivery of a new aircraft, that unit consisted of two parts, one being the basic aircraft and the other the "built-in overhaul" that came with it. As we utilized the aircraft, we used up that built-in overhaul that had been a substantial part of the total cost of the aircraft. Therefore, from the very first hour of flight, I had accrued an airworthiness reserve equal to $100 per air-time hour flown to account for this actual cost, which otherwise would not have been reflected in the operating statements submitted to shareholders. From inception of operations through 1977, we had incurred accruals to the airworthiness reserve account of $7.75 million, of which $1.1 million was still there as of December 31, 1977. With a twelve-aircraft fleet and plans already in place to replace our three original aircraft prior to their scheduled heavy-maintenance overhauls, it seemed appropriate to me to go from an "accrual basis" to an "as-incurred basis," beginning with the year 1978 rather than the originally planned date of January 1, 1979. This revised plan had been presented to and approved by our public accountants, Arthur Young & Co.

My revised plan now was to amortize the remaining reserve over the twelve months of 1978. Our original 1978 forecast of operating results showed that these reserve accruals during 1978 would exceed actual expenditures for heavy maintenance, due to the newness of our fleet, by $1.275 million. Therefore, the change in accounting procedure as of January 1, 1978, rather than January 1, 1979, would give us a $2.397 million start on 1978 results before flying the first mile that year. Add to this the planned $3 fare increase as of midyear, which was being announced in our 1977 annual report to shareholders, and 1978 was really going to be a piece of cake, exclusive of the multimillion-dollar profit to be realized on the sale of the three original aircraft. Total 1978 income promised to, in fact, exceed $15 million. The immediate importance of this change was that our reported earnings for the first quarter of 1978 would be well ahead of the first quarter of 1977, as opposed to my original forecast of a down quarter, taking the pressure off King's ill-advised sale of 5,000 shares. This policy change was fully discussed in my memos to directors dated March 8 and 16, 1978.

My son, Mike, had for some time been negotiating with Gary Barron, an attorney with Herb Kelleher's firm of Oppenheimer, Rosenberg, Kelleher and Wheatley, Inc., to join the Southwest management team as a senior executive in charge of administration, one of the duties that Mike was then performing. Since arranging financing for our rapid expansion had become a full-time job, he needed help in this other area. I sent a March 23, 1978, memo to "All Southwest Employees," with a copy to the board of directors, announcing the appointment of Barron as VP-administration and Mike Muse's change in title from VP–finance and administration to senior VP-finance. Additionally, a separate memo announced the promotion of Ed Lang from assistant VP–human resources to VP-marketing, replacing Jess Coker, who had resigned to accept an ownership position with Tuesday Morning.

This announcement gave Rollin King another leg up to allege that I was trying to make my son the heir apparent to the presidency of Southwest. This was totally untrue. Had I not included the word "senior" in Mike's title, the change would have appeared to be a demotion, which was certainly not the case.

My real long-range plan had been set in concrete during January when I made a deal with George Schrader, then Dallas's city manager, a man liked and respected across the political spectrum, to join Southwest as its president and chief operating officer effective July 1, 1978. The delay was to allow him to remain with the city until after a June referendum to approve the largest bond issue in the city's history, an issue designed to take care of the next two decades of its capital needs. The bonds would provide funding for the widening into boulevards of all major east-west thoroughfares north of downtown Dallas, and an expansive new city hall. Announcement of our arrangement prior to the bond election could have had an adverse effect on the vote, so there was to be no word of our agreement till after it was over.

I felt that there was only one member of our board whom I could trust with the information on my agreement with Schrader. So in a private conversation with John Murchison, I explained my detailed plan for the future management scheme of Southwest and its subsidiary, Midway (Southwest). Simultaneous with the appointment of Mr. Schrader as president and chief operating officer of Southwest, I would be officially named chairman of the board and CEO of Southwest Airlines and additionally as president and CEO of our subsidiary, Midway (Southwest). I planned to move to Chicago for an extended period and take Mike along with me as number-two man; when I returned to Dallas, he would be named president and chief operating officer of the Chicago operation. All of this was on the assumption that the deregulation bill would finally die in committee and the two corporate structures would continue to be required. Murchison stated that he considered my plan an ideal solution to the management strengthening that the board seemed to desire and was very complimentary of my selection of George Schrader. This private meeting occurred sometime during January 1978; I did not keep a record of the exact date.

There was one other exchange of correspondence with Rollin King during the first half of March, this time regarding his ill-advised sale of Southwest common stock, after which I took my family on a fast trip to Snowbird for some spring skiing. I made up my mind that, one way or the other, Rollin King and I were parting ways. Upon my return to the office on March 24, without really much thought and without clearly stating that it was either him or me—a big mistake—I dispatched the following letter to the board on my personal stationery:

March 24, 1978
TO THE MEMBERS OF THE BOARD OF DIRECTORS:
Recent events force me to make a decision which should have undoubtedly been made long ago. I choose not to stand for election, nor will I serve as a Director of Southwest Airlines following my current term which expires at the annual meeting of shareholders scheduled for Tuesday, April 25, 1978.
Since this action violates the second sentence of paragraph 2 of my current employment agreement, I herewith offer my resignation as an employee of Southwest Airlines, to be effective, with limitations, at the pleasure of the Board. The limitations are as follows:
Termination shall be effective either:
a. Immediately

b. One calendar month from today

c. On December 31, 1978 or December 31, 1979, provided that all benefits currently provided me are continued with an adjustment in the annual cash salary from the present $60,000 to $100,000.

A prompt decision by the Board as to your wishes relative to the above four choices would be greatly appreciated. Otherwise, I will assume that April 24, 1978, will be my final day as a Southwest employee and will act accordingly.

I sincerely appreciate the opportunities you have made available to me over the past seven plus years. They have been the most productive and rewarding of my business career, in spite of the obstacles.

Cordially,

Herb Kelleher had often told me that if I ever left the company, he would be gone at the same time. After dispatching my message to the board, Barbara and I took off for a long weekend at our house on Lake Palestine. After arriving there, I received a phone call saying there was a telegram from Herb that read:

EFFECTIVE IMMEDIATELY, I HEREBY RESIGN AS A DIRECTOR, SECRE-TARY AND GENERAL COUNCIL OF SOUTHWEST AIRLINES CO. IT HAS BEEN A PLEASURE WORKING WITH YOU AND I WISH EACH OF YOU AND THE COMPANY THE VERY BEST. SINCERELY HERB KELLEHER.

I immediately called Herb's office in San Antonio, but Colleen advised me that he was taking no calls that weekend. End of conversation.

Then came another telegram, this one from Sam Barshop:

WE SHOULD NOT ACCEPT HERB KELLEHER'S RESIGNATION UNTIL WE HAVE A CHANCE TO DISCUSS FULLY WITH MR. KELLEHER HIS REASONS FOR RESIGNING.

I was puzzled and remain so to this date. Kelleher surely had received my letter before sending his telegram. I can only conclude that Barshop probably hadn't before sending his telegram.

I am not really sure how it got called, but there was a board meeting set up for 1:00 P.M on March 28, 1978, the day Barbara and I returned from our long weekend at the lake. I understood that Adger was coming into Dallas on the flight that arrived at 10:50 A.M. Since he probably had no transportation over to the office, I went to the terminal to meet him and get a quick bite to eat before the meeting. He advised me, though, that Rollin King was meeting him, and then I saw King standing over in a corner just waiting for me to get out of the way, which I did. When I returned from lunch, the board members had gathered in Rollin King's unused office for the meeting—which itself seemed strange. Since I had always acted as chairman, I said at the outset, "Well, Mr. King, this meeting was apparently called by you. What do you want to talk about?"

The response came instead from John Murchison, the one man on the board I trusted implicitly. He said, "Well, the first thing we need to do is accept Lamar's resignation."

That statement coming from John Murchison knocked me for a loop. I just stared at him for a few seconds in disbelief, but he refused to make eye contact, instead looking off across the room. Then I said that if that was the way it was, they had no further need of me in their meeting. I picked up the file I had brought to the meeting and left. Back in my office, I put in a call to Barbara, asking her to come and pick me up, that I was no longer an employee of Southwest Airlines and thus had no transportation home.

Bob Wylie and Stan Cobb, the sales representatives from Boeing, had been in my office that morning to execute the contract for the six Boeing 737-200 aircraft scheduled for early 1979 delivery at 1978 prices for our planned Midway operation. While there, they had invited Barbara, Lisa, and me to dinner that evening. Being perfect gentlemen, they kept the appointment (and also confirmed their earlier invitation for a week's salmon fishing the next summer in British Columbia on their company yacht, the *Malibu*). As can be imagined, though, the dinner was not the celebration that had been planned. It was more like a wake. I think we were all glad when it was over.

16. THE LUV YEARS —

The Aftermath

I had been in attendance at the March 28 board meeting for no more than a few minutes, but I was convinced that Herb Kelleher had been present and a participant. Nevertheless, I made a determined effort to maintain a cordial relationship with him via correspondence (which he seldom acknowledges), office visits around annual meeting time, and occasional meetings for lunch. It therefore came as a surprise when, at one of our lunch meetings at The Palm in Dallas during May 2001, Herb asked me what the big argument had been between the board members and me at that March 28 meeting. I couldn't understand why he was asking me that question when he knew that I had been present for only a couple of minutes. He then told me that he and Colleen had been in Houston taking care of some legal business at the University of Houston when he had received a call from Sam Barshop telling him to get to Dallas as quickly as he could because of a big argument going on between me and the other board members.

Until that moment over lunch, I had never taken seriously his telegram resigning all his connections with Southwest. I now explained that there had been no discussion whatsoever at that meeting, that I had asked Rollin what he wanted to talk about,

194

and John Murchison had popped up with his motion to accept my resignation.

Thereafter, I reedited that part of the manuscript to reflect Herb's statement that he had not been present. Sometime later, *Fortune* magazine featured Katrina Brooker's big front-cover story on Herb Kelleher, in which he was quoted in great detail about the March 28 directors meeting at which he, reluctantly, and the other members of the board supported John Murchison's motion. This was, of course, a complete contradiction of what he had told me. I arranged another appointment with Herb, primarily to deliver to him a copy of my manuscript and request that he consider writing the foreword to it but also to clear up the discrepancy about who was where at that March 28, 1978 meeting.

He said that after our lunch it had worried him that we remembered the events differently, and when he concentrated on the matter, he remembered that Rollin King, in addition to calling the special meeting of all the directors, had also apparently arranged for a rump meeting of those directors not named Muse or Kelleher to precede the called meeting. It was during or at the conclusion of that rump meeting that Sam Barshop had phoned Herb and told him that Rollin was setting himself up to be nominated president and CEO by John Murchison, and if Kelleher didn't want that calamity to happen, he had better get his tail up to Dallas for the 1:00 P.M meeting, since his resignation had not been accepted.

After I had finally been disposed of, including an honest attempt by Herb to bring me back to the meeting, panic apparently prevailed, because Rollin King had stashed his own lawyer and CPA at the nearby Brookhollow Country Club, awaiting instructions to join the meeting and negotiate his employment contract as the company's new president and CEO. Since apparently only two of the board members wanted that to happen (John Murchison and Sid Adger), Sam Barshop needed Herb there to be the hit man. I later learned that John owed a very serious personal debt to Rollin King that Rollin had called in on this occasion. Why else would an intelligent businessman favor such a ruinous change in the direction of the company? The meeting wound up with Herb assuming my duties as CEO. As a temporary measure, Bill Franklin was named general manager to handle day-to-day operations. Mike Muse was terminated without notice. Rollin King never flew another trip as an employee of Southwest, obtaining in lieu thereof some kind of short-term consulting agreement. The search for a new president was begun.

Meanwhile, at the Muse domicile, the damn phone was ringing off the wall. Barbara took more than 200 messages from reporters, friends, the curious, concerned investors, and potential employers. I composed a brief statement for those who called:

> I felt that recent questionable conduct by one of our directors was of such import that I could not in good conscience continue to serve on the same board with him. Since refusing to serve violated my employment contract, I offered my resignation as an employee to be effective at the pleasure of the board. In other words, it was either him or me. In the collective infinite wisdom of the Southwest board of directors, they kept Mr. Rollin King and fired me. I slept well last night. I hope they did.

Herb Kelleher was on the phone the next day. Southwest was due to release the 1977 annual report, which contained an article entitled "Justification for a 1978 Fare Increase," but it was absolutely imperative that at least the chairman of the TAC be advised of this planned fare increase before it was released to the public through the annual report. Since Herb knew none of the factors involved in the rate increase, he wanted me to accompany him to the office of the TAC chairman, David Witts, in downtown Dallas and sell him the package. I was more than happy to do this for him.

Additionally, since oral argument before the members of the Civil Aeronautics Board on the Midway Project was being held the following week in Washington, Herb wanted my presence at that argument to show the board that my leaving Southwest had not changed anything. Why he wanted this, I could never quite figure out, as (1) he refused to complete negotiations with me to allow me to take over the Midway (Southwest) project and then (2) subsequently announced publicly that Southwest was abandoning the project and had sold to the Federal Express

Company the six valuable Boeing 737-200 delivery positions I had obtained in exchange for the piddling $150,000 we had paid for them. Yes, the same $150,000 that Rollin King had made such a big issue of, and which I had mistakenly decided not to address with my draft letter dated January 6, 1978.

While in Washington, I had the opportunity to meet Travis C. Johnson, an El Paso attorney whom Herb had recruited to take my place on the board of directors, and to renew my acquaintance with Rollin's ex-wife, Marsha. At lunch, after the oral argument before the CAB members, we all agreed that Marsha and I had something in common. We had both been screwed by Rollin King.

The negative repercussions to the board's action were not long in coming. By late 1979 and the early 1980s, Southwest was scrambling frantically for aircraft to take advantage of the many opportunities handed to them on a silver platter by the Congress's passage of the deregulation bill, signed into law by the president during November 1978. The company was forced to pay fantastic lease rates for every available Boeing 737 in the world, no matter what condition. They even broke Southwest's cardinal simplicity rule of using only one type of aircraft by—of all things—leasing a Boeing 727, with its three-man cockpit crew and four-girl cabin crew, from—of all people—Braniff Airways, to take some of the pressure off the burgeoning Love Field–Hobby market. In the end, Southwest actually paid dearly for those six aircraft, the only problem being that FedEx held valid title to them, thanks to Rollin King.

While Kelleher was telling the "Fellow Members of the Southwest Team" that "Your company will continue in the direction he [Lamar Muse] charted for us, and therefore his departure will not affect our philosophy, policies and operating procedures," Bill Franklin changed all of them at the very first staff meeting after my departure. He announced that Lamar's cap on the number of employees at no more than 1,000 for our current operation was no longer in effect; all supervisors were henceforth permitted to add whatever new positions they deemed appropriate. With that single announcement, the stringent cost and budget controls I had insisted on from the very inception of operations went out the window, and there was a wild scramble to build empires and throw money after nonessentials. Unfortunately, with my change in accounting for the airworthiness reserve, I had given them a $2.4 million kitty to play with during the remaining nine months of 1978.

While it was obvious that members of the Southwest board of directors were not my most enthusiastic supporters, others saw things differently. My nemesis in the courtroom, S. G. (John) Johndroe Jr., Fort Worth's ever-present city attorney, wrote: "I just want to tell you that I really enjoyed working in cases with you. I have great respect for you. Everyone is fully aware of the plain and simple fact that now that you have done all of the work in building from scratch a most productive and viable operation against what would seem to have been almost overwhelming odds, others would seek to claim and reap all of the benefits of your efforts. Don't ever worry about it, you did a terrific job." He added this P.S.: "I didn't say 'cockroaches' but admit to 'termites.'" This referred to the fact that after the loss of each court proceeding to Southwest, John was reported to have said that the president of Southwest was a liar, and/or that Southwest was just a bunch of cockroaches and termites. It was nice to know at last that I was at least not a cockroach—just a termite!

The letter from Harry I. Martin, publishing vice president of *Air Transport World*, said, "I have just seen the preliminary figures which show that you have a profit picture that is unprecedented. The reason behind your success is very apparent, at least to Don Bondlow and myself. The enthusiasm we saw displayed between you, Barbara and Lisa during our dinner discussion certainly becomes contagious, not only to your employees, not only to your passengers, but to the people in the industry."

Richard J. Sterne, VP–corporate planning of Merrill Lynch in New York, wrote, "You are the best chief executive officer I have had the privilege to know. I am sad for Southwest to see you leave." Bert Fingerhut, the dean of airline analysts and a VP of Oppenheimer & Co., wrote on March 30, "Just a short note to again say how sorry I am about recent developments." He enclosed a copy of a short report that his company had just published, which removed Southwest common stock from their "Emphasis and Recommended Lists" as a result of my departure. On April 18 Bert wrote again. "The newspapers are filled with stories about your possibly trying to re-enter Midway. In that regard, I certainly wish you success. I just wanted you to know that we at Oppenheimer would be most interested in trying to help in any manner." Peter K. Nevitt, president of BankAmeriLease Group, said, "Certainly the success of Southwest Airlines, which proceeded on the precise timetable you originally outlined, is one of the outstanding achievements in business history." F. Rockwell Lowe, VP at Continental Bank–Chicago, wrote, "Our bank has a lot of confidence in you, and we are dismayed at the possible impact of your exit on the existence of a bankable Midway project, i.e. the necessary management is separated from necessary capital."

James Campbell, executive director of the Ad Hoc Committee for Airline Regulatory Reform in Washington, D.C., had this to say: "I was very sorry to see that you and Mike will be leaving Southwest Airlines. I had just finished reading a transcript of your testimony at the CAB in the Midway Low-Fare Proceeding. Fine testimony in a blizzard of baloney. The more I have been involved with Congress and the companies which depend upon the favor of the Federal Government, the more disappointed I have become. Your efforts up here, and the company you have built in Texas, have been one of the very few hopeful signs."

Harold Collum, realtor-developer-investor, wrote: "I have very much enjoyed flying 'Your Airline.' I very much hope to see you do the same thing with a new national airline. If you decide to organize another company, I would be pleased if you would list me as one of your potential investors. In the meantime, we would be pleased to furnish you office space of up to 600 sq. ft. absolutely free for your use." Robert Walker, president of a local fire insurance company, offered his "sincere help and possible financial help in regard to your purchase of Midway Airway." Ken Gordon of Control Data Cybersearch wrote: "The massive earthquake your resignation created is applauded by your fans and followers, of whom I've been one for several years. We know that it took 'guts.' Talent and ability is a rare combination to beat." Charles Wesley Goyer Jr. wrote: "The bombshell news of yesterday prompts me to write this long-intended letter. I have enjoyed watching Southwest's burgeoning growth and silently extended my congratulations to you—daily. You have

199

accomplished magnificent things, and I stand with the cheering crowds."

James M. Tanner, Ph.d., of Birmingham, Alabama, who had helped me when I was at Southern trying to get Tom Grojean started on his highly successful airline career, wrote: "I was distressed to learn of your resignation from Southwest. I am reminded of the satisfaction I have enjoyed as a stockholder and the vicarious pride I have experienced in observing your success." David and Carolyn Allex—David was past president of the Harlingen Chamber of Commerce—wrote to Barbara and me: "I hope the Valley holds a warm spot in your hearts besides the money angle. Both of you have many *close* friends in Harlingen—that respect you—have confidence in you—and love you. Please don't stay away."

Durwood Fleming, president of Southwestern University in Georgetown, Texas, my alma mater, wrote, "I have identified with the trauma that has been the experience for you and your lovely wife, as well as your son, and can only express regrets, especially for Southwest Airlines, that what we believe was the wrong decision was made. I fully understand the position you were in and salute the incredible courage you had in taking your stand. While I was not surprised that you took such a stand, knowing you to be a man of impeccable integrity and strength, I can only say you set an example for a lot of weak-kneed Texans and society in general. Frank Smith sent me a copy of the article from the *Houston Business Journal* entitled 'A Tribute to Lamar Muse.' I think in summary he sort of put it all together for us. I wish I could have said it half as well."

The one I appreciated the most, however, was the piece of David Witts' personal stationery, on which with a felt pen he had drawn a heart with an arrow piercing it. Inside the heart were written the letters "DW + LM." Together David Witts, the TAC chairman, and I had conquered Braniff and Texas International.

Of the nearly 1,000 Southwest officers and employees, I only received messages from two, both women, neither of them an officer. I won't embarrass them by saying who they were. So much fear had gone through that organization in such a short period of time!

Prior to leaving Southwest, I had agreed to be the luncheon

speaker on May 3, 1978, at Southern Methodist University's Beta Gamma Sigma luncheon. On that day, Robert O. Harvey introduced me in this way:

> Our speaker today has been in the news.
> His biography is written for you to peruse.
> To his directors he said, "you must choose!"
> "Pilot error" was the word in the morning reviews.
>
> Air service he created for transients to use,
> Carried for aisle sitters magnificent views.
> The profits he generated, they'll try not to lose,
> But they worry about his offer they decided to refuse.
>
> The moral of this saga, aspiring youths?
> Even the righteous and talented may temporarily lose.
> An earnest life pledged to honor and truths
> Oft times carries burdensome dues.
>
> I'm privileged to introduce Mr. M. Lamar Muse.

As you can well imagine, that speech started off with tears in this speaker's eyes.

R. Jerry Falkner, CFA, a senior analyst with Underwood, Neuhaus & Co. in Houston, was a staunch supporter of Southwest stock even at its lowest point of $2 per share after the initial offering price of $11. I got a note from him that just said, "Couldn't let you leave without saying goodbye." Attached was the following "Editorial Comment" on Underwood, Neuhaus & Co. stationery and distributed to all their clients, entitled "A Tribute to Lamar Muse." It was later picked up as the lead editorial in the *Houston Business Journal*.

Editorial Comment   April 3, 1978
SOUTHWEST AIRLINES, INC. ($16 ½)
A Tribute to M. Lamar Muse

Last week, Lamar Muse resigned as President and Chief Executive Officer of Southwest Airlines. This particular writer will miss him. As investors, we should regret the fact that this colorful businessman will no longer be at the controls of such an exciting airline. As American citizens, we have lost a man who brought the cost of airline transportation in Texas down dramatically, and he was working to do so nationwide. While he will probably take a well-deserved rest from the business arena, we are all made a little poorer by his leaving, and his shoes will be hard to fill.

This is not to say that Southwest Airlines as a company faces any operating or financial difficulties. It does not. In fact, travelers have responded so strongly to Southwest's low fares and on-time service that earnings for the first quarter will probably be better than expected. With a fare increase anticipated this Summer, profits for the year may very well exceed $13.5 million, or $4.50 per share (vs. a record $2.52 earned in 1977). The operating management recruited under Lamar Muse's leadership remains largely intact, and Southwest should continue to realize its potential for further significant growth within the State of Texas.

Lamar Muse believed that if you gave the public a bargain, you could make a fortune. He proved the worth of that philosophy in an industry which had always responded to its problems by raising fares. Southwest's cut-rate prices, on the other hand, were even competitive with automobile travel and often below bus fares. Earth-bound travelers from the commuting businessman to the seldom-visited grandmother and the budget-strapped student responded enthusiastically. While investors in Southwest stock have profited greatly, the real beneficiaries were the citizens of Texas and those visiting our State.

Lamar Muse believed in the free enterprise system. He wasn't real strong on government regulation. It seems he didn't consider it in the best interests of the traveling public or of the airlines themselves. He always felt that if you concentrated on controlling your costs, instead of relying upon government-approved higher ticket prices, your profits would increase while stimulating further market growth. We call it "real" growth—and it can be applied to the economics of managing the smallest company or an entire nation. He also believed that incentives would improve productivity at all levels within the Company. Every employee of Southwest understood that higher profits for the airline meant more money in their pockets. Regular bonuses were paid to all employees based upon a profit-sharing formula. He made the free enterprise system work for everyone involved. It came as little surprise to us that Southwest's operating costs per trip were far below those of other airlines, despite the expenses associated with rapid fleet expansion.

Finally, we will miss Lamar because it just won't be as much fun without him around. This writer has followed many companies as an investment analyst during the past nine years. But he has never come across a group of employees so totally devoted to the success of the Company. They started with an idea and fought to realize its potential against enormous odds. Not only was their own industry trying to prevent this maverick from succeeding, but many local politicians acted somewhat contrary to "the public interest" in order to stifle Southwest's growth. Lamar was never what one could call "modest" and seldom refrained from speaking his mind. As a result, some folks were not too fond of him. But every mechanic, flight hostess, secretary and pilot that this writer ever met exhibited what can be termed no less than the greatest respect for their "boss." His office was filled with mementos of appreciation and reminders of the battle scars which were suffered trying to get a new airline started. Under Lamar's guidance, Southwest Airlines was a challenging and fun company to follow from an investment point of view.

We don't know why he really resigned. Maybe we never will. (The official news release stated "for personal reasons.") We just know that he will be missed — even by those who never knew him.

R. Jerry Falkner, C.F.A.
"Eagles don't flock — you have to find them one at a time."

Probably the best reporting in a concise manner of my separation from Southwest was the lead article in the April 3, 1978, *Aviation Daily*. It is reprinted here in its entirety:

SOUTHWEST PRESIDENT SAYS HE LOST "POWER PLAY"

M. Lamar Muse resigned as president of Southwest Airlines after he tried a "power play" and lost the last major round in a series of disagreements with Southwest board member and major stockholder Rollin W. King. Muse told the *Daily*, "The reason I left is because I had all of Rollin King I could take. I did a power play to make it either Rollin King or Lamar Muse and I was the loser. I decided I was too old and too rich to put up with it any more."

Muse's resignation was accepted by the board of directors at a meeting Tuesday afternoon. Muse said he had decided to submit a letter of resignation and force a showdown. "I decided to leave it up to the board—either King or Lamar Muse. They apparently think Rollin King is more valuable to the company than Lamar Muse. I never dreamed the board would feel that way." Muse refused to discuss specifics of his dispute with King except to say that King had written letters to directors criticizing Muse. He said King "wanted from the outset to be chief executive and worked diligently to get me out of the way." Muse has no immediate plans for new business ventures. He is still working on a financial settlement with Southwest.

Southwest issued a statement late last week emphasizing there would be no change in operations or policy. "We fully intend to carry on the highly successful pricing and service policies instituted under the leadership of M. Lamar Muse. We do not contemplate any changes whatsoever in the management philosophy, operational methods, or policies and procedures."

Southwest's stock dropped over two points after word spread of Muse's resignation. Subsequent statements from both Muse and Southwest appear designed to assure investors there will be no major changes in the company. Muse said Friday there is no reason why Southwest should not earn $13 million this year.

After leaving Southwest, it was necessary for me to resign my position as an officer and member of the Downtown Rotary Club of Dallas, since I could no longer fill a classification. Sometime thereafter, I was invited to be the luncheon speaker at Houston's Rotary Club, which met at the Shamrock Hotel. Instead of talking about Southwest, I chose to speak about a visit I had recently made to Cape Canaveral. The tour group I was with had observed a missile coming out of the ocean depths from a submerged submarine some ten miles out from the cape, and afterward we were privileged to tour the entire submarine, including the center missile storage and launch area. We were advised that one submarine had more firepower than had been expended by both sides during World War II. And here we were, as a nation, with hundreds of the damn things. I was not impressed, just disgusted, and I said so in my remarks to Houston's Rotary Club.

Afterward, Leroy Melcher, then president of the Rotary Club of Houston, wrote to say, "I want to express my appreciation on your splendid speech before our club. Several other members of Rotary all share my enthusiasm about your fine address. You have won the respect, confidence and admiration of all the people in this area in your business endeavors, and you have every right to be proud of the reputation you have earned." Braxton Thompson wrote, "Just a note to tell you on behalf of the entire Houston Rotary Club how much we appreciated your thoughts with us last Thursday. A speaker's message is always taken to heart by his listeners when it is obvious that the speaker feels deeply about the message he is bringing. I can't recall any of our speakers about whom this was more true than last Thursday's meeting. Many of our members have commented to me how much they appreciated your visit." A close friend of mine, Jick Kenderdine, wrote, "Just a note to tell you again what a great job you did in your speech to the Houston Rotary Club yesterday. I have never seen a more attentive audience as I looked out over the group. Your ending was truly a dramatic close, and you couldn't have improved if you had rehearsed it a thousand times, which, of course, you had not done or expect to do. ... In fact, I did not sleep worth a damn last night when I started thinking about 'The thing more tragic than defeat is victory.' There has got to be an end somehow in this maddening, stupid, futile arms race the world is in." I never heard or read a single negative comment from any source about my subject.

After my departure from Southwest, the hardest things for me were (1) learning to sleep late and (2) hearing those Southwest 737s going over our house every few minutes when using the north-south approach pattern—which was most of the time. We solved the second problem by moving lock, stock, and barrel to our home on Lake Palestine as soon as school was out in late May. We bought a nice little fifty-five-acre ranch, and I traded in the Lincoln Mark V the company had given me for a fancy new Ford pickup truck and set about trying to forget about my first love—Southwest Airlines.

The company honored my employment contract and continued granting positive-space annual passes to Barbara and me, though Herb insisted that I not trespass on company property without invitation. My big fight over Midway became a non-event when Congress finally passed in late 1978 the Airline Regulatory Reform Bill, on which I had spent so much of my time during the previous three years. This effectively gave Southwest the right to go anywhere they wanted to, except from Dallas Love Field, and man, have they! More power to them. I'll say this for Herb Kelleher: except for a few minor things that probably had to be changed due to the company's routes getting so far-flung, he has been true to his word not to change the "management philosophy, operational methods, policies or procedures" that I had established during the company's formative years. Until recently, he didn't even change the paint design on the aircraft, and then only changed the colors to celebrate the company's thirtieth anniversary. (That is generally one of the very first things a new airline CEO does, as I myself did at both Central and Universal.) Keep up the good work, Herb, for as long as you damn well please. (Postscript: Herb gave up the CEO and president titles on the company's thirtieth anniversary to James Parker and Colleen Barrett, respectively.)

Finally, I just can't leave the Southwest portion of this book without commenting on the period subsequent to my unceremonious departure. So many fabulous things have happened for Southwest in the years since the passage of the Airline Regulatory Reform Act in late 1978 (which year I claim for myself) through the turn of the century, and even in 2001, the year of turmoil highlighted by the September terrorist attacks.

The 3 million common shares that were outstanding on December 31, 1978, had a book value of $42.9 million, or $14.30 per share—$5.67 of which had been earned that very year—with a market capitalization of $58.9 million ($19 ⁵/₈ per share), reflecting a price-earnings ratio of only 3.5/1 versus the 29.3/1 on December 31, 2001. On that date, after twelve stock splits, those 3 million shares, belonging to several thousand shareholders including all eligible Southwest employees, represented 481 million, or 62.6 percent, of the 776.8 million shares outstanding. Those 481 million shares had a market value on December 31, 2001, of $8,880,000,000, or $2,960 for each one of those 3 million original shares. From under $20 to almost $3,000 makes Microsoft look not so hot. The Southwest management team and all employees should be proud of that accomplishment.

It seems almost sacrilegious to suggest that results could have been even better, but I will give it a try. Through the remainder of 1978, the company ran on the momentum created prior to my dismissal. During November 1978, a United Airlines marketing executive named Howard Putnam was brought in as president and CEO, with Kelleher continuing as chairman of the board. Putnam was employed under a three-year agreement to accomplish two major functions. Only one of those functions was spelled out in the agreement, and it was to make sure that not one single facet of Southwest's highly successful formula for profits was disturbed or allowed to founder. The other function, unknown to Putnam, was to teach Kelleher enough about the airline business so that he could legitimately take over Putnam's position at the end of his initial agreement, which he did when Putnam "resigned" to go to the badly faltering Braniff Airways. Herb Kelleher disputes my version of the Putnam affair, but it just seems totally illogical to me for a totally logical man to leave the CEO job of a fabulously successful company to go to the same position in a company inevitably headed for bankruptcy. Putnam did what he agreed to do, retaining the extremely high productivity of the Southwest employees—3,100 to 3,200 passengers per year per employee—and with a lower but still healthy 13 percent of revenues carrying through to the bottom line, as shown in the line graph on page 208.

With the deregulation of the airlines at the end of 1978,

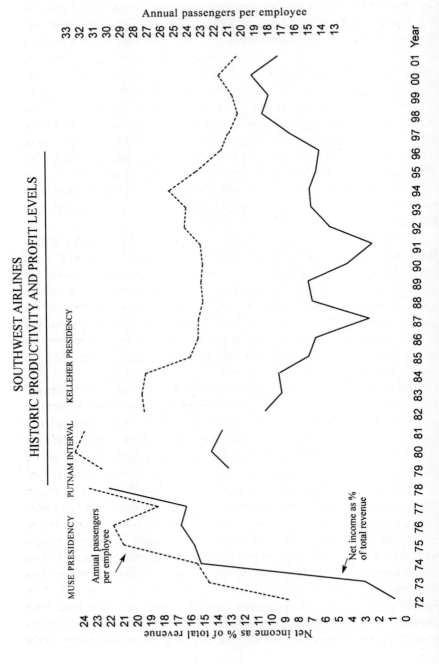

SOUTHWEST AIRLINES
HISTORIC PRODUCTIVITY AND PROFIT LEVELS

MUSE PRESIDENCY   PUTNAM INTERVAL   KELLEHER PRESIDENCY

Annual passengers per employee

Annual passengers
per employee

Net income as %
of total revenue

Net income as % of total revenue

72 73 74 75 76 77 78 79 80 81 82 83 84 85 86 87 88 89 90 91 92 93 94 95 96 97 98 99 00 01 Year

Southwest was permitted to pick and choose markets throughout the forty-eight states, a situation totally unlike the pitched battles we had experienced up to that time to expand only within the state of Texas. The fleet grew from 15 Boeing 737-200s, all equipped with 112 seats, to 355 Boeing 737-200, -300, -500, and -700 series models, equipped with from 118 to 137 seats. I see those twenty-three years as three different periods — the three Putnam years, Herb's learning decade, and finally the ten years ending on December 31, 2001, during which great opportunities have presented themselves, including the aftermath of 9/11. The tabulation on the next page compares mythical average years for those three described periods with the actual year of 1978, the first full year of operations for the nine-city Texas network we had developed over the previous seven years.

First, the Putnam years. Both service provided and utilization thereof increased approximately two-thirds. With a 50 percent increase in average fare, the company was able to maintain the 50 percent break-even load factor, even though fuel costs per gallon more than doubled and as a percent of operating costs went from 27.5 to 37.8 percent. Employee productivity remained reasonably constant in all categories, with an increase in annual operating income per employee of 20 percent, to $22,565. Overall, it was an excellent record.

During the decade beginning with Mr. Kelleher's assumption of direct management, an average year showed further growth, as the company expanded to the West Coast and acquired both Muse Air and Morris Air. Trips flown almost tripled, and seat-miles quadrupled, reflecting the addition of one row of seats into the aircraft, the new stretched versions of the 737 aircraft, and the approximately 100-mile-longer average stage length of each flight. The problem was that the traffic volumes didn't cooperate. The average load factor declined from 66.7 to 60.1 percent, and because of substantial increases in controllable costs, the break-even load factor increased from 50.7 to 56.9 percent, even though average passenger fares were up another 63 percent and fuel prices were down 15 percent. The profit spread of 17.7 percent that Mr. Putnam enjoyed had shrunk to only 5.8 percent, not much better than the competition. This shrinkage was reflected in the price of the company's

SOUTHWEST AIRLINES CO.–LUV

FINANCIAL AND OPERATING HISTORY, 1978–2001

	Muse	Putnam	Kelleher		1992–2001 Multiple of 1978
Responsible CEO	Muse	Putnam	Kelleher		
Avg. 12-month period	1978	1979–81	1982–91	1992–01	
Number of years	1	3	10	10	
Trips flown	54,816	92,427	257,883	732,723	13.37
Avail. seat miles (millions)	1,556	2,974	11,801	42,806	27.51
Avg. lgth. of flight*	253	273	366	410	1.62
Passengers carried	3,528	5,923	14,330	49,055	13.89
Rev. psgr. miles (millions)	1,049	1,973	7,095	28,760	27.43
Avg. lgth. psgr. haul (miles)	297	332	495	577	1.94
Avg. psgr. fare ($)	21.99	32.78	53.28	71.27	3.24
Yld. per psgr. mile (cents)	7.4	9.84	10.76	12.31	1.66
Psgr. load factor (%)	67.4	66.7	60.1	66.8	0.99
Break-even load factor (%)	49.9	50.7	56.9	60.4	1.21
No. of emp. at year-end	1,119	1,866	5,979	22,459	20.07
Productivity per emp.:					
Trips flown	49	49.5	43.1	33	0.67
ASMs (000)	1,391	1,594	1,974	1,889	1.36
Psgrs. carried	3,153	3,174	2,397	2,198	0.71
RPMs (000)	937	1,057	1,187	1,263	1.35
Operating revenues	72,444	110,668	132,430	161,800	2.23
Operating expenses	53,568	88,103	120,680	139,794	2.61
Operating income	18,876	22,565	11,750	22,006	1.17
Net income	15,196	19,562	7,670	14,172	0.93
Net income as % of operating revenues	21.0	17.7	5.8	8.8	0.42
Avg. fuel cost per gallon (cents)	38.2	81.99	70.12	60.48	1.58
Fuel as % of oper. costs	27.5	37.8	21.9	14.7	0.53

*1978 is actual. Other periods' plane miles were not available. Estimates based on estimated average seating capacity of aircraft of 125, 120, and 125, respectively.

stock. While the stock had gone up a couple of thousand percent between 1972 and 1978, and another 500 percent during the three Putnam years, it was up just another 500 percent during the next decade. Pretty good for most outfits, but not Southwest.

During the last decade, though, many good things have fallen into Southwest's lap. First, USAir bought PSA. Then American bought Air California and Delta bought Western Airlines, and none of the three purchasers knew a thing about running the outfits they had purchased. They tried to meld them into their highly inefficient operating mode, but in a surprisingly short period of time, the markets those three independent carriers had operated profitably were simply handed to Southwest on a silver platter. This, together with Southwest's delayed development of the Chicago Midway market and the company's invasion of the East Coast, where their principal competition was that pitiful USAir with fares twice as high as the rest of the industry, meant that things couldn't help but get better.

Southwest is a different animal in today's world than it was in 1978. Back then, we were a low-fare, high-frequency air carrier in small markets made into large markets by our innovative two-level class fares. While the company still does what we did in 1978, by combining short- and long-haul flights as through-flights, or by operating two medium-haul flights in tandem, they now also compete in the same long-haul markets as the trunk carriers. An example of this is the service Southwest provides the passenger who boards Southwest's flight 169 in Ft. Lauderdale at 7:40 A.M. and arrives in Seattle at 12:30 P.M., with only a single thirty-minute stop in Nashville. That's from the southeastern corner of the United States to its northwestern corner. Similarly, a passenger can board Southwest flight 294 in Providence (a better way to Boston) at 8:20 A.M and arrive in Los Angeles at 1:00 P.M. after a thirty-minute stop in Kansas City. This takes him from the northeastern corner of the USA to its southwestern corner. Try to match those two services with anything the major trunk airlines offer! As a bonus, compare the price you would pay.

This invasion by Southwest of the trunk carriers' territory was primarily the result of the conniving of trunk airline industry executives. With their political power and their big guns sighted on Southwest, they persuaded the Congress to change the flat transportation tax, which had been based on a carrier's passenger revenues (10 percent thereof), to a formula that severely penalized all low-fare, short-haul carriers—a flat amount of $3 per passenger leg flown, be it 200 miles or 2,000 miles, plus 7.5 percent of the fare charged. Southwest warned the trunks when they were pushing for this change that if they pursued this policy, they would force Southwest to enter their long-haul markets and divert traffic to Southwest, using the draw of its lower fares and superior service.

And they have done just that. The effect of the longer stage lengths has been to reduce seat-mile costs. However, this also has reduced revenue per passenger-mile flown even more, resulting in a reduction of profits per passenger flown. In 1978 the 3,528,000 passengers carried flew an average of 297 miles each, producing $4.82 net income from a $21.99 fare, or 22 percent. In 2001 the 64,446,773 passengers carried flew an average of 690 miles each (more than twice as far), but they produced only $7.93 of net income from an average fare of $83.46, or 9.5 percent. In 1978 dollars, that $7.93 would be something less than $3.

Maybe the size and complexity of today's operation make it inevitable that profit margins shrink—that seems to be the history of American business—but I personally don't buy that. The philosophy of "Keep it simple, Stupid" still rings true. Southwest no longer offers a clearly delineated Executive Class fare on short-haul flights operated between 6:30 A.M and 6:59 P.M. on weekdays—serving free cocktails—or Pleasure Class flights at all other times including all weekend flights. Instead there is a confusing conglomeration of as many as ten different fares in a single market, with every passenger trying to finagle the lowest one. So-called "yield management" departments try to fine-tune every flight throughout the day every day of the week to produce the highest load factor, but not necessarily the best financial result. While I don't know exactly how many flight departures Southwest now operates on a weekday, I do know, from studying one of their recently published schedules, that 1,982 of the flights each day serving 130 different markets and involving well over 80 percent of the total passengers carried could be operated in the Executive/Pleasure class format utilized so successfully during the late 1970s and early '80s. If your rates are low enough and your service is better than that of the competition, as Southwest's were back then, you don't have to jump through hoops like "yield management" to make a fancy return. Of course, you must have low costs to justify low fares. But just because Southwest's fares are among the lowest in the industry, that does not mean they are as low as they should be. Everybody always blames high costs on the price of fuel, but Southwest's average fuel cost per gallon is 26 percent lower than it was during Putnam's reign, and as a percent of total operating costs, fuel has dropped from 37.8 percent to only 14.7 percent. What that says is that all other costs have just ballooned, and many of them are or were controllable.

One of the major economies we enjoyed during the 1970s and early '80s that has not been available since Southwest's expansion to both coasts was the single base for all cockpit crews and flight attendants as well as aircraft maintenance operations. That single base was also a major factor for building the great group spirit that permeates the Southwest organization. Today's pilots, flight attendants, and mechanics living and working in or out of Phoenix, Seattle, Baltimore, and so forth can't have the feeling of family that is present in employees located in Dallas.

A wonderful opportunity presented itself a couple of years ago when Legend Airlines began operations out of Love Field in Dallas. They were using reconfigured DC-9s that seated only fifty-six passengers to provide service to destinations beyond the "neighboring states restriction" created by the Wright Amendment applicable only to Dallas's Love Field. At that time, Bob Crandall of American Airlines put tremendous pressure on the City of Dallas and Southwest Airlines to obtain two of Southwest's gates at Love Field so that they could offer a competing service.

I strongly suggested to Herb Kelleher that agreeing to help Mr. Crandall could be a real bonanza for Southwest to at least partially reverse the multiple-base problem and at the same time substantially cut Southwest's unit costs and increase profits—all at American's expense. My suggestion was to tell Crandall that Southwest would give American the exclusive use of two of its gates at Love Field if he would provide the same consideration to Southwest at one of its DFW terminals. Of course, Crandall would immediately want to know what the hell Kelleher wanted with two of his gates at DFW. After hearing the answer, he probably would have decided that he didn't want to fly out of Love Field as badly as he thought he did.

The plan? Ultimately, fly one trip in and out of DFW from each gate each hour throughout the day and night, a total of forty-eight arrivals and departures, to and from every major city served by Southwest outside the permitted area of the Wright Amendment. Each inbound flight would be operated by a crew going off duty and would leave with a fresh crew, both of which would be Dallas-based. All aircraft due a major maintenance function would be ferried to Love Field and replaced by a fresh aircraft from that maintenance facility. Just the major savings of eliminating a flock of crew bases and their attendant costs for supervision, reserve crews, and overnight accommodation, together with the centering of all major maintenance functions at Love Field, would go a long way toward paying the direct flight costs of these trips.

Revenues would be secondary, but very substantial, creating abnormally high profit margins. There are thirteen cities on or near the West Coast that could be given service at a one-way unrestricted fare of $99, as could seven cities in the northeastern U.S. Seventeen additional cities in a belt beginning in south Florida, extending through the Midwest, and ending in Tucson, Arizona, could be served at a one-way unrestricted fare of $79. These cities would account for thirty-seven of the forty-eight daily roundtrips, leaving eleven roundtrips as second roundtrips for the most promising markets or for convenience of crew scheduling. The flexibility that this type of operation would provide for aircraft utilization, maintenance, and crew scheduling, and the consolidation of a much larger proportion of the total employee complement in the Dallas area, would perform miracles for both unit costs (which is the name of the game) and morale (which makes things tick). Without question, the longer-haul, low-fare trips into DFW would sustain average passenger load factors in excess of 80 percent, and the night trips particularly would be loaded with mail and cargo.

214

Possibly because of the source of this recommendation, nothing ever came of my proposal, and eventually American got two undesirable gates over in another wing at Love Field. However, my plan is just as good (or bad) today, maybe even more so. Now that Herb has released his titles of president and CEO, just maybe there could be a more unbiased response sometime in the future. The stockholders should certainly hope so.

Be all that as it may, Southwest is a fabulous success story of which Herb and every other Southwest employee, past and present, should be and rightfully are very proud. What began as a little three-aircraft airline, which Harding Lawrence of Braniff Airways—as well as many other so-called experts—forecast would not last more than ninety days back in 1971, came through something as debilitating to an industry as 9/11 was without laying off a single employee or canceling a single flight other than during the three days following 9/11 forced upon the company by the FAA. And Southwest achieved a market capitalization exceeding that of the rest of the industry combined during the recent difficult period. A lot of people have got to be doing something right. As Herb has often said, "It's not so important that you do things right, but rather that you do the right things," or words to that effect.

After 9/11, Southwest's management did not forget lessons we learned in the early days about leverage in the airline business—that is, that you can add service to an existing base at very low cost. On the other hand, if you are forced to cut service, the reduction in costs is negligible, causing break-even load factors to rise very rapidly and employee morale to hit bottom. In other words, the airline industry is a capital-intensive, high-fixed-cost business in which leverage can make you or break you. It's too bad the rest of the industry, with their 10 to 20 percent cuts after 9/11, have never learned that basic fact.

It is therefore my considered opinion that, at this point in time, Southwest has the potential for the greatest profitable growth of its thirty-one-year operating history if it will just take advantage of it by accelerating delivery of new aircraft rather than the current practice of delaying such deliveries and parking brand-new aircraft in the Arizona desert. Such action would permit the company to begin serving the pick of the many markets that have been cut back or abandoned by other companies. That action, together with a DFW operation, would, within a relatively short period of time, double Southwest's net income and resultant market capitalization once again.

The serious drawbacks to accomplishing that goal are twofold. First, top management of the company is in a state of flux and will continue to be until the new president finishes receiving all the honors she is collecting and has fulfilled all the invitations to speak before women's groups she will receive, at which time hopefully she will relinquish her honorary position and permit the company's executive VP–finance, Gary Kelly, to assume the all-important position of president and chief operating officer. The company's formative years were under the direction of a CEO with a financial background, and then it passed for three years to an expert in marketing, who incidentally was smart enough to bring along with him a finance man, and during the last twenty-one years the company has been controlled by a couple of attorneys, both from the same firm. It is time to get back to basics, get costs under control, be the low-fare carrier in fact rather than fiction, and stay the course.

The second drawback is, as usual, our federal government. Bureaucrats capitalized on the events of September 11, 2001, to put a burden on the airline industry as well as our nation that effectively makes bin Laden's al-Qaeda network the winner. The airlines had absorbed for the last twenty-eight years the security costs required of them by the FAA because a nut named D. B. Cooper decided to jump out of a Boeing 727-100 with a parachute, creating some 27,000 jobs for people who would otherwise have most likely been on welfare and establishing a new "security" division for the Federal Aviation Administration. That was child's play, though, compared to what has occurred as a result of 9/11. Instead of 27,000 minimum-wage employees, we are now going to have 72,000 "government security agents" making several times the rate of pay previously standard for the positions. The majority of the original 27,000 will qualify for the new positions, since (1) the government doesn't fire people, and (2) so that they won't have to fire them, the requirements of U.S. citizenship and a high school education have been eliminated.

The secretary of transportation appointed by President Bush is a defeated congressman from California who, with his family, was detained in an American internment camp throughout World War II due to his Japanese ancestry. As a result, he considers profiling to be a mortal sin and will not permit its use in airport security matters. But with pressure from the Congress and other uninformed Americans, he had to do something to at least give the semblance of tightened security, so he came up with "random" security. That's what they call these hamburger flippers you see at the gate who randomly pick out unsuspecting grandmothers, soldiers in uniform, and even pregnant ladies to harass with their probes, sticky fingers, and embarrassing questions, resulting in delayed flights. If you are one of the every fifteenth passenger selected, you are guilty until proven innocent. Immediately after Congress passed security legislation, the FAA testified that it would take 54,000 government agents to handle security, which just happens to be 27,000 multiplied by two, and then, when they came up with the "random" ploy for each individual departure, the personnel count went on up to 72,000. What a shame!

Flights of 200 to 300 miles requiring from forty-five minutes to one hour will become a thing of the past if the ridiculous security requirements presently in place and to be implemented before year-end 2002 are permitted to become permanent. When you have to spend one and a half to two hours to get to the airport and endure all the lines and harassment involved, then an hour on the plane, plus thirty minutes to get to baggage claim, retrieve your luggage, and hail a very expensive taxi, you are really better off to just hit the interstates and have the convenience of your car when you get to your destination. That, together with the outrageous cost of short-haul transportation, will very shortly jam the interstates and force us to do what should have been done decades ago: rapid surface transport in all short-haul markets, utilizing the maglev principle developed by the Germans.

I know that it is hard to believe, but back when I ran Southwest Airlines, you could buy a refundable, unrestricted roundtrip ticket from Love Field in Dallas to Hobby Airport in Houston, or vice versa, for travel on weekday evenings and all day Saturday and Sunday for the total sum of $30, of which we kept $26.55, gave Uncle Sam $2.73, and contracted out the stupid security boondoggle for $.72. Today, to buy the exact same package, a refundable, unrestricted roundtrip ticket, you will pay, instead of $30, the sum of $193, of which Southwest keeps $169.30, gives the government $18.70 transportation tax, and the current $5 security fee, which will right soon go up to $10.

Legislation recently passed by Congress permits airport-assessed passenger facility charges (PFC) of up to $18 and government-imposed post–September 11 security fees of up to $10 for each roundtrip. That is a total of $28 in just fees for short-haul transportation charged directly to the customer, versus the $.72 Southwest absorbed as security costs back in 1978. Is it any wonder the airline industry is going broke?

Now the government is considering, with presidential support, a $900 million program with continuing annual costs of $200 million to put pistols in the hands of qualified airline pilots. Shortly after 9/11, I dispatched the following handwritten fax to Herb Kelleher: "Here's what I would do right now if I was in your shoes. First, I would install a temporary fix on the cockpit door so that it could not be opened. Second, I would install as permanent equipment in the cockpit two .38 revolvers loaded with bullets that would not penetrate the fuselage. Third, I would install stun guns as permanent equipment in each galley. Fourth, I would tell the FAA to go f--- themselves, and finally, I would advertise the hell out of it, and just dare terrorists to try something. I guarantee you, passengers will swarm to your flights." Herb never took action. Now our great protector, Uncle Sam, is going to take care of the problem, for an inflated price.

It seems to me that Peter's Laws should come into effect at this time. Number 15 says, "Bureaucracy is a challenge to be conquered with a righteous attitude, a tolerance for stupidity, and a bulldozer when necessary." All that is needed is a senior industry executive who has credibility—and the guts to tell the government to butt out.

17. THE MUSE AIR YEARS —

A Storybook Retirement Interrupted

Since the summer of 1978, when we left Dallas to try to forget Southwest, I have resided in seven different homes located in the Texas Hill Country, our two homes on Lake Palestine, at Walden Country Club on Lake Conroe, at PGA West at La Quinta in the California desert, at Pender Harbour on the Sunshine Coast of beautiful British Columbia, and on St. Simons Island in Georgia. I have also made my home on the *Holy Moses*, a fifty-three-foot, twin-screw, diesel, trawler-type yacht that winters in LaConner, Washington, and summers in the waters between Pender Harbour, British Columbia, and Skagway, Alaska. Barbara and I have covered North America on a touring Yamaha motorcycle, having visited Cabo San Lucas and Guadalajara, Mexico; Vancouver, Lake Louise, Banff, and Montreal, Canada; and Key West, Florida, with lots of stops in between, including Denver, Salt Lake City, the Napa Valley, Yellowstone (both by motorcycle in the summer and snowmobile in the winter), Glacier National Park, Mount Rushmore, Maine, New Hampshire, and Vermont during the fall colors, the Blue Ridge Mountains, Atlanta, and New Orleans. Also, we took a ten-day trip on a BMW cruising bike through Austria, the Swiss Alps, northern Italy, Liechtenstein, France, and Bavaria.

We spent several weeks flying around the world in a Muse Air MD-80 as the guests of McDonnell Douglas, who had chartered the aircraft for a tour to show that beautiful airplane to the air carriers of the world. Along with cruises in the Mediterranean, from New York to Montreal, in Bermuda and the Caribbean, through the Panama Canal, and from Bombay to Singapore, together with a month in Australia and New Zealand, we have pretty well seen and experienced it all.

Besides all the above, I bought and operated a small truck line for a couple of years just so I could drive a big eighteen-wheeler. Additionally, I spent a great week of instruction at and graduated from the Bondurant race car–driving school in Phoenix, Arizona. However, I would have traded all of the above in a New York minute for another seven years (until age sixty-five) as CEO of Southwest Airlines.

From the moment President Carter signed the Airline Regulatory Reform Bill in November 1978, my son, Mike, who had returned to Price Waterhouse & Co.'s Dallas office as a tax manager, saw the opportunity to form a new airline providing low-fare, high-frequency scheduled service. It would be headquartered in Houston, Texas, rather than Dallas, due to Love Field's Wright Amendment restricting destinations from that airport, and would serve all the major cities of the central and midwestern portion of the U.S. as far north as Minneapolis, Minnesota. Mike's practical side told him, though, that such a project could not be accomplished without the aid, encouragement, and support of his old dad. I utilized the "no-compete" clause of my termination agreement with Southwest to avoid having to say no for as long as I could. That excuse expired on October 1, 1980, and as that date approached, I ran out of excuses. Since it was extremely important to me to maintain the tenuous relationship I had with my son, I acquiesced by handing over to him as a loan the remaining 15,000 shares of Southwest stock I had put away for my old age. This would provide the walking-around money for his new company, Muse Air Corporation. The market value of this block of shares was then something over $400,000. I encouraged him to use the shares only as collateral for a loan, but he was convinced that the shares would go down in value and thus cashed them in with a market order the following morning. I hasten to add that the note Mike signed for the shares at their then market value was paid off in accordance with its terms.

While I was to be chairman of the board of Muse Air, Mike was to be president and was to run the show. Other than assisting in the raising of our initial capital requirements, I wanted to keep a very low profile. Mike did a great job of lining up a really first-class cadre of management people, and they in turn hired a staff of some 200 employees unmatched in the industry. Ed Lang from Southwest joined us as senior VP-marketing, James T. Ferguson, who had been a senior captain with TI, agreed to head up our flight and dispatch operations, and Buford Minter, formally VP-maintenance at Braniff, moved to Muse Air in the same role. Doug Lane, former director of purchasing for Southwest, Universal, and TI, joined us in our new venture as VP-purchasing, and Jim Thompson left his job as assistant treasurer at Southwest to become Muse Air's comptroller. Kelleher obviously realized that Bill Franklin and Bud Herring would also be joining our new company but kept them by offering five-year employment contracts with a substantial back-end cash bonus.

Elliott Bradley, a VP at E. F. Hutton & Co., convinced his firm to be the lead underwriter for a public offering of a package of securities consisting of 2.2 million common shares of Muse Air Corporation stock, plus five-year warrants for an additional 1.1 million shares. The initial public offering was consummated in late April 1981 at a unit-offering price of $17.50 for one share of common plus one-half of a stock warrant. Bradley told the media that the Muse Air offering "represented something very unusual in the investment world in that his company underwrote the stock offering even though Muse Air had no history of operation, no earnings, no revenue—not even a plane in the air." The offering netted the company $35.5 million after all fees that at the time were deemed sufficient to tide the company over until profitable operations were experienced.

An additional $75 million in capital was provided by McDonnell Douglas in the form of $17.7 million of subordinated debt, and $57.8 million of senior debt by Continental Illinois Bank of Chicago and First National Bank of Dallas. By far, Muse Air was the best-financed airline startup in the history of the aviation industry.

Ray Trapp, formerly our account executive at the Bloom Agency, was now president of the Texas division of the Keller Crescent Agency, owned by American Standard Co. His exceptional performance for Southwest made our selection of an advertising agency an easy decision. In spite of my expressed desire to remain in the background, their presentation of the theme they wanted to use for the introduction of hourly service between Dallas's Love Field and Houston's Hobby Airport centered around me dressed in a three-piece dark suit with a gold watch chain across the vest, Daddy Warbucks style. The headline read, "Big Daddy Is Back." By this time it was too close to our planned inauguration of service to develop a new advertising campaign from scratch, so I reluctantly authorized the program. In my view, this whole presentation was not getting the project off to a very good start, but only time would tell. And it did. That presentation brought Muse Air the undeserved nickname "Revenge Air."

I had an agreement with Mike that if I was lending my name and reputation to his airline, then every facet of it had to be an improvement over Southwest—equipment utilized, service provided, presentation, and, hopefully, profits generated. The major service improvements I demanded were leather upholstery over the finest seats available and assigned seating in aircraft cabins that were totally smoke-free. We were to be the very first nonsmoking airline in the world.

The equipment had to be the latest technology, which obviously was McDonnell Douglas's DC-9 Super 80, subsequently designated the MD-80. This 155-passenger airliner, with its high bypass, fuel-efficient, extremely quiet Pratt & Whitney engines, clearly was the only choice, particularly with fuel costs approaching $1.50 per gallon at that time and seemingly headed for

$2 or more. I calculated that at jet fuel prices of $1.50 to $2 per gallon, the cost saving of these fuel-efficient engines would more than offset the much higher capital cost of these $20 million-plus aircraft. And it would have, had fuel prices stayed in that range. But they didn't. Within a year, jet fuel was abundant at prices well below $1. My first big mistake!

Since the MD-80 was in high demand, with the Long Beach production line being clogged with American Airlines MD-80s, the backbone of their current fleet, the earliest delivery positions we could obtain were during the last half of 1982. We were able to obtain a one-year lease, however, on two aircraft ordered by a South American carrier with financial problems and thus willing to delay their delivery.

On the Sunday morning in mid-July 1982 immediately preceding the Monday-morning inaugural flights, one of our two leased aircraft took off from Houston Hobby Airport destined for New Orleans, Louisiana, with Barbara and me as hosts to a planeload of Houston dignitaries and travel industry representatives. Simultaneously, the other half of our fleet departed Dallas's Love Field with Mike and his wife, Diane, as hosts to a similar Dallas group heading for New Orleans. The planes arrived within minutes of each other at Moisant Airport. After being greeted by New Orleans dignitaries, including Jack McIlhenny of Tabasco Sauce fame, the group of some 250 guests climbed into charter buses, to be delivered to the Royal Orleans Hotel Ballroom for libations and a Sunday brunch-to-end-all-brunches, to the accompaniment of Pete Fountain's fine sextet. New Orleans and a three-hour concert by that great artist gained the company some good TV coverage on the Sunday-night news immediately preceding our first scheduled flight.

I did not maintain a detailed history of events at Muse Air as I had during the eight years I was at Southwest, so I will only hit the high spots in this narrative. Suffice it to say that Southwest Airlines was and is a tough competitor. Whereas during the 1970s Southwest, as the David, pretty well controlled the agenda against the Goliath, Braniff Airways, in the 1980s Southwest, the Goliath, absolutely controlled the agenda against Muse Air, the David. At every market move Muse Air made, Southwest trumped it by reducing the going fare in that market by $10. During our first year, when Muse Air only served the one market from Dallas to Houston, Southwest's only $35 fare was in that market. If you wanted to fly from Dallas to Austin or Houston to San Antonio, both being markets under 200 miles versus the 241 miles between Love Field and Hobby Airport, you paid Southwest's fare of $45. At normal passenger load factors, that $10 was the difference between profit and loss.

Sometime before the scheduled delivery of our own four MD-80s in 1982, the FAA's flight controllers union called an illegal strike, after which President Reagan, utilizing that illegality factor, stupidly refused to selectively take back the many fine people who had dedicated their careers to this all-important job. Instead, the FAA filled these thousands of positions with people off the street who didn't understand the intricacies of the flight controllers' responsibilities—and many still don't. The totally inadequate training they received then and continue to receive now has crippled the industry for the last two decades. Even today, it is absolutely impossible to maintain any semblance of a scheduled operation at many of the major airports of this nation. This is one of the principal reasons that Southwest, as well as Muse Air, historically has chosen secondary airports where available and adequate. Thanks, President Reagan.

This action created a new word in the aviation dictionary: *slots*. Slots are pieces of time and airspace that nobody owns but possession of which has been usurped by the FAA and grandfathered out to the established carriers who were utilizing them at the time of the strike. This action, and the continued control over slots to this day, effectively negated the congressional deregulation of the industry by replacing the CAB with the Department of Transportation's Federal Aviation Administration, a much more pervasive regulation insofar as new entrants are concerned.

The immediate effect on Muse Air was that we had two $22 million aircraft parked up against the fence because the FAA would not grant additional slots to the company. We had planned to inaugurate service to Tulsa, Oklahoma, and Midland-Odessa, Texas, with these two aircraft. The only thing that permitted us to do so was the timely discontinuance of flight operations by Braniff Airways when they filed for bankruptcy. At that point, the FAA had no leg to stand on in continuing to deny the company the slots it required to efficiently operate the additional aircraft. Incidentally, when Muse Air began service to these two markets, Southwest's former $45 fare magically became a $35 fare, while fares from Dallas to Oklahoma City and to Lubbock, similar but shorter markets, remained at $45.

At a slightly later date, Mike decided to begin service from both Houston and Dallas to Little Rock, Arkansas. His only mistake was that he let that decision become public knowledge prior to negotiating a lease agreement for terminal space with the Little Rock Airport Authority. Southwest immediately jumped in and leased every available square foot of terminal space at the Little Rock Airport. Do I blame them? Hell, no, I'd have done the same thing; when you have the competition on the run, keep tightening the screws.

As more aircraft were delivered, service was extended west from Houston and Austin to Las Vegas, Nevada, and the California cities of Los Angeles, Ontario, and San Jose. Aircraft for this service took more capital, however, and with the losses Muse Air was incurring, and with the Muse Air shares down around the $3.50 level with the options underwater, the only funds available were subordinated debentures carrying a fixed interest rate of 18 percent. I vividly remember the conference-call directors meeting to approve these debentures. I was aboard the *Holy Moses*, anchored out at the Royal Victoria Yacht Club in British Columbia, all guest spaces having been previously occupied. I had gone ashore to participate in the meeting at a pay phone about ten feet from where I had tied up my dingy. I tried to explain to the other directors that at 18 percent interest, all we would ever be doing with those airplanes was to bore holes in the sky—they could never be a profitable investment. The final vote almost an hour later had one dissenting vote—me. The reason I remember this incident so vividly is that I could hear my dingy crunching on the rocks as the sixteen-foot tides normal for that area did their thing. By the time the meeting was over, my dingy was high and dry, and I had to wait for the next rising tide before I could return to the *Holy Moses*.

Incidentally, to get two slots to land and take off at Los Angeles (LAX), the company had to purchase two old, worn-out ten-passenger aircraft at a ridiculous price from a third-level carrier which, on the day the controllers strike was called, happened to be operating two flights that they now wanted to abandon. About a year later, the company managed to dump the two crates for less than half of what had been invested in them. If this makes absolutely no sense to you, then you are beginning to get the picture of airline economics since the FAA took over.

In the Love-Hobby market, Muse Air had slightly less than one-third of the flights but was carrying somewhat more than one-half of the local traffic volume. There were several factors contributing to this, among them the ambience of the Muse Air aircraft and boarding procedure versus the cattle-car treatment at Southwest, and the knee room on Muse Air aircraft as opposed to the crunch on Southwest. After my termination, Southwest had stuffed the cabin with another row of seats, increasing the capacity from 112 to 118. But the biggest factor was the fresh, clean air in the cabin. In fact, the surveys we conducted proved that our original decision to be a nonsmoking airline was a winner. These surveys showed that five out of ten passengers would wait up to an additional thirty minutes to fly Muse Air, which only had flights every hour, rather than take Southwest, which provided flights every half-hour. For four out of ten, the fact that we were nonsmoking made no difference to their choice of airline, which meant that only one out of ten flew Southwest because of Muse Air's nonsmoking policy. I told our people that I'd take five-to-one marketing odds any day of the week! It took the rest of the industry five more years—and then only with the prodding of government—to see the light.

During the summer of 1984, Barbara and I flew down from Seattle to the La Costa Airline Golf Classic sponsored by McDonnell Douglas, and my son, Mike, met us for the tournament. One night he knocked on my door to see if I would take a look at an upcoming schedule change being considered. I told him that the system schedule was so screwed up that tinkering with it around the edges was useless. "You just can't make a mink coat out of a sow's ear," I said. "You are going to have to start from scratch." That was the last time I had a civil conversation with my son for a number of very troubled years.

By September 1984 the financial situation at Muse Air had

226

become so bad that the word *bankruptcy* was being mouthed by the board. I then made big mistake number two, that being to convince the board that new top management was absolutely necessary and further recommending who it should be, after only the most cursory examination of my candidate's credentials. Sam Coats had been a state legislator and more recently had experience in public relations activities with Braniff and, after that company's bankruptcy, as principal spokesman for Southwest. I just figured that if Southwest had hired him, he had to be good. Coats became president and chief operating officer, with Mike accepting the title of vice chairman and chief financial officer. As it turned out, I had obviously done Southwest a big favor by taking Coats off their hands.

It wasn't only schedules that needed a complete overhaul. While I had the greatest respect for Ray Trapp, Keller Crescent's main office was remote, and their product, at least for Muse Air, seemed to be just run-of-the-mill, lacking creativity. Coats and I agreed that we needed to make a change in advertising agencies. Stan Richards' company, the Richards Group, was the agency for the Mercantile National Bank in Dallas, and I thought they were extremely creative in the presentation and delivery of the bank's theme of "momentum." Besides that, Stan was a great guy with whom I knew we could work very effectively, particularly with his total operation located in Dallas. And like the Bloom Agency back in early 1971, they seemed especially excited about the opportunity to become the advertising agency for Muse Air. We agreed that they were the obvious choice. Later, when I became CEO, Stan named me as the company spokesman for all of our TV and radio commercials, kind of like Colonel Sanders of Kentucky Fried Chicken and Dave of Wendy's. I guess it was the right decision, since one of *D Magazine's* selections of the fifty best things in Dallas for the year 1985 was "the honest and straight-forward TV commercials by Lamar Muse."

On a beautiful fall day in November 1984, Barbara and I were guests of Harold and Annette Simmons, along with Norman and Nancy Brinker — Norman being one of Muse Air's directors — and Harold's principal stockbroker (name escapes me) in the Simmons' skybox at Texas Stadium for a Cowboys football game. The course of the conversation, on the way from the Simmons' home to the stadium, led the stockbroker to remark that everything Harold touched seemed to turn to gold. I came back with, "I wish to hell he would touch Muse Air, then." During the course of the game, that remark turned into a three-way conversation between Norman, Harold, and me and resulted in Simmons infusing $16 million into Muse Air, his only stipulation being that I assume the position of CEO and devote 100 percent of my energies to removing the company from the jaws of the bankruptcy courts.

At the time I took over as the active CEO, Sam Coats was in the process of filing schedules to provide service from both Dallas and Houston to San Antonio, right on top of the now predominant carrier, Southwest. Realizing that such action on our part would just result in another low-fare war with Southwest, I canceled that plan. What we needed to do was to take some action that Southwest, which was bent on bankrupting us, would be unable to trump. I then remembered from my days at Southwest that, of the Rio Grande Valley traffic carried by Southwest through the Harlingen airport, only 18 percent actually came from the Harlingen area. The balance was drawn there from the upper Valley area, which would be better served through the airport located in McAllen, and from the lower Valley and Padre Island, which would be better served through the Brownsville airport.

In my scheming mind, the quickest way for Muse Air securities to gain market value and for Barbara and me to get the hell out of the coming Texas summer's 100-plus degrees of heat would be to convince Southwest's board of directors that it would be cheaper to buy us out than continue to fight us. Especially since the infusion of Simmons' $16 million had now eliminated the specter of a Muse Air bankruptcy. Meanwhile, that pesky gnat Muse Air was causing Southwest many more millions of dollars in lost revenue each year than Muse Air itself was losing, and we were killing them in their previous monopoly market of Love Field–Hobby Airport. So they just might begin to get our message if we inaugurated a Rio Grande Valley operation serving the Brownsville and McAllen airports, which would have the effect of eliminating more than half of their Harlingen market.

So we did it, and our Rio Grande Valley operation was profitable from the very first month. I was not at all surprised when one February 1985 morning I received a call from Herb Kelleher, who asked me just one question. "Lamar," he said, "would you rather be spending next summer on the *Holy Moses* fishing for salmon in 70 degree weather, or be here in sweltering Dallas running Muse Air?"

I responded, "Herb, I know you well enough to know that you would never ask that question if you didn't already know the answer."

"Well," said Herb, "why don't we have breakfast together tomorrow morning at my condo and talk about it?"

"What time?" was my only response.

Since Herb's long list of accomplishments did not include cooking, it was not much of a breakfast, but that meeting did include some very interesting conversation. He advised me that Southwest would like to purchase Muse Air and continue to have it operate as a separate company, with some obvious schedule changes—such as the duplication of flights in the Love-Hobby market and the unnecessary service to the Rio Grande Valley. His proposal was a figure somewhat in excess of both the book and market value of the company, but I advised him that I was in no position to consider any offer without the full participation of Harold Simmons, who, as he knew, now owned a substantial interest in Muse Air. I recommended a subsequent meeting that would include Simmons. Herb agreed, and a couple of days later the three of us met in Simmons' office.

I always considered myself to be a fairly good negotiator, but compared to Harold Simmons, I was like Ned in the First Reader. Harold made it perfectly clear to Herb that under no condition would he consider a buyout by Southwest that did not include for his interests a 100 percent gain on their investment. A few calculations revealed that this meant a combination of cash, Southwest common stock, and five-year warrants to purchase additional shares at a fixed price would have to be valued at approximately $72 million. Within forty-eight hours, we had a signed agreement to that effect, subject, of course, to the approval of both companies' boards of directors and the Department of Transportation in Washington.

Several months elapsed while we awaited government action on our petition for approval of the purchase by Southwest, but the agreement was finally consummated on June 30, 1985. Prior to that time, I donated 20,000 shares of my Muse Air stock to my alma mater, Southwestern University in Georgetown, Texas, so as to eliminate any profit from Muse Air for my account. I felt very bad that many people had purchased shares of Muse Air in the initial public offering at $17.50, based on trust in my previous reputation, and then later found it necessary to sell those shares for as low as $3.50 each.

The Muse Air shareholders who participated in the sale of the company did okay, provided they sold their warrants to purchase Southwest shares promptly. Those, like me, who held them for the five-year period found them to be of no value at expiration, since during the five-year period from 1985 to 1990, the value of Southwest common stock went absolutely nowhere.

On the afternoon of June 30, 1985, Barbara and I caught a flight to San Francisco, where I was scheduled to be the luncheon speaker the following day for the Northern California Association of Hospital Administrators, who were just getting their first glimmer of the competitive world in which they would soon find themselves. They wanted to hear from somebody who knew the meaning of the word *competition*. I really don't remember what I told them, except that hospitals should look upon doctors, who bring them the bulk of their business, pretty much the same way airlines looked upon the travel agent industry — with great suspicion.

The very next day we flew on to Seattle and boarded the *Holy Moses*, thus resuming retirement for the third and final time.

EPILOGUE

I have spent forty-four years in the business world, thirty-seven of those years as the chief financial, planning, or executive officer of seven different commercial airlines. Since Barbara and I headed for the *Holy Moses* via our one day in San Francisco on June 30, 1985, I've had seventeen years to review those thirty-seven years, and when I do, I dwell primarily on the mistakes made, and I sometimes play "what if."

"What if" I had ignored the advice of the PSA executives who recommended 25-minute turn times at the gate for our three Boeing 737s and from the first day of Southwest's operations, utilizing our famous ten-minute turns, operated flights every hour in the Dallas-Houston market and every two hours in the Dallas–San Antonio market with only the three aircraft we originally contracted for? The question of taking delivery of that fourth aircraft as of October 1, 1971, would have never been raised, an event that precipitated Wesley West's resignation from Southwest's board and his quest to get his original investment back rather than the $2 billion-plus that investment would have been worth at the end of the year 2001.

And "what if" I had thought like a Dallas business executive rather than a citizen of Houston and had chosen the close-in Hobby Airport in Houston from the very beginning rather than the new Intercontinental Airport—even though it was necessary to chase the bats out of the old terminal building? Our early operating costs would have been lower and our initial passenger loads and operating revenues would have been much higher, resulting in greatly reduced initial operating losses.

Also, "what if" we had realized right from the beginning that to exponentially expand markets and provide a real service to our state, there were two distinct markets to serve? Rather than the one-price fare of $20 with which we began service and almost went broke, what if right from the beginning we had charged $25 on weekday business-hour flights and only $15 on evening flights and all flights operated during weekends? Unquestionably, Southwest Airlines would have been profitable, not from March 1973 forward, but rather from the very first full month of operations in July 1971, as has been the case in every route expansion since then once the company got the cookie-cutting machine into operation and kept it well greased with its "Southwest Airlines Employees Profit Sharing Plan." Instead, we put in twenty-one months of ... experimenting is the nice word, but fumbling around is probably more accurate.

And from a personal standpoint, "what if" I had gone ahead and mailed to the directors a finished copy of my draft letter dated December 6, 1977, regarding King's continual misguided harassment? Just maybe I would have been able to stick around and had the fun and riches that Herb Kelleher has so relished in my stead. In that connection, since 1991, shares totaling 6.1 percent of the present shares outstanding, representing $873 million of the market value, have been exercised from "off the books" options granted earlier to Southwest executives at then-market value, including options to Mr. Kelleher, largely at $1 per share (before stock splits). That's $873 million of operating expense never recorded on the books or reported to shareholders in other than small-print footnotes included in the annual reports, even though those costs were utilized to further reduce the company's federal income tax liabilities. And those are only the options that have been exercised through December 31, 2001. There are many more still outstanding. The value of the options exercised exceeds the company's net income during the first five years of the decade.

And finally, "what if" I had kept those last 15,000 shares of Southwest common stock stashed away for my old age rather than handing it over to my son, Mike, for his walking-around money to start Muse Air? Those shares, which at the time had a market value of a little over $400,000, in today's market represent 1,622,006 shares, worth almost $30 million. Of course, as Mike paid off his note, I could have reinvested the funds in Southwest common, but that just didn't happen. And if the last two paragraphs sound to you like sour grapes, I can't say you are wrong.

During the last fifteen years, based on my experience with the airlines, I've thought a lot about our government and how it can screw up as much as or more than reasonably intelligent businessmen do in the corporate world. And it all boils down to the basic principles that I believe hold true in both spheres: (1) management or government operated by committee creates mediocrity, and (2) incentives can do their job of good or bad depending on the direction they are pointed.

Most corporate boards of directors are nothing more nor less than committees, and when they succeed in running the show, you can expect mediocrity. Southwest's board attempted to do that throughout my tenure as CEO, but I resisted with every fiber of my body and it eventually cost me my job. During the following decade, the Southwest board exerted great influence on the interim president, Howard Putnam, and continued to do so during early years while Herb Kelleher was learning the business. But during the last five or six years, it is obvious that Herb learned the secret that I never learned: how to make your board an asset rather than a liability. Just a glance at the line graph on page 208, which pictures the continuing decline in productivity as well as net income as a percent of total revenues with improvement during the last five years, makes this assumption perfectly obvious.

This thesis is further substantiated by the public perception of Southwest Airlines, as demonstrated by the market price of its security, LUV, from inception in the early 1970s through the year 2001. There were fourteen stock splits through 2001, and from January 1, 1972, through December 31, 1978, when I was CEO, the stock went from $.01 to $.13 with a high of $.19, adjusted for the fourteen stock splits, a compound annual growth rate of 90 percent. During Putnam's three years—he was also an independent soul—the stock proceeded on up to $.51 with a high of $.80, representing an annual growth rate of 58 percent. Mr. Kelleher's first decade saw the shares further increase from $.51 to $2.25, a compound rate of only 16 percent, but during the next ten years, through December 31, 2001, that rate jumped 50 percent, to 23.3 percent, even after the disastrous effect on the entire industry of the World Trade Center and Pentagon calamities, at which time Southwest stock hit a low of $11.25 per share versus the high of $22 reached earlier in the year. I attribute the very poor performance during the first ten years of Herb's reign principally to two things: first, meddling in management's area of responsibility by the board, and second, competition from Muse Air, which was so efficient that the Southwest board was willing to pay an exorbitant price to eliminate the most effective competition the company had ever faced.

But man alive, with the competition out of the way, look what happened during the next ten years of Kelleher's leadership! LUV went from an adjusted $2.25 per share all the way to $18.48 as of December 31, 2001. Obviously, Herb had effectively harnessed Rollin King by late 1990, something I was never able to do.

Southwest's profit-sharing plan was an incentive that was certainly pointed in the right direction and has produced fabulous results for the company. On the other hand, a pension plan inevitably would have been pointed in the wrong direction. Few people realize that Southwest Airlines is probably the only major American corporation that has not a single pension plan, unless you call their tax-advantaged 401K plans one. And there can be no better example of proper incentives to the public than the low-fare, high-frequency operations of Southwest for purposes of both market expansion and the common good.

Now take a look at our government. Everything starts with the Congress. It's not just a committee; it's two of them with hundreds of subcommittees. Double trouble! Each committee or house has to make compromises to get agreement between the opposing factions, and then committees of those committees have to compromise further to get something together that they can send to the president for ratification. At that point, the really big committee takes over, consisting of the Congress, the White House, and the Supreme Court, each of which is a committee in its own right. So is it any wonder that nothing really productive ever comes out of Washington? Conversely—and this is our government's one saving grace—nothing really horrible ever comes out of Washington, either, unless it was Johnson's Great Society, Papa Bush's Iraqian fiasco, or his son's Afghanistan boondoggle.

Barbara and I ended our forty-one-year relationship, twenty-three years as husband and wife, in 1997 by divorce. It was not her fault. I was the moving party. We maintain a cordial relationship. I subsequently was married to Pat Cords of Lufkin, Texas, for a tumultuous three years. Another divorce. What's that popular new law about the third time and you are out? I think that is me. I'm eighty-two, still in good health, have a great bachelor pad in The Woodlands, am not worried about where my next meal is coming from, and am sincerely thankful to whatever it is that has granted me the full and exciting life I have lived.

INDEX

242